THE HUMANISTIC TRADITION

SECOND EDITION

1

Origins of the Humanistic Tradition:
The First Civilizations
and the Classical Legacy

THE HUMANISTIC TRADITION

SECOND EDITION

1

Origins of the Humanistic Tradition: The First Civilizations and the Classical Legacy

Gloria K. Fiero

University of Southwestern Louisiana

WCB Brown & Benchmark
PUBLISHERS

Madison, Wisconsin • Dubuque, Iowa

Book Team
Associate Publisher   *Rosemary Bradley*
Senior Developmental Editor   *Deborah Daniel Reinbold*
Publishing Services Manager   *Sherry Padden*

**WCB Brown &
Benchmark**
A Division of Wm. C. Brown Communications, Inc.

Executive Vice President/General Manager   *Thomas E. Doran*
Vice President/Editor in Chief   *Edgar J. Laube*
Director of Marketing   *Eric Ziegler*
Vice President of Production   *Vickie Putman Caughron*
Director of Custom and Electronic Publishing   *Chris Rogers*

Wm. C. Brown Communications, Inc.

President and Chief Executive Officer   *G. Franklin Lewis*
Corporate Senior Vice President and Chief Financial Officer   *Robert Chesterman*
Corporate Senior Vice President and President of Manufacturing   *Roger Meyer*

The credits section for this book begins on page 154 and is considered an extension of the copyright page.

A Times Mirror Company

Library of Congress Catalog Card Number: 94–072136

ISBN 0–697–24217–X

This book was designed and produced by
CALMANN & KING LTD
71 Great Russell Street, London WC1B 3BN

Designer   *Karen Osborne*
Cover designer   *Karen Stafford*
Picture researcher   *Carrie Haines*
Maps by Oxford Illustrators Ltd.
Timeline artwork by   *Richard Foenander*

Typeset by Bookworm Typesetting, Manchester, UK
Printed in Singapore

10 9 8 7 6 5 4 3 2

Front cover
Main image: Epicetus, Cup (detail), ca. 510 B.C.E. Diameter 13 in. Reproduced by courtesy of the Trustees of the British Museum, London.
Insets: (top) Detail of South rose window, Chartres Cathedral, France, thirteenth century. Photo: Sonia Halliday, Weston Turville.
(center) Raphael, *The School of Athens* (detail), 1509–1511. Fresco, 26 ft. × 18 ft. Stanza della Segnatura, Vatican, Rome. Scala/Art Resource, New York.
(bottom) *Shiva Nataraja* from Chidambaram, ca. eleventh century. Bronze, height 21¼ in. Museum van Asiatische Kunst Amsterdam.
Photo: Bildarchiv preussischer kulturbesitz, Berlin.

Frontispiece
Detail of Scene of Fowling, from the Tomb of Neb-amon at Thebes, Egypt, ca. 1400 B.C.E. Painting on stucco, height 32¼ in.
Reproduced by courtesy of the Trustees of the British Museum, London.

Series Contents

Book 1
Contents

PART II

The Classical
Legacy 55

MUSIC LISTENING SELECTION

Preface

"It's the most curious thing I ever saw in all my life!" exclaimed Lewis Carroll's Alice in Wonderland, as she watched the Cheshire Cat slowly disappear, leaving only the outline of a broad smile. "I've often seen a cat without a grin, but a grin without a cat!" A student who encounters an ancient Greek epic, a Yoruba mask, or a Mozart opera – lacking any context for these works – might be equally baffled. It may be helpful, therefore, to begin by explaining how the artifacts (the "grin") of the humanistic tradition relate to the larger and more elusive phenomenon (the "cat") of human culture.

The Humanistic Tradition and the Humanities

In its broadest sense, the term *humanistic tradition* refers to humankind's cultural legacy – the sum total of the significant ideas and achievements handed down from generation to generation. This tradition is the product of responses to conditions that have confronted all people throughout history. Since the beginnings of life on earth, human beings have tried to ensure their own survival by controlling nature. They have attempted to come to terms with the inevitable realities of disease and death. They have endeavored to establish ways of living collectively and communally. And they have persisted in the desire to understand themselves and their place in the universe. In response to these ever-present and universal challenges – *survival*, *communality*, and *self-knowledge* – human beings have created and transmitted the tools of science and technology, social and cultural institutions, religious and philosophic systems, and various forms of personal expression, the sum total of which we call culture.

Even the most ambitious survey cannot assess all manifestations of the humanistic tradition. This book therefore focuses on the creative legacy referred to collectively as *the humanities*: literature, philosophy, history (in its literary dimension), architecture, the visual arts (including photography and film), music, and dance. Selected examples from each of these disciplines constitute our *primary sources*. Primary sources (that is, works original to the age that produced them) provide first-hand evidence of human inventiveness and ingenuity. The primary sources in this text have been chosen on the basis of their authority, their beauty, and their enduring value. They are, simply stated, the masterpieces of their time and, in some cases, of all time. Because of their universal appeal, they have been imitated and transmitted from generation to generation. Such works are, as well, the landmark examples of a specific time and place: they offer insight into the ideas and values of the society in which they were produced. *The Humanistic Tradition* surveys these landmark works, but joins "the grin" to "the cat" by examining them within their political, economic, and social contexts.

The Humanistic Tradition explores a living legacy. History confirms that the humanities are not frivolous social ornaments, but rather, integral forms of a given culture's values, ambitions, and beliefs. Poetry, painting, philosophy, and music are not, generally speaking, products of unstructured leisure or indulgent individuality; rather, they are tangible expressions of the human quest for the good (one might even say the "complete") life. Throughout history, the arts have served the domains of the sacred, the ceremonial, and the communal. And even in modern times, as these domains have come under assault and as artists have openly challenged time-honored traditions, the reciprocal relationship between artist and community prevails. Unquestionably, the creative minds of every age both reflect and shape their culture. In these pages, then, we find works made by individuals with special sensitivities and unique talents for interpreting the conditions and values of their day. The drawings of Leonardo da Vinci, for example, reveal a passionate determination to understand the operations and functions of nature. And while Leonardo's talent far exceeded that of the average individual of his time, his achievements may be viewed as a mirror of the robust curiosity that characterized his time and place – the Age of the Renaissance in Italy.

The Scope of the Humanistic Tradition

The humanistic tradition is not the exclusive achievement of any one geographic region, race, or class of human beings. For that reason, this text assumes a global and multicultural rather than exclusively Western perspective. At the same time, Western contributions are emphasized, first, because the audience for these books is predominantly Western, but also because in recent centuries the West has exercised a dominant influence on the course and substance of global history. Clearly, the humanistic tradition belongs to all of humankind, and the best way to understand the Western contribution to that tradition is to examine it in the arena of world culture.

As a survey, *The Humanistic Tradition* cannot provide an exhaustive analysis of our creative legacy. The critical reader will discover many gaps. Some aspects of culture that receive extended examination in traditional Western humanities surveys have been pared down to make room for the too often neglected contributions of Islam, Africa, and Asia. This book is necessarily selective – it omits many major figures and treats others only briefly. Primary sources are arranged, for the most part, chronologically, but they are presented as manifestations of *the informing ideas of the age* in which they were produced. The intent is to examine the evidence of the humanistic tradition thematically and topically, rather than to compile a series of mini-histories of the individual arts.

Studying the Humanistic Tradition

To study the creative record is to engage in a dialogue with the past, one that brings us face to face with the values of our ancestors, and, ultimately, with our own. This dialogue is (or should be) a source of personal revelation and delight; like Alice in Wonderland, our strange, new encounters will be enriched according to the degree of curiosity and patience we bring to them. Just as lasting friendships with special people are cultivated by extended familiarity, so our appreciation of a painting, a play, or a symphony depends on close attention and repeated contact. There are no shortcuts to the study of the humanistic tradition, but there are some techniques that may be helpful. It should be useful, for instance, to approach each primary source from the triple perspective of its *text*, its *context*, and its *subtext*.

The Text: The *text* of any primary source refers to its *medium* (that is, what it is made of), its *form* (that is, its outward shape), and its *content* (that is, the subject it describes). All literature, for example, whether intended to be spoken or read, depends on the medium of words – the American poet Robert Frost once defined literature as "performance in words." Literary form varies according to the manner in which words are arranged. So poetry, which shares with music and dance rhythmic organization, may be distinguished from prose, which normally lacks regular rhythmic pattern. The main purpose of prose is to convey information, to narrate, and to describe; poetry, a form that assumes freedom from conventional patterns of grammar, is usually concerned with expressing intense emotions. Philosophy (the search for truth through reasoned analysis) and history (the record of the past) make use of prose to analyze and communicate ideas and information. In literature, as in most kinds of expression, content and form are usually interrelated. The subject matter or the form of a literary work will determine its *genre*. For instance, a long narrative poem recounting the adventures of a hero is an *epic*, while a formal, dignified speech in praise of a person or thing constitutes a *eulogy*.

The visual arts – painting, sculpture, architecture, and photography – employ a wide variety of media, such as wood, clay, colored pigments, marble, granite, steel, and (more recently) plastic, neon, film, and computers. The form or outward shape of a work of art depends on the manner in which the artist manipulates the formal elements of color, line, texture, and space. Unlike words, these formal elements lack denotative meaning. The artist may manipulate form to describe and interpret the visible world (as in such genres as portraiture and landscape painting); to generate fantastic and imaginative kinds of imagery; or, to create nonrepresentational imagery – that is, without identifiable subject matter. In general, however, the visual arts are all spatial in that they operate and are apprehended in space.

The medium of music is sound. Like literature, music is durational: that is, it unfolds over the period of time in which it occurs, rather than all at once. The formal elements of music are melody, rhythm, harmony, and tone color – elements that also characterize the oral life of literature. As with the visual arts, the formal elements of music are without symbolic content, but while literature, painting, and sculpture may imitate or describe nature, music is almost always nonrepresentational – it rarely has meaning beyond the sound itself. For that reason, music is the most difficult of the arts to describe in words, as well as (in the view of some) the most affective of the arts. Dance, the artform that makes the human body itself a medium of expression, is, like music, temporal and performance-oriented. Like music, dance exploits rhythm as a formal tool, but like painting and sculpture, it unfolds in space as well as time.

In analyzing the text of a work of literature, art, or music, we might ask how its formal elements contribute to its meaning and affective power. We might examine the ways in which the artist manipulates medium and form to achieve a characteristic manner of execution and expression that we call *style*. We may try to determine the extent to which a style reflects the personal vision of the artist and the larger vision of his or her time and place. Comparing the styles of various artworks from a single era, we may discover that they share certain defining features and characteristics. Similarities (both formal and stylistic) between, for instance, Golden Age Greek temples and Greek tragedies, between Chinese lyric poems and landscape paintings, and between postmodern fiction and pop sculpture, prompt us to seek the unifying moral and aesthetic values of the cultures in which they were produced.

The Context: We use the word *context* to describe the historical and cultural milieu. To determine the context, we ask: In what time and place did the artifact originate? How did it function within the society in which it was created? Was the purpose of the piece decorative, didactic, magical, propagandistic? Did it serve the religious or political needs of the community? Sometimes our answers to these questions are mere guesses. Nevertheless, understanding the function of an artifact often serves to clarify the nature of its form (and vice-versa). For instance, much of the literature produced prior to the fifteenth century was spoken or sung rather than read; for that reason, such literature tends to feature repetition and rhyme, devices that facilitated memorization. We can assume that literary works embellished with frequent repetitions, such as the *Epic of Gilgamesh* and the Hebrew Bible, were products of an oral tradition. Determining the original function of an artwork also permits us to assess its significance in its own time and place: The paintings on the walls of Paleolithic caves, which are among the most compelling animal illustrations in the history of world art, are not "artworks" in the modern sense of the term; cave art was most probably an extension of sacred hunting rituals, the performance of which was essential to the survival of the community. Understanding the relationship between text and context is one of the principal concerns of any inquiry into the humanistic tradition.

The Subtext: The *subtext* of the literary or artistic object refers to its secondary and implied meanings. The subtext embraces the emotional or intellectual messages embedded in, or implied by, a work of art. The epic poems of the ancient Greeks, for instance, which glorify prowess and physical courage, carry a subtext that suggests such virtues are exclusively male. The state portraits of the seventeenth-century French ruler, Louis XIV, carry the subtext of unassailable and absolute power. In our own century, Andy Warhol's serial adaptations of soup cans and Coca-Cola bottles offer wry commentary on the supermarket mentality of postmodern American culture. Analyzing the implicit message of an artwork helps us to determine the values and customs of the age in which it was produced and to test these values against others.

Beyond *The Humanistic Tradition*

This book offers only small, enticing samples from an enormous cultural buffet. To dine more fully, students are encouraged to go beyond the sampling presented at this table; and for the most sumptuous feasting, nothing can substitute for first-hand experience. Students, therefore, should make every effort to supplement this book with visits to art museums and galleries, concert halls, theaters, and libraries. *The Humanistic Tradition* is designed for typical students, who may or may not be able to read music, but who surely are able to cultivate an appreciation of music in performance. The clefs that appear in the text refer to the forty-five Music Listening Selections found on two accompanying cassettes, available from Brown and Benchmark Publishers. Lists of suggestions for further reading are included at the end of each chapter, while a selected general bibliography of humanities resources appears at the end of each book.

The Second Edition

The second edition of *The Humanistic Tradition* broadens the coverage of non-European cultures, while emphasizing the fertile, reciprocal nature of global interchange. This edition also gives increased attention to the contributions of women artists and writers. Selections from the writings of the Han historian, Ssu-ma Ch'ien; from Li Ju-chen's eighteenth-century satire, *Flowers in the Mirror*; and from modern Chinese and Japanese poetry enhance our appreciation of the Asian literary tradition. A new, more graceful and precise translation of the Koran appears in Book 2. Three Native American tales have been added to Book 3. Short stories by Isabel Allende (Chile) and Chinua Achebe (Africa) now enrich Book 6, which has been updated to include a section on sexual orientation, AIDS art, and the most recent developments in global culture. In response to the requests and suggestions of numerous readers, we have added literary selections from the works of Cervantes, Pushkin, Frederick Douglass, Dostoevsky, Nietzsche, Kate Chopin, and Gwendolyn Brooks; and we have lengthened the excerpts from the *Iliad*, Virgil's *Aeneid*, the Gospel of Matthew, the writings of Augustine, Dante's *Inferno*, *Sundiata*, Chaucer's *Canterbury Tales*, Milton's *Paradise Lost*, and Whitman's *Leaves of Grass*.

The second edition offers a larger selection of high quality color illustrations and a number of new illustrations, some representative of the rich legacy of Japanese art. Expanded timelines and glossaries, updated bibliographies, and color maps provide convenient study resources for readers. In Book 3, materials on the Euro-American encounter have been augmented with text and illustrations. To facilitate the transition from Book 3 to Book 4, we have added to the latter an introductory summary of the Renaissance and the Reformation. Other changes of organization and emphasis have been made in response to the bountiful suggestions of readers.

Acknowledgments

Writing *The Humanistic Tradition* has been an exercise in humility. Without the assistance of learned friends and colleagues, assembling a book of this breadth would have been an impossible task. James H. Dormon read all parts of the manuscript and made extensive and substantive editorial suggestions; as his colleague, best friend, and wife, I am most deeply indebted to him. I owe thanks to the following faculty members of the University of Southwestern Louisiana: for literature, Allen David Barry, Darrell Bourque, C. Harry Bruder, John W. Fiero, Emilio F. Garcia, Doris Meriwether, and Patricia K. Rickels; for history, Ora-Wes S. Cady, John Moore, Bradley Pollack, and Thomas D. Schoonover; for philosophy, Steve Giambrone and Robert T. Kirkpatrick; for geography, Tim Reilly; for the sciences, Mark Konikoff and John R. Meriwether; and for music, James Burke and Robert F. Schmalz.

The following readers and viewers generously shared their insights in matters of content and style: Michael K. Aakhus (University of Southern Indiana), Vaughan B. Baker (University of Southwestern Louisiana), Katherine Charlton (Mt. San Antonio Community College), Bessie Chronaki (Central Piedmont Community College), Debora A. Drehen (Florida Community College – Jacksonville), Paula Drewek (Macomb Community College), William C. Gentry (Henderson State University), Kenneth Ganza (Colby College), Ellen Hofman (Highline Community College), Burton Raffel (University of Southwestern Louisiana), Frank La Rosa (San Diego City College), George Rogers (Stonehill College), Douglas P. Sjoquist (Lansing Community College), Howard V. Starks (Southeastern Oklahoma State University), Ann Wakefield (Academy of the Sacred Heart – Grand Coteau), Sylvia White (Florida Community College – Jacksonville), and Audrey Wilson (Florida State University).

The University of Southwestern Louisiana facilitated my lengthy commitment to this project with two Summer Faculty Research Grants. I am indebted also to the University Honors Program and to the secretarial staff of the Department of History and Philosophy. The burden of preparing the second edition has been considerably lightened by the able and spirited assistance of Rosemary Bradley, Associate Publisher at Brown and Benchmark; and by the editorial efficiency of Melanie White at Calmann and King Limited. Finally, I am deeply grateful to my students; their sense of wonder and enthusiasm for learning are continuing reminders of why this book was written.

In the preparation of the second edition, I have benefited from the suggestions and comments generously offered by numerous readers, only some of whom are listed below. I am indebted to the various members of four fine Humanities "teams" – those at Hampton College (Hampton, Virginia), Kean College (Union, New Jersey), Thiel College (Greenville, Pennsylvania), and Tallahassee Community College (Florida). Special thanks go to Enid Housty at Hampton, James R. Bloomfield at Thiel, and Jim Davis and Roy Barineau at Tallahassee. Useful guidance for the revision was provided by other members of these departments including Muntaz Ahmad and Mabel Khawaja (Hampton); Elizabeth Kirby, Ursula Morgan, and Elizabeth Stein (Tallahassee); and also Elizabeth Folger Pennington (Santa Fe Community College).

Special thanks also to anthropologists Karen Davis (Marygrove College) and Jon Gibson (University of Southwestern Louisiana) for updating the pages on pre-history; and to Charles Muenchow (Tallahassee Community College) for his keen insights into the religious life of the ancient world; also to Nina R. Ritchie (Carl Albert State College) and Bruce W. Hozeski (Ball State University) for reviewing the final manuscript of Book 1.

SUPPLEMENTS FOR THE INSTRUCTOR

A number of useful supplements are available to instructors using *The Humanistic Tradition*. Please contact your Brown & Benchmark representative or call 1-800-338 5371 to obtain these resources, or to ask for further details.

Audiocassettes

Two ninety-minute audiocassettes containing a total of forty-five musical selections have been designed exclusively for use with *The Humanistic Tradition*. Cassette One corresponds to the music listening selections discussed in Books 1–3 and Cassette Two contains the music in Books 4–6. Each selection on the cassettes is discussed in the text and includes a voice introduction for easier location. Instructors may obtain copies of the cassettes for classroom use by calling 1-800-338 5371. Individual cassettes may be purchased separately; however, upon the request of instructors who place book orders, Cassette One or Two can be packaged with any of the six texts, so that students may use the musical examples *along with* the text.

Slide Sets

A set of 50 book-specific slides is available to adopters of *The Humanistic Tradition*. These slides have been especially selected to include many of the less well-known images in the books, and will be a useful complement to your present slide resources. Please contact your Brown & Benchmark representative for further details.

A larger set of 200 book-specific slides is available for purchase from Sandak, Inc. For further information, please contact Sandak, 180 Harvard Avenue, Stamford, CT 06902 (phone 1-800-343-2806, fax 203-967-2445).

Instructor's Resource Manual

The Instructor's Resource Manual, written by Paul Antal of Front Range Community College, Boulder, and Regis University, Denver, is designed to assist instructors as they plan and prepare for classes. Course outlines and sample syllabi for both semester and quarter systems are included. The chapter summaries emphasize key themes and topics that give focus to the primary source readings. The study questions for each chapter may be removed and copied as handouts for student discussion or written assignments. The *Factual Questions* allow students to recapture the important points of each chapter, while the *Challenge Questions* force students to think more deeply and critically about the subject matter.

The Test Item File, previously at the end of the manual, has been revised and expanded, and is now divided by chapter. Each chapter also has a correlation list that directs instructors to the appropriate music examples, slides, transparencies, and software sections of the other supplements. A list of suggested videotapes, recordings, videodiscs and their suppliers is included.

MicroTest III

The questions in the test item file are available on MicroTest III, a powerful but easy-to-use test generating program by Chariot Software Group. MicroTest is available for DOS, Windows, and Macintosh personal computers. With MicroTest, an instructor can easily select the questions from the test item file and print a test and answer key. You can customize questions, headings, and instructions, you can add or import questions of your own, and with the Windows and Macintosh versions, you can print your test in a choice of fonts if your printer supports them. Instructors can obtain a copy of MicroTest III by contacting your local Brown & Benchmark sales representative or by phoning Educational Resources at 1-800-338-5371.

Call-In/Mail-In/Fax Service

You may use Brown & Benchmark's convenient call-in/mail-in/FAX service to generate tests. Using this test item file, select the questions to include in the customized test. Then simply call (1-800-338-5371), mail (Brown & Benchmark Publishers/25 Kessel Court/Madison, WI 53711), or FAX (608-277-7351) your request to Educational Resources. Within two working days of receiving your order, Brown & Benchmark will send by first-class mail (or FAX), a test master, a student answer sheet, and an answer key for fast and easy grading.

Brown & Benchmark *Humanities Transparencies*

A set of 71 acetate transparencies is available with *The Humanistic Tradition*. These show examples of art concepts, architectural styles, art media, maps, musical notation, musical styles, and musical elements.

Culture 2.0 ©

Developed by Cultural Resources, Inc., for courses in interdisciplinary humanities, Culture 2.0 © is a fascinating journey into humanity's cultural achievements on Hypercard © software. Available in either IBM PC or Macintosh formats, this seven-disk program allows students to explore the achievements of humanity through essays, almanacs, visual, or musical examples. Each time period contains historical, political, religious, philosophical, artistic, and musical categories, creating an interactive, Socratic method of learning for the students. Culture 2.0 © also features note-taking capabilities, report capabilities, and a student workbook for more guided learning. Contact your Brown & Benchmark representative for preview disks or ordering information.

	To 10,000 B.C.E.	8000	4000	2000	1000

WORLD EVENTS

PALEOLITHIC culture
5 million–10,000
Australopithecus uses
stone tools and weapons

ICE AGE ca. 3 million–10,000

NEANDERTHAL culture
ca. 30,000–10,000

Evolution of
Homo sapiens
ca. 35,000

NEOLITHIC culture:
food produced,
villages formed,
pottery invented ca. 5000

Birth of
civilization |—— BRONZE AGE ——|
Bronze weapons developed   Hittites introduce iron
                                      |———— IRON AGE ————▶

Mesopotamia: |—— SUMER PERIOD ——|—— BABYLONIAN PERIOD ——

Egypt (Kingdoms): |— OLD —|— MIDDLE —|— NEW —

Crete: |—— MINOAN ——|
                        Dorian
                        migrations

Greece: |— MYCENAEAN —|
                    Trojan War

Canaan: |————————
Hebrews migrate   Moses   Solom
to Canaan

India: |— INDUS CIVILIZATION —|—— EARLY ——
          Aryan   VEDIC AGE
          invasion   Sanskrit
                     caste system

China: |—— YELLOW RIVER VALLEY ——|—— SHANG DYNASTY ——
                CIVILIZATION
             Chinese calligraphy

Migrations to the
Americas ca. 12,000

The Americas: |——————— PRE-COLUMB

LITERATURE AND PHILOSOPHY

Pictographic   *Epic of Gilgamesh*   *Babylonian Creation*
script

Hieroglyphs   Hammurabi's
  Cuneiform script   Code

Pyramid texts   Egyptian Book   Linear B
of Egypt   of the Dead   Script
                                                 in Crete and
  Hymn to the Aten   Greece

Vedas in India

Oracle bones in China

VISUAL ARTS AND ARCHITECTURE

Cave art at   Stonehenge
Lascaux and Altimira   Palette of   Sumerian ziggurats   Portrait of
30,000–10,000   Narmer   *Standard of Ur*   Nefertiti
                                       Statues at Tell
"Venus of   Neolithic   Egyptian   Asmar   Coffin of
Willendorf"   beaker from   Pyramids   Tutankhamen
                        Susa
                                                Palace at   Lion Gate
                                                Knossos   at Mycenae

                                       Cycladic figure   *Minoan
                                                          Priestess*

                                                Chinese   Chinese ritual
                                                jade disks bronzes

MUSIC AND DANCE

Sumerian and   *Hymn to the Aten*
Egyptian
rattles, harps,
and lyres

Vedas (sung recitation)

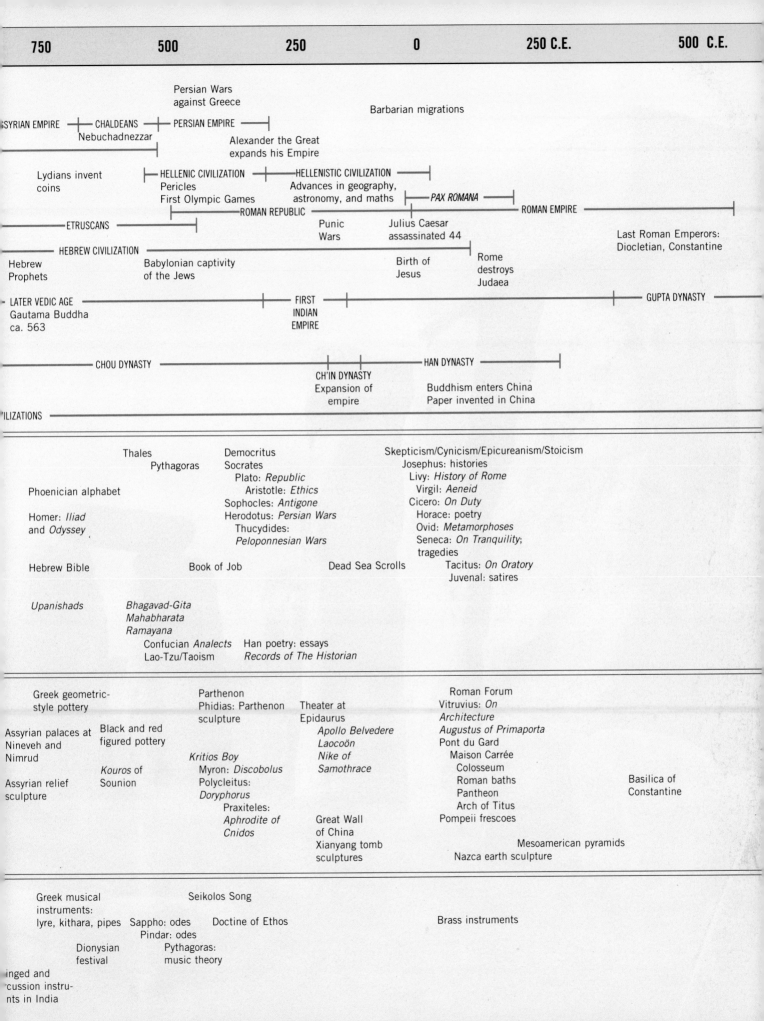

| 750 | 500 | 250 | 0 | 250 C.E. | 500 C.E. |

Persian Wars against Greece

Barbarian migrations

ASSYRIAN EMPIRE — CHALDEANS — PERSIAN EMPIRE
Nebuchadnezzar
Alexander the Great expands his Empire

Lydians invent coins
HELLENIC CIVILIZATION — HELLENISTIC CIVILIZATION
Pericles
First Olympic Games
Advances in geography, astronomy, and maths
PAX ROMANA
ROMAN EMPIRE
ROMAN REPUBLIC
ETRUSCANS
Punic Wars
Julius Caesar assassinated 44
Last Roman Emperors: Diocletian, Constantine

HEBREW CIVILIZATION
Hebrew Prophets
Babylonian captivity of the Jews
Birth of Jesus
Rome destroys Judaea

LATER VEDIC AGE
Gautama Buddha ca. 563
FIRST INDIAN EMPIRE
GUPTA DYNASTY

CHOU DYNASTY
CH'IN DYNASTY
Expansion of empire
HAN DYNASTY
Buddhism enters China
Paper invented in China

CIVILIZATIONS

Thales
Pythagoras
Democritus
Socrates
Plato: *Republic*
Aristotle: *Ethics*
Sophocles: *Antigone*
Herodotus: *Persian Wars*
Thucydides: *Peloponnesian Wars*
Skepticism/Cynicism/Epicureanism/Stoicism
Josephus: histories
Livy: *History of Rome*
Virgil: *Aeneid*
Cicero: *On Duty*
Horace: poetry
Ovid: *Metamorphoses*
Seneca: *On Tranquility*; tragedies

Phoenician alphabet

Homer: *Iliad* and *Odyssey*

Hebrew Bible
Book of Job
Dead Sea Scrolls
Tacitus: *On Oratory*
Juvenal: satires

Upanishads
Bhagavad-Gita
Mahabharata
Ramayana
Confucian *Analects*
Lao-Tzu/Taoism
Han poetry: essays
Records of The Historian

Greek geometric-style pottery

Assyrian palaces at Nineveh and Nimrud

Assyrian relief sculpture

Black and red figured pottery

Kouros of Sounion

Parthenon
Phidias: Parthenon sculpture

Kritios Boy
Myron: *Discobolus*
Polycleitus: *Doryphorus*
Praxiteles: *Aphrodite of Cnidos*

Theater at Epidaurus
Apollo Belvedere
Laocoön
Nike of Samothrace

Great Wall of China
Xianyang tomb sculptures

Roman Forum
Vitruvius: *On Architecture*
Augustus of Primaporta
Pont du Gard
Maison Carrée
Colosseum
Roman baths
Pantheon
Arch of Titus
Pompeii frescoes

Mesoamerican pyramids
Nazca earth sculpture

Basilica of Constantine

Greek musical instruments: lyre, kithara, pipes
Sappho: odes
Pindar: odes
Dionysian festival
Seikolos Song
Doctine of Ethos
Pythagoras: music theory
Brass instruments

stringed and percussion instruments in India

PART

I

PREHISTORY AND THE FIRST CIVILIZATIONS

The first chapters in the history of human life are often regarded as the most exciting. They present us with a gigantic puzzle that requires piecing together numerous fragments of information, most of which, like buried treasure, have been dug out of the earth. Reassembled, these fragments reveal the progress of humankind from its prehistoric beginnings through the cultural history of the ancient civilizations of Egypt, Mesopotamia, India, and China. The individual histories of these civilizations will not concern us here; rather, we shall review patterns of culture that shaped the humanistic tradition.

Chapter 1 deals with prehistory – the period before written records – and with the major features surrounding the birth of civilization. The development of an increasingly sophisticated technology and the evolution of early forms of social and religious organization proceeded from our early ancestors' efforts to meet the challenges of their environment and to ensure human survival.

Chapter 2, "Ancient Civilizations: People and the Gods," examines the ways in which the people of ancient Egypt, Mesopotamia, India, and China tried to explain the origins of life, the operations of nature, and the mysteries of death. It surveys the nature deities of Egypt and Mesopotamia, and compares the attitudes of each civilization toward the question of life after death. Chapter 2 also explores Hebrew monotheism, Hindu pantheism (as it evolved in ancient India), and Taoism, which emerged in ancient China.

The third chapter, entitled "Ancient Civilizations: People and the Law," investigates various early forms of political authority and individual systems of law and order. It examines ancient Egyptian, Babylonian, Hebrew, and Chinese efforts to establish meaningful bonds between the secular and spiritual realms, between rulers and their subjects, and among the inhabitants of civilized communities. Literature, architecture, and art – the rich legacies of ancient history – provide the primary sources for our understanding of the dynamic interaction between people and nature, people and the gods, and people and the law.

(opposite) Detail of Figure 1.10 Stonehenge, Wiltshire, England, ca. 2000 B.C.E. © English Heritage Photographic Library.

1

Prehistory and the Birth of Civilization: People and Nature

Whether one believes that the beginnings of life were divinely generated or came about spontaneously, it is clear that human beings emerged as part of a long evolutionary process. The story of human evolution is a record of the behavioral adaptation of human beings to our surroundings. It is the last chapter in a long history that begins with the simplest forms of life that lived in the primeval seas hundreds of millions of years ago and culminates in the astonishing achievements of modern human beings. Throughout our short history on this planet, human beings have faced the challenges of the environment and of an often hostile geography and a threatening climate. Meeting such environmental challenges was the primary occupation of the earliest inhabitants.

Prehistory

The study of history before the appearance of written records, a discipline that originated in France around 1860, is called **prehistory**. In the absence of written records, prehistorians draw on the disciplines of geology, paleontology, anthropology, archeology, and ethnography. Each of these disciplines provides a unique kind of information about the past. Using instruments that measure the radioactive atoms remaining in the organic elements of the earth's strata, geologists are able to determine the approximate age of the earth. They estimate that our planet is about 4.5 billion years old. Paleontologists examine fossil remains and describe the nature of earth's earliest living creatures. Anthropologists study human biology, society, and cultural practices throughout all times and places: archeologists uncover, analyze, and interpret the material remains of past societies in order to determine how such people lived. Finally, a special group of cultural anthropologists known as ethnographers study surviving, preliterate societies. All of these specialists contribute to producing a detailed picture of humankind's first environment.

Geologists report that the earliest organic remains in the earth's strata are almost four billion years old. From one-celled organisms that inhabited the watery terrain of the ancient planet, higher forms of life evolved. Some hundred million years ago, dinosaurs stalked the earth, becoming extinct possibly because they failed to adapt to climatic changes. Eighty million years ago, mammals roamed the earth, and although even approximate dates are much disputed, it is generally agreed that between five million and ten million years ago, ancestral humans first appeared in eastern and southern Africa. The exact genealogy of humankind is still a matter of intense debate. However, in the last fifty years, anthropologists have clarified some aspects of the relationship between human beings and earlier primates – the group of mammals that today includes monkeys, apes, and human beings. Fossil evidence reveals structural similarities between human beings and chimpanzees (and other apes); and biochemical research indicates that human beings and chimpanzees share genetic similarities and identical hemoglobin.

Paleolithic ("Old Stone Age") Culture* (ca. 5 million – 10,000 B.C.E.**)

Early in the twentieth century, anthropologists discovered the fossil remains of **hominids**, protohuman creatures who walked the earth some five or more million years ago. Hominids lived in packs; they gathered seeds, berries, wild fruits, and vegetables, and possibly even hunted the beasts of the African savannas. Between two and three million years ago, a South African variety of hominid known as *Australopithecus*

---

*The terms Paleolithic and Neolithic do not describe uniform time periods, but, rather, cultures that appeared at different times in different parts of the world.
**Dates are designated as B.C.E., "Before the Christian (or Common) Era," or C.E., "Christian (or Common) Era."

were using sharp-edged pebbles for chopping and skinning. *Australopithecus* flourished for three million years with very little change, but eventually early human beings with larger brain cavities and greater locomotive abilities emerged. These creatures, of the genus *Homo* and the species *habilis* (thus "tool-making human"), fashioned stone and bone tools to serve specific purposes. Tool making represents the beginning of **culture**, which, in its most basic sense, proceeds from the manipulation of nature. The making of tools — humankind's earliest technology — constitutes the primary act of extending control over nature and the most basic example of problem-solving behavior.

Approximately 1.7 million years ago, *Homo erectus* ("upright human") was making tools that were more varied and efficient than those used by earlier human beings. These included hand-axes, cleavers, chisels, and a wide variety of choppers. The hand-axe became the standard tool for chopping, digging, cutting, and scraping. Fire, too, became an important part of the early culture of humankind, providing safety, warmth, and a means of cooking food. Although it is still not certain how long ago fire was used, *Homo erectus* sites outside of Africa suggest that fire was a regular feature in the hearths of caves in Europe and East Asia. Some one hundred thousand years ago, a group of human ancestors with anatomical features and brain-size similar to our own appeared in the Neander Valley in Düsseldorf, Germany. The burial of human dead among Neanderthal folk and the practice of including tools, weapons, and flowers in a number of Neanderthal graves are evidence of self-conscious, symbol-making humans known as *Homo sapiens*. Characterized by memory and foresight, these archaic forerunners of modern-day humans were the first to demonstrate — by their ritual treatment of the deceased — a self-conscious concern with human mortality. That concern may have involved respect for or fear of the dead and the anticipation of life after death.

The development of the human brain in both size and complexity was integral to the evolution of *Homo sapiens*: Over millions of years, the average brain size of the human being grew to roughly three times the size of the gorilla's. Equally critical were changes that included the growth of more complex motor capacities. Gradually, verbal methods of communication complemented the nonverbal ones shared by animals and protohumans. We do not know at what point speech replaced more primitive sound codes, but over a process of time our prehistoric ancestors came to use spoken language to objectify experience and transmit patterns of culture for use in future generations. Capable of communicating abstract concepts to others by means of language, *Homo sapiens* distinguished themselves from other primates. Chimpanzees are capable of binding two poles together to gather a bunch of bananas hanging at the top of a tree, but, short of immediate physical demonstration, they have no means of passing on this technique to subsequent generations of chimpanzees. *Homo sapiens*, on the other hand, have produced symbol systems that enable them to transmit culture. Thus, in the fullest sense, culture requires both the manipulation of nature and the formulation of a symbolic language for its transmission.

Paleolithic culture evolved during a period of climatic fluctuation called the Ice Age. Between roughly three million and ten thousand years ago, at least four large glacial advances covered the area north of the equator. As hunters and gatherers, Paleolithic people were forced to either migrate or to adapt to changing climatic conditions. Ultimately, the ingenuity and imagination of *Homo sapiens* were responsible for the fact that they fared better than other creatures, many of whom became extinct during this era.

Early modern humans devised an extensive technology of stone and bone tools and weapons that increased their comfort, safety, and, almost certainly their confidence. A seven-foot stone-tipped spear enabled a hunter to attack an animal at a distance of six or more yards. Other spear-throwing devices increased the leverage of the arm and thus doubled that range. Spears and harpoons, and — toward the end of the Ice Age — bows and arrows, extended the efficacy and safety of Paleolithic people, just as axes and knives enhanced their food-preparing abilities.

During the last fifty years, archeologists have discovered paintings and carvings on the walls of caves and the surfaces of rocks at Paleolithic sites in Europe, Africa, Australia, and North America. Over one hundred cave dwellings in southwestern France include paintings that reveal a high degree of artistic and technical sophistication. Executed ten to thirty thousand years ago, these images provide a visual record of such long-extinct animals as the hairy mammoth and the woolly rhinoceros; but equally important, they document the culture of a hunting people. Colored with earth pigments and shaded with bitumen and burnt coal, the realistically-depicted animals are often shown wounded by spears and lances (Figure **1.1**). What was the purpose and function of these vivid images, often drawn one over another, with no apparent regard for clarity or composition? Located in the most inaccessible regions of the caves, it is unlikely that they were intended as decorations or even as records of the hunt. It seems likely that, like tools and weapons, cave art reflects the human attempt to control nature. The role of cave art as part of a hunting ritual is suggested by the following description of Pygmy life in the African Congo recorded by the twentieth-century German ethnographer Leo Frobenius.

Figure 1.1 Hall of Bulls, left wall, Lascaux caves, Dordogne, France, ca. 15,000—10,000 B.C.E. French Government Tourist Office.

READING 1
The Story of Rock Picture Research

In 1905 we obtained further evidence from a Congo race, hunting tribes, later famous as the "pygmies," which had been driven from the plateau to the refuge of the Congo [an area in South-central Africa bordering the Congo River]. We met in the jungle district between Kassai and Luebonn. Several of their members, three men and a woman, guided the expedition for almost a week and were soon on friendly terms with us. One afternoon, finding our larder rather depleted, I asked one of them to shoot me an antelope, surely an easy job for such an expert hunter. He and his fellows looked at me in astonishment and then burst out with the answer that, yes, they'd do it gladly, but that it was naturally out of the question for that day since no preparations had been made. After a long palaver they declared themselves ready to make these at sunrise. Then they went off as though searching for a good site and finally settled on a high place on a nearby hill.

As I was eager to learn what their preparations consisted of, I left camp before dawn and crept through the bush to the open place which they had sought out the night before. The pygmies appeared in the twilight, the woman with them. The men crouched on the ground, plucked a small square free of weeds and smoothed it over with their hands. One of them then drew something in the cleared space with his forefinger, while his companions murmured some kind of formula or incantation. Then a waiting silence. The sun rose on the horizon. One of the men, an arrow on his bowstring, took his place beside the square. A few minutes later the rays of the sun fell on the drawing at his feet. In that same second the woman stretched out her arms to the sun, shouting words I did not understand, the man shot the arrow and the woman cried out again. Then the three men bounded off through the bush while the woman stood for a few minutes and then went slowly towards our camp. As she disappeared I came forward and, looking down at the smoothed square of sand, saw the drawing of an antelope four hands long. From the antelope's neck protruded the pygmy's arrow.

I went back for my camera intending to photograph the drawing before the men returned. But the woman, when she saw what I was up to, made such a fuss that I desisted. We broke camp and continued our march. The drawing remained unphotographed. That afternoon the hunters appeared with a fine "buschbock," an arrow in its throat. They delivered their booty and then went off to the hill we had left behind us, carrying a fistful of the antelope's hair and a gourd full of its blood. Two days passed before they caught up with us again. Then, in the evening, as we were drinking a foamy palm wine, the oldest of the three men —

I had turned to him because he seemed to have more confidence in me than the others — told me that he and his companions had returned on the scene of their preparations for the hunt in order to daub the picture with the slain antelope's hair and blood, to withdraw the arrow and then to wipe the whole business away. The meaning of the formula was not clear, but I did gather that, had they not done as they did, the blood of the dead antelope would have destroyed them. The "wiping out," too, had to take place at sunrise.

———————◆———————

As Frobenius' observations suggest, the ritual enactment of the hunt — accompanied by the proper images, words, and gestures — was a form of sympathetic magic invoked to bring about a successful result. It is likely that cave paintings once were a part of collective rituals similarly designed to control nature. Securing the name or physical likeness of an object allowed one to exercise control over that object. Such faith in the power to alter reality through symbols has been basic to religious ceremonies throughout the history of humankind, but it was especially important to a culture in which control over nature was crucial to physical survival. A motif commonly found on cave walls is the image of the hunter's hand, created in negative relief by blowing or splattering color around a real human hand placed against the walls surface (Figure 1.2). Since the hand was the hunter's most powerful ally in making and wielding the weapon, it is fitting that it appears enshrined in the sacred precinct amidst the quarry of the hunt. Although the precise meaning of many of the markings on prehistoric cave walls remains a matter of speculation, cave art may be understood as our early ancestors' attempts to control their environment and thus ensure their survival.

Along with representations of animals and hands, images of women appear frequently in Paleolithic art. Females contributed to the process of securing food and provided for the well-being of the tribe. The Pygmy ritual described by Frobenius suggests a clear division of labor even in the performance of ritual: As the male shoots the arrow into the image of the antelope, his female companion issues special words and gestures. Similar kinds of shared responsibility probably characterized humankind's earliest societies, where women served as healers and nurturers. Moreover, since the female assured the continuity of the tribe by her role as childbearer, she assumed a special importance within the community. In ancient mythology, the earth

Figure 1.2 Spotted Horses and Negative Hand Imprints, Pech-Merle caves, Lot, France, ca. 15,000–10,000 B.C.E. Length 11ft. 2in. Studio Laborie, Bergerac.

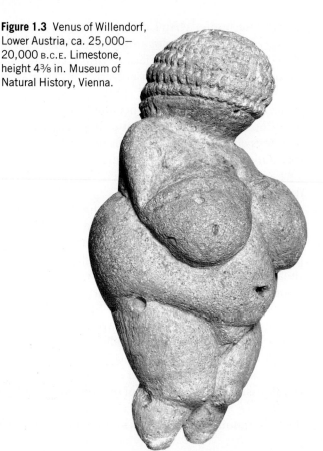

Figure 1.3 Venus of Willendorf, Lower Austria, ca. 25,000–20,000 B.C.E. Limestone, height 4⅜ in. Museum of Natural History, Vienna.

mother or mother-goddess epitomized the procreative force. Her association with fertility is suggested by the numerous examples of female statuettes with swollen breasts and large abdomens, indicating pregnancy (Figure 1.3).

Neolithic ("New Stone Age") Culture (ca. 8000 – 4000 B.C.E.)

Paleolithic people lived at the mercy of nature. However, during the transitional (or Mesolithic) phase that occurred shortly after 10,000 B.C.E., people discovered that the seeds of wild grains and fruits might be planted to grow food. Between roughly 10,000 and 8000 B.C.E., hunters and gatherers became farmers and food producers. A dynamic new phase in the development of human culture – Neolithic (or New Stone Age) culture – emerged. Food production enabled groups of people to settle in one place, to raise crops such as wheat and barley, to build permanent shelters, and to establish farming communities. Neolithic folk domesticated wild animals. They raised goats, pigs, cattle, and sheep that provided regular sources of food and valuable by-products like wool. The transition from the hunting-gathering phase of human subsistence to the agricultural-herding phase was a revolutionary

Figure 1.4 Isometric reconstruction of Neolithic house at Hassuna (level 4). The Oriental Institute, The University of Chicago.

HOUSE
AT LEVEL IV
SUGGESTED RECONSTRUCTION.

sickles. Polished stone tools, some designed especially for farming, replaced the cruder, less sophisticated tools of Paleolithic people. Ancient Japanese hunter-gatherers seem to have produced the world's oldest known pottery – handcoiled and fired clay vessels. But it was in the Neolithic Near East that the domestic crafts of pottery and weaving came to flourish. Clay receptacles, often decorated with abstract motifs (Figure 1.5), were used to preserve surplus foods for the lean months, and woven rugs provided comfort against the wind, rain, and cold. Homemakers, artisans, and shepherds played significant roles in Neolithic society.

Agricultural life stimulated a new awareness of the seasons and seasonal change and a keen preoccupation with such powers of nature as the sun and rain. The earth's fertility and the natural cycle of birth and death were the principal concerns of the farming culture. A hand-modeled clay figurine from a Neolithic grave in Tlatilco in central Mexico presents an astonishing image of the eternal duality of life and death (Figure 1.6). On one side, the realistically modeled figure appears plump and vigorous, but on the other, the flesh is stripped away to reveal the skeletal remains of the body. Although the precise function of this object

Figure 1.5 Beaker painted with goats, dogs, and long-necked birds, Susa, S.W. Iran, ca. 5000–4000 B.C.E. Baked clay, height 11¼ in. Louvre, Paris. Photo: © R.M.N.

development in human social organization because it marked the shift from a nomadic to a sedentary way of life.

Neolithic sites excavated by archeologists in the Near East (especially Israel, Jordan, Turkey, Iran, and Iraq), the Far East (China and Japan), and some dating as late as 1000 B.C.E. in Meso-America, reveal villages incorporating a number of mud- and limestone-faced huts, humankind's earliest architecture (Figure 1.4). At Jericho, in present-day Israel, massive defense walls surrounded the town. In Jarmo, in northern Iraq, a community of more than 150 people farmed with stone

Figure 1.6 Eternal duality of life and death, figurine, Tlatilco, Mexico, 1700–1300 B.C.E. Clay, height approx. 12 in. Museo Regional de Antropologia e Historia, Villahermosa, Tabasco. Richard Stirling/Photo © Ancient Art and Architecture Collection, Harrow.

Figure 1.7 Cycladic figurine, 2400–2000 B.C.E. Marble, height 30¼ in. Reproduced by courtesy of the Trustees of the British Museum, London.

remains a mystery, its startling reference to the interrelationship of life and death reflects a profound sensitivity to temporal decay and to the cyclical aspect of nature.

The large number of female statuettes found in Neolithic graves suggests that Neolithic religion featured the worship of fertility goddesses along with rites focusing on seasonal regeneration. We can only guess at how such statues were used, but they may have been associated with fertility cults that ensured successful childbirth and bountiful crops. In contrast with the so-called Venus of Willendorf (see Figure 1.3), whose sexual characteristics are deliberately exaggerated, a marble statuette from the Cyclades (a group of Greek islands in the Aegean Sea) takes an abstract and highly stylized form (Figure **1.7**). Though lacking the expressive fleshiness of the Paleolithic Venus, the Cycladic figure probably played a similar role in rituals that sought the blessings of mother earth.

To farming peoples, seasonal change – a primary fact of subsistence – was associated with death and rebirth. The dead, whose return to the earth put them in closer touch with the forces of nature, received careful burial. Neolithic folk marked graves with crudely cut stones that form a womblike superstructure (Figure **1.8**). **Megaliths**("great stones") might be placed upright in circles or multiple rows and capped by horizontal slabs, a system exemplary of the most basic type of architectural construction: **post and lintel** (Figure **1.9 a** and **b**). Such structures seem to have served both as burial sites and as temple sanctuaries. At Stonehenge, in southeast England, an elaborate group of stone circles forms one of the most mysterious and impressive monuments of the Neolithic Era (Figures

Figure 1.8 Neolithic burial site, Dolmen (upright stones supporting a horizontal slab), Great Ormes Head, Wales. Ancient Art and Architecture Collection, Harrow.

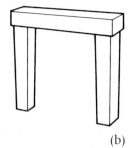

(a)

(b)

Figure 1.9 Stonehenge, Salisbury Plain, Wiltshire, England, ca. 2000 B.C.E. Diameter, 97 ft. Aerofilms Ltd., London. (Right) Post and lintel construction.

Figure 1.10 Stonehenge trilithons (lintel-topped pairs of stones at center). Height approx. 24 ft. (including lintel). © English Heritage Photographic Library.

1.9a and **1.10**). Twenty-foot megaliths, some weighing four tons, were dragged hundreds of miles to complete a temple complex used to predict the movements of the sun and moon – information that would have been essential to an agricultural society. A special stone that stands apart from the complex marks the point at which the sun rises at the midsummer solstice (the longest day of the year). Other Neolithic projects are equally monumental. In the coastal deserts of Peru, enormous earthwork lines form geometric figures, spirals, and bird, animal, and insect designs the meaning and function of which are yet to be deciphered (Figure **1.11**). So extraordinary are these earthworks that some modern writers have attributed their existence to the activity of beings from outer space – just as medieval people thought Stonehenge the work of Merlin, a legendary magician. The total evidence of Neolithic ingenuity, however, severely challenges the credibility of such theories. Indeed, recent scholarship suggests that the Peruvian earthworks may have served as starmaps or astronomical calendars designed to help ancient farmers determine dates for planting crops.

The Birth of Civilization

Around 4000 B.C.E., a new chapter in the history of humankind began. As Neolithic villages grew in population and size and produced surplus food and goods, they began to trade with neighboring villages. The demands of increased production and trade went hand in hand with the division and specialization of labor and with the development of such technological inventions as the wheel, the plow, and the solar calendar, all of which spurred economic efficiency. By 4000 B.C.E., wheeled carts transported people, food, and goods, and sailboats used the natural resources of wind and water for similar purposes. Simple Neolithic villages grew in size and complexity to become cities.

The momentous birth of civilization occurred earliest in Mesopotamia, a fertile area that lay between the Tigris and Euphrates Rivers of the Near Eastern land mass (Map 1.1). Mesopotamia formed the eastern arc of the Fertile Crescent which stretched westward to the Nile delta. At the southeastern perimeter of the Fertile Crescent, about a dozen cities made up the territories of

Figure 1.11 Monkey figure, Nazca Valley, Peru, ca. 100 B.C.E. Photo: © Tony Morrison, South American Pictures.

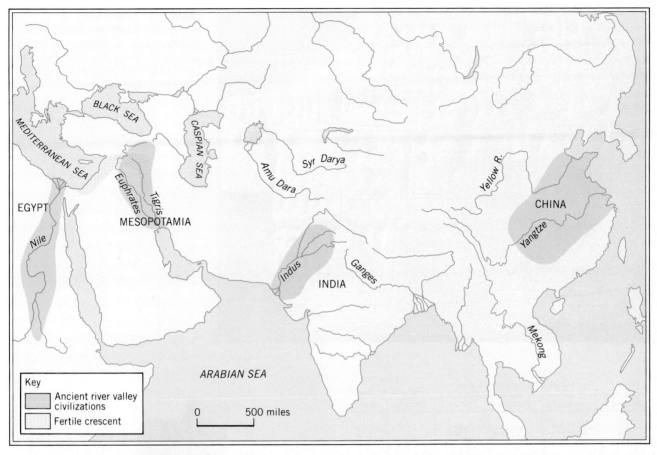

Map 1.1 Ancient River Valley Civilizations.

Sumer, the earliest civilization known to history. Soon after the rise of Sumer, around 3500 B.C.E., Egyptian civilization emerged along the Nile River in northeast Africa. In India, the first cities arose in the valley of the Indus River that runs through the northwest portion of that continent. Chinese civilization was born in the northern part of China's vast central plain, watered by the Yellow River. The shift from village to city life in these four river valleys was not simultaneous. In China, this development seems to have taken place at least a thousand years later than in the ancient Near East.

The cultural patterns of early civilizations were more complex than those of Neolithic villages. Specialization and division of labor enhanced productivity and encouraged trade. Trade became basic to urban economy; and as the numerous transactions of a flourishing economy could not be committed to memory, it became necessary to devise some method of record keeping – hence, the invention of writing. The earliest form of writing comes from Sumer around 3500 B.C.E., where simple drawings, or **pictographs**, were inscribed on clay tablets (Figure **1.12**). By 1900 B.C.E., these marks were transformed into wedge-shaped signs comprising a **cuneiform** script (Figure **1.13**). Of the thousands of clay tablets found in ancient

Mesopotamia, the largest number bear notations concerning production and trade. In addition to these inventories and business accounts, there are cuneiform texts that commemorate special events, record religious practices, and describe political life.

The development of a written language is often regarded as the defining feature of "civilization," but it is only one of many inventions mothered by necessity. At approximately the same time that systems of writing emerged, metal began to be used in place of stone and bone. Metallurgy, first practiced in Asia Minor around 4000 B.C.E., afforded a significant extension of control over nature by providing harder and more durable tools and weapons. At first, copper ore was extracted from surface deposits, but eventually metalsmiths devised methods of mining and smelting ores. The result was bronze, an alloy of copper and tin that proved far superior to stone or bone in strength and durability. Since metal resources were often located far apart, travel and far-flung trade were essential to Bronze-Age cultures. Moreover, metallurgy was a time-consuming process that required specialized training and the division of labor. Bronze weapons, therefore, were costly, hence available only to a small and well-to-do minority of the population. This minority formed a

Figure 1.12 Reverse side of a pictographic tablet from Jamdat Nasr, near Kish, Iraq, ca. 3000 B.C.E., listing accounts involving animals and various commodities including bread and beer. Ashmolean Museum, Oxford.

Earliest pictographs (3000 B.C.)	Denotation of pictographs	Pictographs in rotated position	Cuneiform signs ca. 1900 B.C.	Basic logographic values	
				Reading	Meaning
	Head and body of a man			lú	Man
	Head with mouth indicated			ka	Mouth
	Bowl of food			ninda	Food, bread
	Mouth + food			kú	To eat
	Stream of water			a	Water
	Mouth + water			nag	To drink
	Fish			kua	Fish
	Bird			mušen	Bird
	Head of an ass			anše	Ass
	Ear of barley			še	Barley

Figure 1.13 The development of Sumerian writing from a pictographic script to cuneiform script to a phonetic system. Adapted from Samuel Noah Kramer, "The Sumerians," Copyright © 1957 by Scientific American, Inc. All rights reserved.

Figure 1.14 Ceremonial vessel with a cover, Late Shang Dynasty, China, ca. 1000 B.C.E. Bronze, height 20 1/16 in. Freer Gallery of Art, Smithsonian Institution, Washington, D.C. Accession No. 30.26 AB.

Figure 1.15 The King of Lagash Leads His Phalanx into Battle. Detail of Eannatum's Stele of Victory from Telloh (Lagash), ca. 2800 B.C.E. Louvre, Paris. Giraudon/Art Resource, New York.

military elite who wielded power by virtue of superior arms. As the victory monument pictured in Figure **1.15** indicates, ancient Mesopotamian warriors were outfitted with bronze shields, helmets, and lances.

The technology of bronze casting spread throughout the ancient world. In ancient China, ritual vessels of bronze were used to offer food and drink to ancestral spirits. Such vessels were cast in sectional molds assembled around a solid central core (Figure 1.14). Legs and handles were cast separately and soldered on,

and all surfaces were ornamented with fantastic mythical animals. The stylized ducks, dragons, and mazelike spirals that adorn the surface of the wine vessel pictured in Figure 1.14 vividly convey the ancient Chinese view of the universe as animated by natural spirits.

Specialization of labor encouraged the development of different classes of workers with different types of authority. In early civilizations, the magician-priest who prepared the wine in the ritual vessel, the soldier

Figure 1.16 The Standard of Ur,
ca. 2700 B.C.E. Panel inlaid with shell,
lapis lazuli, and red limestone, approx. 8 × 19 in.
Reproduced by courtesy of the Trustees of the British Museum, London.

who protected the city, and the farmer who cultivated the field represented fairly distinct groups of people with unique duties and responsibilities to society as a whole. The "Standard of Ur," an object whose precise function in unknown, illustrates this division of labor in Mesopotamia around 2700 B.C.E. (Figure **1.16**). The three registers of this double-sided panel, executed in shell, mother-of-pearl, and **lapis lazuli**, describe events commemorating a Sumerian victory. On one side, the top and middle strips show the ruler and his soldiers taking prisoners, while the bottom one depicts horse-drawn chariots trampling the victims of war. On the reverse side of the panel, the rulers of the Sumerian community lift their goblets at a celebratory banquet

whose entertainers include a harpist and his female companion. The bottom registers record the transportation of goods and animals – the booty of war.

The birth of civilization came about not as a fleeting moment of change, but as a slow process of urban growth. As the political, economic, and religious institutions of ancient civilizations grew more complex, palaces, temples, and military defenses became essential to community welfare, as did irrigation, road building, and a wide variety of other activities. Civilization was made possible only by cooperation among those whose individual tasks – governing, trading, farming, and so on – contributed to communal survival.

The Iron Age

Any radical change in the technology of a given society has wide-reaching effects. Such was the case when the Hittites, a nomadic tribe using horse-drawn chariots and iron weapons, entered Asia Minor around 2000 B.C.E. The chariot gave Hittite warriors speed and mobility, while their iron weapons, which were cheaper to produce and more durable than those made of bronze, gave them clear military superiority. More durable tools meant increased agricultural production, which in turn supported increased population. And cheaper and stronger weapons meant larger, more efficient armies. By the first millennium B.C.E., war was no longer the monopoly of the elite. Equipped with iron weapons, the armies of the Assyrians (ca. 750–600 B.C.E), the Chaldeans (ca. 600–540 B.C.E), and the Persians (ca. 550–330 B.C.E.) conquered vast portions of Mesopotamia. One after the other, they imposed political control over territories outside their own natural boundaries – a practice known as **imperialism**. War and slavery – two salient characteristics of ancient history – were enterprises undertaken by human beings to establish control not simply over their environments, but over each other.

In the wake of the Iron Age, numerous small states emerged in ancient Mesopotamia. Some of these civilizations made major contributions to world culture. By 1000 B.C.E., the Phoenicians, an energetic trading culture located on the Mediterranean Sea, developed an alphabet of twenty-two signs that eventually replaced pictographic script. The Lydians, who succeeded the Hittites in Asia Minor, began the practice of minting coins during the seventh century B.C.E. And the Hebrews, whose history will be treated in the next chapters, developed unique religious beliefs and a code of moral law, both of which have survived for centuries.

SUMMARY

The story of our humanistic tradition begins in an unrecorded past, in the prehistory of our earliest ancestors as they struggled for survival in an environment they sought to control. Unlike lower forms of life, early human beings developed the ability to transmit information from generation to generation. Not only did these creatures manipulate nature to shape culture, but they devised ways of passing on that culture to their heirs.

Paleolithic people were tribal hunters and gatherers who controlled nature by means of stone and bone tools and weapons. Neolithic folk exercised considerably greater control over nature by learning how to produce food. Farming freed Neolithic people from the perils and uncertainties of nomadic life. After 4000 B.C.E., at the birth of civilization, river valleys in Mesopotamia, Egypt, northern India, and central China began to support urban centers with trading economies. Written systems of record keeping and a bronze technology are two hallmarks of these early civilizations. The development of iron around 2000 B.C.E. in ancient Mesopotamia represented yet another technological leap in the human extension of control over nature. By the operation of an increasingly refined abstract intelligence, and by means of ingenuity, imagination, and cooperation, the earliest human beings triumphed over nature and laid the foundations for our humanistic tradition.

GLOSSARY

culture   the sum total of those things (including traditions, techniques, material goods, and symbol systems) that people have invented, developed, and transmitted

cuneiform   ("wedge-shaped") a system of writing used in the ancient Near East and consisting of wedge-shaped characters impressed into clay by means of a reed stylus

hominid   any of a family of bipedal primate mammals, including modern humans and their ancestors, the earliest of which is *Australopithecus*

imperialism   the practice of extending rule or authority over the political and economic life in areas outside of one's natural or linguistic boundaries

lapis lazuli   a blue-colored semiprecious stone

megalith   a large, roughly shaped stone, often used in ancient architectural construction

pictograph   a pictorial symbol that makes up humankind's earliest systems of writing

post and lintel   the simplest form of architectural construction, consisting of vertical members (posts) and supporting horizontals (lintels); see Figure 1.9

prehistory   the study of history before written records

SUGGESTIONS FOR READING

Brown, M.H. *The Search for Eve.* New York: Harper, 1990.

Chiera, Edward. *They Wrote on Clay: The Babylonian Tablets Speak Today.* Chicago: Chicago University Press, 1938.

Dahlberg, Frances. *Woman the Gatherer.* New Haven, Conn.: Yale University Press, 1971.

Hadingham, E. *Lines to the Mountain Gods: Nazca and the Mysteries of Peru.* New York: Random House, 1987.

Hawkins, G.S. *Stonehenge Decoded.* New York: Dell, 1965.

Leakey, Richard. *Origins Reconsidered: In Search of What Makes Us Human.* New York: Doubleday, 1992.

Redman, C.L. *The Rise of Civilization: From Early Farmers to Urban Society in the Near East.* San Francisco: Freeman, 1987.

Ruspoli, Mario. *The Cave of Lascaux.* London: Thames and Hudson, 1987.

Sandars, N.K. *Prehistoric Art in Europe*, 2nd ed. Baltimore: Penguin, 1985.

Schwartz, Jeffrey. *What the Bones Tell Us.* New York: Henry Holt, 1993.

2
Ancient Civilizations: People and the Gods

The Nature Deities of Egypt and Mesopotamia

Like their Prehistoric ancestors, ancient peoples lived in intimate and dynamic association with nature. They believed that the forces of nature – sun, wind, and rain – were inhabited by spirits, a belief known as **animism**. Just as human beings created tools and weapons that gave them power over nature, so they fashioned explanations that helped them to come to terms with the workings of the universe, its origins, the sources of human life, and other mysterious or unknown matters. Such stories, or **myths**, often featuring superhuman characters, were possibly enacted communally as the spoken part of rituals performed to celebrate seasonal change or to honor the gods.

Figure 2.1 Throne with Tutankhamen and Queen, detail of the back, late Amarna period, New Kingdom, Eighteenth Dynasty, ca. 1360 B.C.E. Wood, plated with gold and silver, inlays of glass paste, approx. 12 × 12 in. Egyptian Museum, Cairo.

In the ancient world, **polytheism**, the belief in many gods, prevailed. Ranked according to their importance to the community, the gods were invisible and immortal. Their specific powers were often associated with those of animals and with the natural elements. In early Egyptian history, goddesses outnumbered gods, and local deities reigned supreme within their own districts. Ancient people forged contractual relationships with their gods: In return for divine benefits, they made human and animal sacrifices, appointed priests and priestesses to tend holy sanctuaries, and lived as they believed the gods would wish.

Egypt: Domain of the Sun God, Gift of the Nile

Geography usually determined the types of deities that the people of the ancient world worshiped. In ancient Egypt, for instance, where a hot, dry North African climate prevailed, the sun god held the place of honor. The sun god, variously called Amon, Ra, or Aten, was considered greater than any other Egyptian deity, and his cult dominated the religious life of ancient Egypt for almost three thousand years. Associated with heat, light, and fertility, the sun god was considered a life force, the "creator of seed," as he is called in "The Hymn to the Aten." Egyptians viewed the sun's daily resurrection in the east as a victory of the forces of light and goodness over those of darkness and evil. In the cyclical regularity of nature evidenced by the daily setting and rising of the sun, the ancient Egyptians perceived the inevitability of death and the promise of rebirth. Not surprisingly, then, a sense of well-being and optimism pervades Egyptian literature and art. "The Hymn to the Aten," a song of praise with many earlier Egyptian antecedents, probably was chanted at fertility rituals and celebrations honoring Egypt's rulers, who were regarded as sons of Amon and earthly representatives of the gods (Figure 2.1).

READING 2

From "The Hymn to the Aten"

You rise in perfection on the horizon of the sky   1
   living Aten,[1] who started life.
Whenver you are risen upon the eastern horizon
   you fill every land with your perfection.
You are appealing, great, sparkling, high over every land;   5
   your rays hold together the lands as far as everything you
     have made.
Since you are Re,[2] you reach as far as they do,

and you curb them for your beloved son.
Although you are far away, your rays are upon the land;
   you are in their faces, yet your departure is not observed.   10
Whenever you set on the western horizon,
   the land is in darkness in the manner of death.
They sleep in a bedroom with heads under the covers,
   and one eye does not see another.
If all their possessions which are under their heads were stolen,   15
   they would not know it.
Every lion who comes out of his cave
   and all the serpents bite,
   for darkness is a blanket.
The land is silent now, because he who made them   20
   is at rest on his horizon

But when day breaks you are risen upon the horizon,
   and you shine as the Aten in the daytime.
When you dispel darkness and you give forth your rays
   the two lands[3] are in festival,   25
   alert and standing on their feet,
   now that you have raised them up.
Their bodies are clean,
   and their clothes have been put on;
   their arms are [lifted] in praise at your rising.   30
The entire land performs its work:
   all the cattle are content with their fodder,
   trees and plants grow,
   birds fly up to their nests,
   their wings [extended] in praise for your Ka.[4]   35
All the Kine[5] prance on their feet;
   everything which flies up and alights,
   they live when you
   have risen for them.
The barges sail upstream and downstream too,   40
   for every way is open at your rising.
The fishes in the river leap before your face
   when your rays are in the sea.

You who have placed seed in woman
   and have made sperm into man,   45
   who feeds the son in the womb of his mother,
   who quiets him with something to stop his crying;
   you are the nurse in the womb,
   giving breath to nourish all that has been begotten.

. . . .

———————◆———————

Second only to the sun as the major natural force in Egyptian life was the Nile, whose annual overflow left a layer of arable soil along the banks of the river, providing the Egyptians with a sense of regularity and material security. Ancient Egyptians derived their explanation of the world's origins from the facts of their environment: The mountainless topography of North

---

[1]The sun disc, worshiped by the pharaoh Akhenaten in the fourteenth century B.C.E., as the sole god in the Egyptian pantheon.
[2]Another name for the sun god, associated with his regenerative powers.

[3]The kingdoms of Upper and Lower Egypt. Lower Egypt comprised the Nile delta north of Memphis; Upper Egypt extended south as far as the first cataract at Syene (Aswan) see Map 2.1.
[4]The governing spirit or soul of a person or god.
[5]Cows.

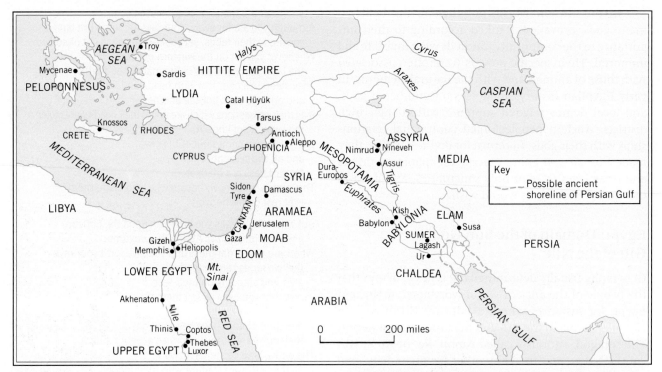

Map 2.1 Ancient Near East.

Africa inspired the Egyptian concept of the universe as a platter resting on the waters of an underworld out of which all life forces had issued spontaneously. At the beginning of time, the Nile's primordial waters were said to have brought forth a mound of silt out of which the sun god arose.

The Egyptians identified the Nile with Osiris, ruler of the underworld and god of the dead. According to Egyptian myth, Osiris was slain by his evil brother, Set, who chopped his body into pieces and threw them into the Nile. But Osiris' loyal wife and sister, Isis, Queen of Heaven, gathered the severed fragments and restored Osiris to life. Isis and the resurrected Osiris then conceived a son, Horus, who ultimately avenged his father by overthrowing Set and becoming King of Egypt. The Osiris myth vividly describes the idea of resurrection that was central to ancient Egyptian religion.

Egyptians regarded their rulers, the pharaohs, as the living representatives of the sun god. Upon his death, the pharaoh would join with the sun to govern Egypt eternally. His body was prepared for burial by means of a special, ten-week embalming procedure that involved removing all of his internal organs and filling his body cavity with preservatives. His corpse was wrapped in fine linen and placed in an elaborately decorated coffin (Figure 2.2), which was floated down the Nile on a royal barge to a burial site along the banks of the Nile. During the first period in Egyptian history, called the Old Kingdom (ca. 2700–2150 B.C.E.), the

Figure 2.2 Egyptian Mummy and Coffin, ca. 1000 B.C.E. Reproduced by courtesy of the Trustees of the British Museum, London.

Egyptians built tombs whose shape – a pyramid – symbolized the mound of silt from which the primordial sun god arose. The burial vault itself was hidden within a series of chambers connected to the exterior by tunnels.

Raised between 2600 and 2500 B.C.E., the pyramids of ancient Egypt are technological wonders and symbols of ancient Egypt's endurance through time (Figure 2.3). Mammoth stone blocks, weighing between two and fifty tons, were assembled without the use of mortar, then faced with finely polished limestone – a feat achieved with stone and copper tools. The Great Pyramid of Khufu stands as part of a large burial complex (Figure 2.4) located in Gizeh, near the southern tip of the Nile Delta (Map 2.1). It consists of more than two million limestone blocks rising to a height of approximately 480 feet and covering a base area of thirteen acres. The tomb was begun when the pharaoh first came to the throne, and it took thirty or more years to complete. A tribute to the ancient Egyptian faith in

Figure 2.3 Great Pyramids of Gizeh: Menkure, ca. 2575 B.C.E., Khafre, ca. 2600 B.C.E., Khufu, ca. 2650 B.C.E. Zefa Picture Library (UK) Ltd., London.

Figure 2.4 Reconstruction of the Pyramids of Khufu and Khafre at Gizeh, ca. 2500 B.C.E. (after Hoelscher). From Horst de la Croix and Robert G. Tansey, *Art through the Ages*, sixth edition, copyright © 1975 Harcourt Brace Jovanovich, Inc., reprinted by permission of the publisher.

1. Pyramid of Khafre
2. Mortuary temple
3. Covered causeway
4. Valley temple
5. Great Sphinx
6. Pyramid of Khufu
7. Pyramids of the royal family and mastabas of nobles

Figure 2.5 Painting from the tomb of Neb-aman, Dra Abu el-Naga, West Thebes, Egypt, 18th Dynasty, ca. 1550—1295 B.C.E In the lower register this painting shows two young girls dancing to the music of the double flute. British Museum, London. Photo: Werner Forman Archive.

the eternal benevolence of the ruler, the royal tomb included the pharaoh's most precious possessions — priceless treasures of jewelry, weapons, and furniture that he might need in the life to come. The chamber walls were painted in **fresco** and carved in low **relief** with scenes illustrating the pharaoh's daily life. **Hieroglyphs**, ancient Egypt's pictographic script, surround the illustrations. They describe the achievements of Egypt's rulers and provide perpetual prayers for the deceased. Tomb paintings reveal much about ancient Egyptian culture. They are, for example, our main source of information about ancient Egyptian music. It is clear that song and poetry were often interchangeable (hymns like that praising the Aten were sung, not spoken), and that musical instruments such as harps, flutes, and rattles (found buried with the dead) accompanied dance and song. Nevertheless, we have no certain knowledge how the music of ancient Egypt actually sounded. Visual representations confirm, however, that music had a special place in religious rituals, in festive and funeral processions, and in many aspects of secular life (Figure **2.5**).

Intended primarily as homes for the dead, the pyramids were built to assure the ruler's comfort in the afterlife. However, in the centuries after their construction, grave robbers despoiled them, and their contents were plundered and lost. The ancient Egyptians turned to other methods of burial, including interment in the rock cliffs along the Nile and in unmarked graves in the Valley of the Kings west of Thebes. In time, these too were despoiled. One of the few royal graves to have escaped vandalism was that of a minor fourteenth-century-B.C.E. ruler named Tutankhamen. Uncovered by the British archeologist Howard Carter in 1922, its contents included riches of astonishing variety, including the solid gold coffin of the young pharaoh (Figure **2.6**).

Such elaborate homes for the dead were reserved for royalty and members of the aristocracy. However,

Figure 2.6 Egyptian cover of the Coffin of Tutankhamen (portion), ca. 1360 B.C.E. Gold with inlay of enamel and semiprecious stones. Egyptian Museum, Cairo. Photo: Wim Swann.

Figure 2.7 Scene from a Funerary Papyrus, or "Book of the Dead," Princess Entiu-ny stands to the left of a set of scales on which Anubis, the jackal-headed god, weighs her heart against the figure of Truth, while Osiris, Lord of the Dead, judges from his throne. His wife, Isis, stands behind the princess. The Metropolitan Museum of Art, New York, Rogers Fund.

Figure 2.8 Scene of Fowling, from the Tomb of Neb-amon at Thebes, Egypt, ca. 1400 B.C.E. Painting on stucco, height 32¼ in. Reproduced by courtesy of the Trustees of the British Museum, London.

the promise of life after death was a concept that dominated Egyptian culture throughout its long history. *The Book of the Dead*, a collection of funerary prayers originating as far back as 4000 B.C.E., describes the manner in which the dead were judged to determine their destinies (Figure **2.7**). The painted **papyrus** shows the enthroned Osiris, god of the underworld, overseeing the ceremony in which the heart of the deceased Princess Entiu-ny is weighed against the figure of Truth. Accompanied by Isis, the Princess watches as the jackel-headed god of death, Anubis, prepares her heart for the ordeal. If the heart is not "found true by trial of the Great Balance" (as the accompanying prayer explains), it will be consumed by the monster, Ament. If pure, it will prevail in a realm where wheat grows high and the dead enjoy feasting and singing.

A sense of order and stability dominates ancient Egyptian art, as it did Egyptian life. In Egyptian art figures are usually sized according to a strict hierarchy, or graded order: Upper-class individuals are shown larger than lower-class ones, and males usually outsize females (Figure **2.8**). However, the consort of the king is occasionally depicted of equal size (see Figures 2.1 and 3.4). All figures are viewed from more than one angle: The upper torso is seen from the front, while the lower is seen from the side; the eyes are frontal, while the head is in profile. The manner in which the human body is rendered is conceptual rather than perceptual. Conceptual is also the Egyptian approach to space: Spatial depth is indicated by placing one figure above the next, often in separate registers. Cast thus in a timeless matrix, human images share the stylized look and symbolic function of the hieroglyphs by which they are surrounded. Indeed, nowhere else in ancient art do we see such a sensitive conjunction of images and words — signs that convey ideas rather than imitate things. Egyptian artists glorified the world of the senses. At the same time, they loved realistic detail, as we see in the hunting scene from the tomb of Neb-amon at Thebes, where both fish and fowl are depicted with extraordinary accuracy (see Figure 2.8).

Egypt was not the only ancient civilization that prepared elaborate burials for its rulers and other exalted members of society. In ancient China, kings and nobles were entombed in magnificent chambers filled with royal goods (see Figure **1.14**), ceramic replicas of domestic and military life (see Figures 7.26, 7.27), as well as captives of war and faithful servants (often buried alive). Likewise, in pre-Inca royal tombs uncovered at Sipán in Peru in 1992 (the richest find of burial contents ever excavated in the Western hemisphere), elaborately crafted objects of gold, silver, and turquoise fill the graves of Moche warrior-priests.

Mesopotamia: The Capricious Gods

While Egypt's climate was regularly hot and dry, that of Mesopotamia — the Fertile Crescent of the Near East — featured fierce changes of weather, including drought, violent rainstorms, flood, wind, and hail. In contrast with the Nile River, which flooded Egyptian soil annually, the rivers essential to food production in Mesopotamia — the Tigris and the Euphrates — overflowed unpredictably, often wiping out whole villages and cities. Moreover, unlike Egypt, whose natural boundaries of desert and water contributed to a condition of relative invulnerability, Mesopotamia suffered the repeated attacks of tribal nomads, who descended from the mountainous regions north of the Fertile Crescent (see Map 2.1). Geography and climate contributed to the mood of fear and insecurity that prevails in all forms of Mesopotamian expression. Mesopotamian deities are pictured as violent and capricious, and Mesopotamian mythology is filled with tales of physical and spiritual woe, of chaos and conflict.

According to *The Babylonian Creation*, a Sumerian poem recorded in the early part of the second millennium, creation obeyed no preordained plan. Rather, at the beginning of time, the universe came about by means of spontaneous generation. *The Babylonian Creation* tells us that when there was neither heaven nor earth, the sweet and bitter waters "mingled" to produce the pantheon of gods. The bitter water, associated with the primeval goddess Tiamat, reigned over a rabble of squabbling gods, until finally, Marduk, the hero-god and offspring of Wisdom, took matters in hand: Destroying Tiamat, and thus ending a long tradition of matriarchial supremacy, Marduk proceeded to establish universal order. He founded the holy city of Babylon as "home of the gods," and, with the following words, created human beings as servants of the gods:

> "Blood to blood I join,
> blood to bone I form
> an original thing,
> its name is MAN,
> aboriginal man
> is mine in making.

> "All his occupations
> are faithful service,
> the gods that fell have rest,
> I will subtly alter
> their operations,
> divided companies equally blest."

Mesopotamia: The Search for Immortality

The theme of human vulnerability dominates Mesopotamian culture. It is central to the first **epic** in world
literature, the *Epic of Gilgamesh*, which was recited
orally for centuries before it was written down late in
the third millennium B.C.E. An epic is a long narrative
poem that recounts the deeds of a hero and his quest for
meaning or identity. The epic hero and his experiences
embody the ideals and values of his culture.

The hero of the *Epic of Gilgamesh* is a semi-historical
figure who probably ruled the ancient Sumerian city of
Uruk around 2800 B.C.E. Described as two-thirds god
and one-third man, Gilgamesh is blessed by the gods
with beauty and courage (Figure **2.9**). When he loses
his dearest companion, Enkidu, he is so distraught that
he resolves to undertake a long and hazardous quest in
search of everlasting life. He meets Utnapishtim, a
mortal whom the gods have rewarded with eternal life
for having saved humankind from a devastating flood.
Utnapishtim helps Gilgamesh locate the plant that
miraculously restores lost youth. But ultimately, a
serpent snatches the plant, and Gilgamesh is left with
the haunting vision of death as "a house of dust" and a
place of inescapable sadness.

READING 3

From the *Epic of Gilgamesh*

O Gilgamesh, Lord of Kullab,[1] great is thy praise. This   1
was the man to whom all things were known; this was the
king who knew the countries of the world. He was wise, he
saw mysteries and knew secret things, he brought us a tale
of the days before the flood. He went on a long journey, was
weary, worn-out with labor, and returning engraved on a
stone the whole story.

When the Gods created Gilgmesh they gave him a
perfect body. Shamash the glorious sun endowed him with
beauty, Adad the god of the storm endowed him with   10
courage, the great gods made his beauty perfect,
surpassing all others. Two thirds they made him god and
one third man.

In Uruk[2] he built walls, a great rampart, and the temple
of blessed Eanna for the god of the firmament Anu, and for
Ishtar the goddess of love.[3]

[Gilgamesh and his bosom companion, Enkidu, destroy
Humbaba, the guardian of the cedar forest, and perform
other heroic deeds. But Gilgamesh spurns the affections of
Ishtar, and in revenge, she takes Enkidu"s life.]

Figure 2.9 Gilgamesh between Two Human-Headed Bulls (top
portion). Soundbox of a Harp, from Ur, Iraq, ca. 2600 B.C.E. Wood
with inlaid gold, lapis lazuli, and shell, height approx. 12 in. The
University Museum, University of Pennsylvania, Philadelphia
(Neg. #T4-109).

---

[1]Park of Uruk.
[2]A city located in Sumer. Gilgamesh was the fifth ruler in the Dynasty of
Uruk after the flood.
[3]Also associated with fertility and war.

Bitterly Gilgamesh wept for his friend Enkidu; he wandered over the wilderness as a hunter, he roamed over the plains; in his bitterness he cried, "How can I rest, how can I be at peace? Despair is in my heart. What my brother is now, that shall I be when I am dead. Because I am afraid of death I will go as best I can to find Utnapishtim whom they call the Faraway, for he has entered the assembly of the gods." So Gilgamesh travelled over the wilderness, he wandered over the grasslands, a long journey, in search of Utnapishtim, whom the gods took after the deluge; and they set him to live in the land of Dilmun,[4] in the garden of the sun; and to him alone of men they gave everlasting life.

At night when he came to the mountain passes Gilgamesh prayed: "In these mountain passes long ago I saw lions, I was afraid and I lifted my eyes to the moon; I prayed and my prayers went up to the gods, so now, O moon god Sin, protect me." When he had prayed he lay down to sleep, until he was woken from out of a dream. He saw the lions round him glorying in life; then he took his axe in his hand, he drew his sword from his belt, and struck and destroyed and scattered them.

So at length Gilgamesh came to that great mountain whose name is Mashu, the mountain which guards the rising and the setting sun. Its twin peaks are as high as the wall of heaven and its paps reach down to the underworld. At its gate the Scorpions stand guard, half man and half dragon; their glory is terrifying, their stare strikes death into men, their shimmering halo sweeps the mountains that guard the rising sun. When Gilgamesh saw them he shielded his eyes for the length of a moment only; then he took courage and approached. When they saw him so undismayed the Man-Scorpion called to his mate, "This one who comes to us now is flesh of the gods." The mate of the Man-Scorpion answered, "Two thirds is god but one third is man."

Then he called to the man Gilgamesh, he called to the child of the gods: "Why have you come so great a journey; for what have you travelled so far, crossing the dangerous waters; tell me the reason for your coming?" Gilgamesh answered, "For Enkidu; I loved him dearly, together we endured all kinds of hardships; on his account I have come, for the common lot of man has taken him. I have wept for him day and night, I would not give up his body for burial, I thought my friend would come back because of my weeping. Since he went, my life is nothing; that is why I have travelled here in search of Utnapishtim my father; for men say he has entered the assembly of the gods, and has found everlasting life. I have a desire to question him concerning the living and the dead." The Man-Scorpion opened his mouth and said, speaking to Gilgamesh, "No man born of women has done what you have asked, no mortal man has gone into the mountain; the length of it is twelve leagues[5] of darkness; in it there is no light, but the heart is oppressed with darkness. From the rising of the sun to the setting of the sun there is no light." Gilgamesh said, "Although I should go in sorrow and in pain, with sighing and with weeping, still I must go. Open the gate of

the mountain." And the Man-Scorpion said, "Go, Gilgamesh, I permit you to pass through the mountain of Mashu and through the high ranges; may your feet carry you safely home. The gate of the mountain is open."

When Gilgamesh heard this he did as the Man-Scorpion had said, he followed the sun's road to his rising, through the mountain. When he had gone one league the darkness became thick around him, for there was no light, he could see nothing ahead and nothing behind him. After two leagues the darkness was thick and there was no light, he could see nothing ahead and nothing behind him. After three leagues the darkness was thick, and there was no light, he could see nothing ahead and nothing behind him. After four leagues the darkness was thick and there was no light, he could see nothing ahead and nothing behind him. At the end of five leagues the darkness was thick and there was no light, he could see nothing ahead and nothing behind him. At the end of six leagues the darkness was thick and there was no light, he could see nothing ahead and nothing behind him. When he had gone seven leagues the darkness was thick and there was no light, he could see nothing ahead and nothing behind him. When he had gone eight leagues Gilgamesh gave a great cry, for the darkness was thick and he could see nothing ahead and nothing behind him. After nine leagues he felt the north wind on his face, but the darkness was thick and there was no light, he could see nothing ahead and nothing behind him. After ten leagues the end was near. After eleven leagues the dawn light appeared. At the end of twelve leagues the sun streamed out.

There was the garden of the gods; all round him stood bushes bearing gems. Seeing it he went down at once, for there was fruit of carnelian with the vine hanging from it, beautiful to look at; lapis lazuli leaves hung thick with fruit, sweet to see. For thorns and thistles there were haematite and rare stones, agate, and pearls from out of the sea. While Gilgamesh walked in the garden by the edge of the sea Shamash[6] saw him, and he saw that he was dressed in the skins of animals and ate their flesh. He was distressed, and he spoke and said, "No mortal man has gone this way before, nor will, as long as the winds drive over the sea." And to Gilgamesh he said, "You will never find the life for which you are searching." Gilgamesh said to glorious Shamash, "Now that I have toiled and strayed so far over the wilderness, am I to sleep, and let the earth cover my head forever? Let my eyes see the sun until they are dazzled with looking. Although I am no better than a dead man, still let me see the light of the sun."

[Gilgamesh meets Siduri, the maker of wine, who advises him to give up his search and value more highly the good things of the earth. Gilgamesh prepares to cross the Ocean, and with the help of the ferryman Urshanabi, finally reaches Dilmun, the home of Utnapishtim.]

"Oh, father Utnapishtim, you who have entered the assembly of the gods, I wish to question you concerning the living and the dead, how shall I find the life for which I

---

[4]The Sumerian paradise, a mythical land resembling the Garden of Eden described in the Hebrew Bible.
[5]Approximately thirty-six miles.

[6]The Semitic sun god.

am searching?"

Utnapishtim said, "There is no permanence. Do we build a house to stand forever, do we seal a contract to hold for all time? Do brothers divide an inheritance to keep for ever, does the flood-time of rivers endure? It is only the nymph of the dragon-fly who sheds her larva and sees the sun in his glory. From the days of old there is no permanence. The sleeping and the dead, how alike they are, they are like a painted death. What is there between the master and the servant when both have fulfilled their doom? When the Annunaki, the judges, come together, and Mammetun the mother of destinies, together they decree the fates of men. Life and death they allot but the day of death they do not disclose." 130

Then Gilgamesh said to Utnapishtim the Faraway, "I look at you now, Utnapishtim, and your appearance is no different from mine; there is nothing strange in your features. I thought I should find you like a hero prepared for battle, but you lie here taking your ease on your back. Tell me truly, how was it that you came to enter the company of the gods and to possess everlasting life?" Utnapishtim said to Gilgamesh, "I will reveal to you a mystery, I will tell you a secret of the gods." 140

[Utnapishtim relates the story of the flood.]

In those days the world teemed, the people multiplied, the world bellowed like a wild bull, and the great god was aroused by the clamor. Enlil heard the clamor and he said to the gods in council, "The uproar of mankind is intolerable and sleep is no longer possible by reason of the babel." So the gods in their hearts were moved to let loose the deluge; but my lord Ea warned me in a dream. He whispered their words to my house of reeds . . . . "Tear down your house, I say, and build a boat. These are the measurements of the barque as you shall build her: let her beam equal her length, let her deck be roofed like the vault that covers the abyss; then take up into the boat the seed of all living creatures . . . ." 150 160

For six days and six nights the winds blew, torrent and tempest and flood overwhelmed the world, tempest and flood raged together like warring hosts. When the seventh day dawned the storm from the south subsided, the sea grew calm, the flood was stilled; I looked at the face of the world and there was silence, all mankind was turned to clay. The surface of the sea stretched as flat as a roof-top; I opened a hatch and the light fell on my face. The I bowed low; I sat down and I wept, the tears streamed down my face, for on every side was the waste of water. 170

[Utnapishtim leads Gilgamesh to Urshanabi the Ferryman.]

Then Gilgamesh and Urshanabi launched the boat on to the water and boarded it, and they made ready to sail away; but the wife of Utnapishtim the Faraway said to him, "Gilgamesh came here wearied out, he is worn out; what will you give him to carry him back to his own country?" So Utnapishtim spoke, and Gilgamesh took a pole and brought the boat in to the bank. "Gilgamesh, you came here a man wearied out, you have worn yourself out; what shall I give you to carry you back to your own country? Gilgamesh, I shall reveal a secret thing, it is a mystery of the gods that I am telling you. There is a plant that grows under the water, it has a prickle like a thorn, like a rose; it 180

will wound your hands, but if you succeed in taking it, then your hands will hold that which restores his lost youth to a man." 190

When Gilgamesh heard this he opened the sluices so that a sweet-water current might carry him out to the deepest channel; he tied heavy stones to his feet and they dragged him down to the water-bed. There he saw the plant growing; although it pricked him he took it in his hands; then he cut the heavy stones from his feet, and the sea carried him and threw him on the shore. Gilgamesh said to Urshanabi the ferryman, "Come here, and see this marvellous plant. By its virtue a man may win back all his former strength. I will take it to Uruk of the strong walls; there I will give it to the old men to eat. Its name shall be 'The Old Men are Young Again'; and at last I shall eat it myself and have back all my lost youth." So Gilgamesh returned by the gate through which he had come, Gilgamesh and Urshanabi went together. They travelled their twenty leagues and then they broke their fast; after thirty leagues they stopped for the night. 200

Gilgamesh saw a well of cool water and he went down and bathed; but deep in the pool there was lying a serpent, and the serpent sensed the sweetness of the flower. It rose out of the water and snatched it away, and immediately it sloughed its skin and returned to the well. Then Gilgamesh sat down and wept, the tears ran down his face, and he took the hand of Urshanabi; "O Urshanabi, was it for this that I toiled with my hands, is it for this I have wrung out my heart's blood? For myself I have gained nothing; not I, but the beast of the earth has joy of it now. Already the stream has carried it twenty leagues back to the channels where I found it. I found a sign and now I have lost it. Let us leave the boat on the bank and go." 210 220

. . . .

———————◆———————

The *Epic of Gilgamesh* involves a mythic quest whose object, personal immortality, is beyond the hero's reach. Nevertheless, the quest drives the hero to discover his human limits. The *Epic of Gilgamesh* is not only the world's first epic; it is the earliest literary effort to come to terms with death, or nonbeing. It reflects the profound human need for an immortality ideology—a body of beliefs, supported by myth, that promised the survival of some aspect of the self in a life hereafter.

The sense of insecurity that is evident in the *Epic of Gilgamesh* is also apparent in Mesopotamian art and architecture. The inhabitants of Uruk and other cities of Sumer honored their gods by building ziggurats— terraced towers of rubble and brick (Figure 2.10). These massive temples, whose steep stairways linked the realms of heaven and earth, were tended by priests who represented the gods on earth. Chambers at the top of the ziggurat were used as shrines dedicated to gods. Ceremonial in function, the ziggurat was the spiritual center of the city-state. Unlike the Egyptian pyramid, which functioned primarily as a tomb, the ziggurat served as a temple sanctuary. Striking similarities exist

Figure 2.10 Ziggurat at Ur (partially reconstructed), Third Dynasty of Ur, Iraq, ca. 2150–2050 B.C.E. © Hirmer Fotoarchiv.

between the ziggurats of Mesopotamia and the stepped platform pyramids of ancient Mexico, built somewhat later (Figure 2.11). Erected atop a rubble mound and shaped like the ziggurat, Mayan and Aztec sanctuaries often covered sacred graves. Whether or not any historical link exists between these Mesopotamian and Native American monuments remains among the mysteries of ancient history.

Figure 2.11 Pyramid of the Magician, Uxmal, Yucatán, Late Classic Maya, ca. 550–900 C.E.

Figure 2.12 Statuettes from the Abu Temple, Tell Asmar, Iraq, ca. 2900–2600 B.C.E. Marble, tallest figure ca. 30 in. The Iraq Musuem, Baghdad and The Oriental Institute, University of Chicago.

In rooms located some 250 feet atop the Mesopotamian ziggurat, local priests stored clay tablets inscribed with records of the city's economic activities, its religious customs, and its rites. The shrine room of the ziggurat at Tell Asmar in Sumer also housed a remarkable group of statues representing men and women of various sizes, with large, staring eyes and hands clasped across their chests (Figure **2.12**). Carved out of soft stone, these figures may represent the gods, or they may depict the townspeople of Tell Asmar in the act of worshiping their local deities. The larger votive figures are perhaps priests, and the smaller figures, layfolk. Rigid and attentive, they stand as if in perpetual prayer. Their enlarged eyes, inlaid with shell and black limestone (Figure **2.13**), convey the impression of dread and awe, visual testimony to the sense of human apprehension in the face of divine power. Mesopotamian art does not share the buoyant confidence that characterizes Egyptian art; rather, it conveys the insecurities of a people whose vulnerability was an ever-present fact of life.

Figure 2.13 Head of a statuette, Tell Asmar, Iraq, ca. 2900–2600 B.C.E. White gypsum with bitumen, height 11¾ in. The Metropolitan Museum of Art, New York, Fletcher Fund, 1940.

Hebrew Monotheism, Hindu Pantheism, and the Tao

The Hebrews: Monotheism and the Covenant

Almost everything we know about the Hebrew people comes from the Bible — a word derived from the Greek *biblia*, meaning "books." The Hebrew Bible is a collection of stories and songs passed down orally for hundreds of years. The first five books of the Hebrew Bible, called the **Torah**, were assembled some time during the fifth century B.C.E. from at least four main sources. Parts of Genesis, the first book of the Torah, belong to a common pool of traditions rooted in Mesopotamia, where the Hebrews originated. Historically, the Bible is — like the *Epic of Gilgamesh* — a conflation of legend and fact. But within Western culture, it remains the central document of two world religions: Judaism and Christianity. It carries a message of faith, even as it records the dramatic history of a people who viewed all history as divinely directed.

The tribal people called by their neighbors "Hebrews" originated in Sumer. Around 2000 B.C.E., they migrated westward under the leadership of Abraham of Ur and settled in Canaan along the Mediterranean Sea (see Map 2.1). In Canaan, according to the Book of Genesis, Abraham received God's promise that his descendants would return to that land and become "a great nation." God's promise to Abraham established the Hebrew claim to Canaan (modern-day Israel). At the same time, the covenant (or contract) between God and the Hebrews ("I will be your God; you will be my people," Genesis 17:7–8) marked the beginning of the Hebrew belief in their destiny as God's Chosen People.

Shortly after 1300 B.C.E., following a traumatic period of enslavement in Egypt, the Hebrew tribes, under a dynamic leader named Moses, abandoned Egypt and headed back toward Canaan — an event that became the basis for Exodus (literally, "going out"), the second book of the Hebrew Bible. Since Canaan was now occupied by local tribes of a sizable military strength, the Hebrews settled temporarily in a region near the Dead Sea. During this period — which archeologists place between roughly 1300 and 1150 B.C.E. — the Hebrews forged the fundamentals of their faith: **monotheism** (the belief in one and only one god); a set of divine commandments for moral and spiritual conduct; and a covenant fixed in laws that bound the Hebrew community to God in return for God's protection.

Hebrew monotheism focused on devotion to a single Supreme Being, the god Moses called Yahweh (or Jehovah). The idea of single creator-god appeared as well in Egypt: by 1350 B.C.E., the pharaoh Amenho-tep IV (Akhenaten) had made the sun god Aten the sole deity of Egypt — a religious reform that did not outlast Akhenaten's reign. Like all Near Eastern gods and goddesses, however, Aten was an arbitary force associated with a specific natural phenomenon, the sun. Yahweh, on the other hand, transcended nature and all natural phenomena. As Supreme Creator, Yahweh preceded nature and was distinct from the physical universe; equally important, the transcendental god of the Hebrews invested the universe with a preconceived moral order. Whereas in the Babylonian creation myth the universe is the product of spontaneous creation, and universal order is initiated out of discord among the gods, the Book of Genesis describes a universe that is systematically planned. The Hebrew cosmos is the miraculous feat of a single, benevolent, all-knowing Being. Further, in contrast to the Babylonian universe, where squabbling gods fashion human beings as their servants, the Hebrew universe is the gift that is given by God, its creator, to God's supreme creation: humankind. Hebrew monotheism stands apart from other ancient Near Eastern conceptions of divine power (including that of Akhenaten's Aten) in still another essential dimension: its ethical charge. Unique to Hebrew monotheism was the regard for Yahweh as the source of ethical and spiritual life. *Ethical monotheism*, the belief that all moral values derive from God, was the most lasting of the Hebrew contributions to world culture.

READING 4A

The Creation

(Hebrew Bible   Genesis 1:26-31;2)

Chapter 1

[26]God said, "Let us make man in our own image, in the likeness of ourselves, and let them be masters of the fish of the sea, the birds of heaven, the cattle, all the wild animals and all the creatures that creep along the ground."

[27]God created man in the image of himself,
in the image of God he created him,
male and female he created them.

[28]God blessed them, saying to them, "Be fruitful, multiply, fill the earth and subdue it. Be masters of the fish of the sea, the birds of heaven and all the living creatures that move on earth." [29]God also said, "Look, to you I give all the seed-bearing plants everywhere on the surface of the earth, and all the trees with seed-bearing fruit; this will be your food. [30]And to all the wild animals, all the birds of heaven and all the living creatures that creep along the ground, I give all the foliage of the plants as their food." And so it was. [31]God saw all he had made, and indeed it was very good. Evening came and morning came: the sixth day.

Chapter 2

¹Thus heaven and earth were completed with all their array. ²On the seventh day God had completed the work he had been doing. He rested on the seventh day after all the work he had been doing. ³God blessed the seventh day and made it holy, because on that day he rested after all his work of creating.

⁴Such was the story of heaven and earth as they were created.

Paradise, and the test of free will

At the time when Yahweh God made earth and heaven ⁵ there was as yet no wild bush on the earth nor had any wild plant yet sprung up, for Yahweh God had not sent rain on the earth, nor was there any man to till the soil. ⁶Instead, water flowed out of the ground and watered all the surface of the soil. ⁷Yahweh God shaped man from the soil of the ground and blew the breath of life into his nostrils, and man became a living being.

⁸Yahweh God planted a garden in Eden, which is in the east, and there he put the man he had fashioned. ⁹From the soil, Yahweh God caused to grow every kind of tree, enticing to look at and good to eat, with the tree of life in the middle of the garden, and the tree of the knowledge of good and evil.

¹⁰A river flowed from Eden to water the garden, and from there it divided to make four streams. ¹¹The first is named the Pishon, and this winds all through the land of Havilah where there is gold. ¹²The gold of this country is pure; bdellium and cornelian stone are found there. ¹³The second river is named the Gihon, and this winds all through the land of Cush. ¹⁴The third river is named the Tigris, and this flows to the east of Ashur. The fourth river is the Euphrates.

¹⁵Yahweh God took the man and settled him in the garden of Eden to cultivate and take care of it. ¹⁶Then Yahweh God gave the man this command, "You are free to eat of all the trees in the garden. ¹⁷But of the tree of the knowledge of good and evil you are not to eat; for, the day you eat of that, you are doomed to die."

¹⁸Yahweh God said, "It is not right that the man should be alone. I shall make him a helper." ¹⁹So from the soil Yahweh God fashioned all the wild animals and all the birds of heaven. These he brought to the man to see what he would call them; each one was to bear the name the man would give it. ²⁰The man gave names to all the cattle, all the birds of heaven and all the wild animals. But no helper suitable for the man was found for him. ²¹Then, Yahweh God made the man fall into a deep sleep. And, while he was asleep, he took one of his ribs and closed the flesh up again forthwith. ²²Yahweh God fashioned the rib he had taken from the man into a woman, and brought her to the man. ²³And the man said:

This one at last is bone of my bones
   and flesh of my flesh!
She is to be called Woman,
   because she was taken from Man.

²⁴This is why a man leaves his father and mother and becomes attached to his wife, and they become one flesh. ²⁵Now, both of them were naked, the man and his wife, but they felt no shame before each other.

———————◆———————

READING 4B

The Decalogue (*Ten Commandents*)

(Hebrew Bible   Exodus 20:1–20)

¹Then God spoke all these words. He said, ²"I am Yahweh your God who brought you out of Egypt, where you lived as slaves.

³"You shall have no other gods to rival me.

⁴"You shall not make yourself a carved image or any likeness of anything in heaven above or on earth beneath or in the waters under the earth.

⁵"You shall not bow down to them or serve them. For I, Yahweh your God, am a jealous God and I punish a parent's fault in the children, the grandchildren, and the great grandchildren among those who hate me; ⁶but I act with faithful love towards thousands of those who love me and keep my commandments.

⁷"You shall not misuse the name of Yahweh your God, for Yahweh will not leave unpunished anyone who misuses his name.

⁸"Remember the Sabbath day and keep it holy. ⁹For six days you shall labour and do all your work, ¹⁰but the seventh day is a Sabbath for Yahweh your God. You shall do no work that day, neither you nor your son nor your daughter nor your servants, men or women, nor your animals nor the alien living with you. ¹¹For in six days Yahweh made the heavens, earth and sea and all that these contain, but on the seventh day he rested; that is why Yahweh has blessed the Sabbath day and made it sacred.

¹²Honour your father and your mother so that you may live long in the land that Yahweh your God is giving you.

¹³"You shall not kill.

¹⁴"You shall not commit adultery.

¹⁵"You shall not steal.

¹⁶"You shall not give false evidence against your neighbour.

¹⁷"You shall not set your heart on your neighbour's house. You shall not set your heart on your neighbour's spouse, or servant, man or woman, or ox, or donkey, or any of your neighbour's possessions."

¹⁸Seeing the thunder pealing, the lightning flashing, the trumpet blasting and the mountain smoking, the people were all terrified and kept their distance. ¹⁹"Speak to us yourself," they said to Moses, "and we will obey; but do not let God speak to us, or we shall die." ²⁰Moses said to the people, "Do not be afraid; God has come to test you, so that your fear of him, being always in your mind, may keep you from sinning." ²¹So the people kept their distance while Moses approached the dark cloud where God was.

———————◆———————

By the start of the first millennium B.C.E., the Hebrews had reestablished themselves in Palestine (as ancient Canaan came to be called following its occupation by powerful tribes of Philistines in the twelfth century B.C.E.). Under the rule of the Hebrew kings, Saul (ca. 1040–1000 B.C.E.), David (ca. 1000–960 B.C.E.), and Solomon (ca. 960–920 B.C.E.), Canaan became a powerful state boasting iron war chariots and a magnificent palace and temple, the latter (no longer standing) built in Jerusalem by King Solomon. Under Solomon, the Hebrew state was divided into a northern portion, Israel, and a southern portion, Judah (hence the name *Jews*). The commercial pursuits of the young Hebrew nation offered numerous material distractions. The sensuous rituals performed by the polytheistic Canaanites in honor of local fertility gods and goddesses drew many Hebrews away from their own rigorous faith. Unlike other Near Eastern religions, the Hebrew faith forbade the visual representation of God.

Moral laxity among the Hebrews moved a special group of people known as *prophets* (literally "those who speak for another") to warn that violations of the covenant would result in divine punishment. Called to be God's spokesmen, the prophets Amos, Hosea, and Isaiah voiced stirring pleas for renewed faith and social justice. The prophet Jeremiah, born almost a century after the fall of the northern kingdom of Israel to the Assyrians in 722 B.C.E., urged the people of Judah to shun the local religious cults, such as that of Baal, the popular fertility god of the Canaanites. Jeremiah warned the Jews to reaffirm the covenant or face God's wrath. Indeed, the Hebrews viewed both the fall of Israel and the subsequent defeat of Judah as divine chastisement. The Hebrew concept of destiny as secular fortune is reaffirmed in Jeremiah's message: God rewards and punishes not in an afterlife, but here on earth. Jeremiah also reawakened the Hebrews to the divine warning (Exodus 20: 2–6; Reading 4B) that the faults of a father would result in punishment to his offspring for generations to come.

READING 4C

Jeremiah and the Observance of the Covenant
(Hebrew Bible   Jeremiah 11: 1–14)

[1]The word that came to Jeremiah from Yahweh, [2]"Hear the terms of this covenant; tell them to the people of Judah and to the inhabitants of Jerusalem. [3]Tell them, 'Yahweh, God of Israel, says this: Cursed be anyone who will not listen to the terms of this covenant [4]which I ordained for your ancestors when I brought them out of Egypt, out of that iron-foundry. Listen to my voice, I told them, carry out all my orders, then you will be my people and I shall be your God, [5]so that I may fulfil the oath I swore to your ancestors, that I may give them a country flowing with milk and honey, as is the case today.'"I replied, "So be it, Yahweh!" [6]Then Yahweh said to me, "Proclaim all these terms in the towns of Judah and in the streets of Jerusalem, saying, 'Listen to the terms of this covenant and obey them. [7]For when I brought your ancestors out of Egypt, I solemnly warned them, and have persistently warned them until today, saying: Listen to my voice. [8]But they did not listen, did not pay attention; instead, each followed his own stubborn and wicked inclinations. And against them, in consequence, I put into action the words of this covenant which I had ordered them to obey and which they had not obeyed.'"

[9]Yahweh said to me, "Plainly there is conspiracy among the people of Judah and the citizens of Jerusalem. [10]They have reverted to the sins of their ancestors who refused to listen to my words: they too are following other gods and serving them. The House of Israel and the House of Judah have broken my covenant which I made with their ancestors. [11]And so, Yahweh says this, 'I shall now bring a disaster on them which they cannot escape; they will call to me for help, but I shall not listen to them. [12]The towns of Judah and the citizens of Jerusalem will then go and call for help to the gods to whom they burn incense, but these will be no help at all to them in their time of distress!

[13]'For you have as many gods
as you have towns, Judah!
You have built as many altars to Shame,
as many incense altars to Baal,
as Jerusalem has streets!

[14]'You, for your part, must not intercede for this people, nor raise either plea or prayer on their behalf, for I will not listen when their distress forces them to call to me for help.'"

———————◆———————

In 586 B.C.E., Judah fell to Chaldean armies led by their mighty king, Nebuchadnezzar. The inhabitants of Jerusalem, a remnant of the Jewish population, were taken into captivity and exiled to Babylon, the restored capital of the old Babylonian Empire. In Babylon, with its resplendent gardens, its entrance portal dedicated to the goddess Ishtar (Figure 2.14), and its towering ziggurat–the model for the Tower of Babel described in Genesis–the Hebrews experienced almost fifty years of exile (586–538 B.C.E.). Their despair and doubt in the absolute goodness of God are voiced in the Book of Job, possibly written in the years after the Babylonian Captivity. The greatest example of wisdom literature in the Hebrew Bible, the Book of Job raises the question of unjustified suffering in a universe governed by a merciful god. The "blameless and upright" Job has obeyed the Commandments and has been a devoted servant of God throughout his life. Yet he is tested unmercifully by the loss of his possessions, his family, and his health. His wife begs him to renounce God, and his friends encourage him to acknowledge his sinfulness. But Job defiantly protests that he has given God no cause for anger. He asks a universal question: If there is no heaven and thus no justice after death, how can a good man's suffering be justified?

Figure 2.14 The Ishtar Gate (restored), Babylon, reign of Nebuchadnezzar II, 604—562 B.C.E. Glazed brick, height 48 ft. Staatliche Museum, Berlin.

READING 4D

Satan tests Job

(Hebrew Bible   Job 1; 2; 3:1–5, 17–21; 13:28; 14; 38:1–18; 42:1–6)

Chapter 1

[1]There was once a man in the land of Uz called Job: a sound and honest man who feared God and shunned evil. [2]Seven sons and three daughters were born to him. [3]And he owned seven thousand sheep, three thousand camels, five hundred yoke of oxen and five hundred she-donkeys, and many servants besides. This man was the most prosperous of all the Sons of the East. [4]It was the custom of his sons to hold banquets in one another's houses in turn, and to invite their three sisters to eat and drink with them. [5]Once each series of banquets was over, Job would send for them to come and be purified, and at dawn on the following day he would make a burnt offering for each of them. "Perhaps," Job would say, "my sons have sinned and in their heart blasphemed." So that was what Job used to do each time.

[6]One day when the sons of God came to attend on Yahweh, among them came Satan. [7]So Yahweh said to Satan, "Where have you been?" "Prowling about on earth," he answered, "roaming around there." [8]So Yahweh asked him, "Did you pay any attention to my servant Job? There is no one like him on the earth: a sound and honest man who fears God and shuns evil." [9]"Yes," Satan said, "but Job is not God-fearing for nothing, is he? [10]Have you not put a wall round him and his house and all his domain? You have blessed all he undertakes, and his flocks throng the countryside. [11]But stretch out your hand and lay a finger on his possessions: then, I warrant you, he will curse you to your face." [12]"Very well," Yahweh said to Satan, "all he has is in your power. But keep your hands off his person." So Satan left the presence of Yahweh.

[13]On the day when Job's sons and daughters were eating and drinking in their eldest brother's house, [14]a messenger came to Job. "Your oxen", he said, "were at the plough, with the donkeys grazing at their side, [15]when the Sabaeans swept down on them and carried them off, and put the servants to the sword: I alone have escaped to tell you." [16]He had not finished speaking when another messenger arrived. "The fire of God", he said, "has fallen from heaven and burnt the sheep and shepherds to ashes: I alone have escaped to tell you." [17]He had not finished speaking when another messenger arrived. "The Chaldaeans," he said, "three bands of them, have raided the camels and made off with them, and put the servants to the sword: I alone have escaped to tell you." [18]He had not finished speaking when another messenger arrived, "Your sons and daughters", he said, "were eating and drinking at their eldest brother's house, [19]when suddenly from the desert a gale sprang up, and it battered all four corners of the house which fell in on the young people. They are dead: I alone have escaped to tell you."

[20]Then Job stood up, tore his robe and shaved his head. Then, falling to the ground, he prostrated himself [21]and said:

Naked I came from my mother's womb,
naked I shall return again.
Yahweh gave, Yahweh has taken back.
Blessed be the name of Yahweh!

[22]In all this misfortune Job committed no sin, and he did not reproach God . . . .

Chapter 2

[1]Another day, the sons of God came to attend on Yahweh and Satan came with them too. [2]So Yahweh said to Satan, "Where have you been?" "Prowling about on earth," he answered, "roaming around there." [3]So Yahweh asked him, "Did you pay any attention to my servant Job? There is no one like him on the earth: a sound and honest man who fears God and shuns evil. He persists in his integrity still; you achieved nothing by provoking me to ruin him." [4]"Skin after skin!" Satan replied. "Someone will give away all he has to save his life. [5]But stretch out your hand and lay a finger on his bone and flesh; I warrant you, he will curse you to your face." [6]"Very well," Yahweh said to Satan, "he is in your power. But spare his life." [7]So Satan left the presence of Yahweh.

He struck Job down with malignant ulcers from the sole of his foot to the top of his head. [8]Job took a piece of pot to scrape himself, and went and sat among the ashes. [9]Then his wife said to him, "Why persist in this integrity of yours? Curse God and die." [10]"That is how a fool of a woman talks," Job replied. "If we take happiness from God's hand, must we not take sorrow too?" And in all this misfortune Job uttered no sinful word.

[11]The news of all the disasters that had fallen on Job came to the ears of three of his friends. Each of them set out from home —Eliphaz of Teman, Bildad of Shuah and Zophar of Naamath— and by common consent they decided to go and offer him sympathy and consolation. [12]Looking at him from a distance, they could not recognise him; they wept aloud and tore their robes and threw dust over their heads. [13]They sat there on the ground beside him for seven days and seven nights. To Job they spoke never a word, for they saw how much he was suffering.

Chapter 3: Job Curses the Day of his Birth

[1]In the end it was Job who broke his silence and cursed the day of his birth. [2]This is what he said:

[3]Perish the day on which I was born
    and the night that told of a boy conceived.
[4]May that day be darkness,
    may God on high have no thought for it,
    may no light shine on it.
[5]May murk and shadow dark as death claim it for their own,
    clouds hang over it,
    eclipse swoop down on it.

. . . .

[17]What are human beings that you should take them so
        seriously,
    subjecting them to your scrutiny,
[18]that morning after morning you should examine them
    and at every instant test them?
[19]Will you never take your eyes off me
    long enough for me to swallow my spittle?
[20]Suppose I have sinned, what have I done to you,
    you tireless watcher of humanity?
Why do you choose me as your target?
    Why should I be a burden to you?
[21]Can you not tolerate my sin,
    not overlook my fault?
For soon I shall be lying in the dust,
    you will look for me and I shall be no more.

Chapter 14

¹A human being, born of woman,
   [his] life is short but full of trouble.
²Like a flower, such a one blossoms and withers,
   fleeting as a shadow, transient.
³And this is the creature on whom you fix your gaze,
   and bring to judgement before you!
⁴But will anyone produce the pure from what is impure?
   No one can!
⁵Since his days are measured out,
   since his tale of months depends on you,
   since you assign him bounds he cannot pass,
⁶turn your eyes from him, leave him alone,
   like a hired labourer, to finish his day in peace.
⁷There is always hope for a tree:
   when felled, it can start its life again;
   its shoots continue to sprout.
⁸Its roots may have grown old in the earth,
   its stump rotting in the ground,
⁹but let it scent the water, and it buds,
   and puts out branches like a plant newly set.
¹⁰But a human being? He dies, and dead he remains,
   breathes his last, and then where is he?
¹¹The waters of the sea will vanish,
   the rivers stop flowing and run dry:
¹²a human being, once laid to rest, will never rise again,
   the heavens will wear out before he wakes up,
   or before he is roused from his sleep.
¹³Will no one hide me in Sheol,
   and shelter me there till your anger is past,
   fixing a certain day for calling me to mind—
¹⁴can the dead come back to life?—
   day after day of my service, I should be waiting
   for my relief to come.
¹⁵Then you would call, and I should answer,
   you would want to see once more what you have made.
¹⁶Whereas now you count every step I take,
   you would then stop spying on my sin;
¹⁷you would seal up my crime in a bag,
   and put a cover over my fault.

¹⁸Alas! Just as, eventually, the mountain falls down,
   the rock moves from its place,
¹⁹water wears away the stones,
   the cloudburst erodes the soil;
   so you destroy whatever hope a person has.
²⁰You crush him once for all, and he is gone;
   first you disfigure him, then you dismiss him.
²¹His children may rise to honours—he does not know it;
   they may come down in the world—he does not care.
²²He feels no pangs, except for his own body,
   makes no lament, except for his own self.

Chapter 38: Job Must Bow to the Creator's Wisdom

¹Then from the heart of the tempest Yahweh gave Job his answer. He said:

²Who is this, obscuring my intentions
   with his ignorant words?
³Brace yourself like a fighter;
   I am going to ask the questions, and you are to inform me!
⁴Where were you when I laid the earth's foundations?
   Tell me, since you are so well-informed!

⁵Who decided its dimensions, do you know?
   Or who stretched the measuring line across it?
⁶What supports its pillars at their bases?
   Who laid its cornerstone
⁷to the joyful concert of the morning stars
   and the unanimous acclaim of the sons of God?
⁸Who pent up the sea behind closed doors
   when it leapt tumultuous from the womb,
⁹when I wrapped it in a robe of mist
   and made black clouds its swaddling bands;
¹⁰when I cut out the place I had decreed for it
   and imposed gates and a bolt?
¹¹"Come so far," I said, "and no further;
   here your proud waves must break!"
¹²Have you ever in your life given orders to the morning
   or sent the dawn to its post,
¹³to grasp the earth by its edges
   and shake the wicked out of it?
¹⁴She turns it as red as a clay seal,
   she tints it as though it were a dress,
¹⁵stealing the light from evil-doers
   and breaking the arm raised to strike.
¹⁶Have you been right down to the sources of the sea
   and walked about at the bottom of the Abyss?
¹⁷Have you been shown the gates of Death,
   have you seen the janitors of the Shadow dark as death?
¹⁸Have you an inkling of the extent of the earth?
   Tell me all about it if you have!

Chapter 42: Job's Final Answer

¹This was the answer Job gave to Yahweh:

²I know that you are all-powerful:
   what you conceive, you can perform.
³I was the man who misrepresented your intentions
   with my ignorant words.
You have told me about great works that I cannot
      understand,
   about marvels which are beyond me, of which I know
      nothing.
⁴(Listen, please, and let me speak:
   I am going to ask the questions, and you are to inform
      me.)
⁵Before, I knew you only by hearsay
   but now, having seen you with my own eyes,
⁶I retract what I have said,
   and repent in dust and ashes.

. . . .

───────────◆───────────

God's answer to Job is an eloquent vindication of unquestioned faith: God's power is immense and human beings cannot expect rational explanations of the divine will; indeed, they have no business demanding such. Proclaiming the magnitude of divine power and the fragility of humankind, the Book of Job confirms the pivotal role of faith (the belief and trust in God) sustaining the Hebrew covenant.

Pessimism and a sense of human vulnerability pervade the Book of Job as they do the *Epic of Gilgamesh*. Both heroes, Job and Gilgamesh, are tested by superhuman forces, and both come to realize that misfortune and suffering are typical of the human condition. Gilgamesh seeks but fails to secure personal immortality; Job fails to secure from Yahweh any promise that once dead, one might return to life. Indeed, Utnapishtim tells Gilgamesh, "There is no permanence," and Job laments that man born of woman "Like a flower, such a one blossoms and withers, . . . He dies, and dead he remains." Such pessimism is characteristic of early Mesopotamian culture, the culture out of which both the *Epic of Gilgamesh* and the Hebrew Bible emerged. The notion of life after death (so prominent in Egyptian religious thought) is not clearly defined in Hebraic literature. Job anticipates final departure to a shadowy underworld, a land of gloom known to the Hebrews as Sheol or Shadowland. Yet, with no promise of reward, Job remains stubbornly faithful to God as his sole protector. Job's tragic vision involves the gradual but dignified acceptance of his place in a divinely governed universe.

The Hebrew Bible played a major role in shaping the humanistic tradition in the West. It provided the religious and ethical foundations for Judaism, and, considerably later, for Christianity. Biblical teachings, including the belief in a single, personal, caring god who intevenes on behalf of a Chosen People, have become fundamental to Western thought. And Bible stories – from the Creation myth to the Hebrew Exodus and the sufferings of Job – have inspired some of the greatest works of art, music, and literature that humankind has produced.

Ancient India: Hindu Pantheism

The civilization of the Indus valley in northwest India contributed religious ideas that were markedly different from those of the ancient Near East. It also contributed the most ancient of today's world religions: Hinduism. (The name comes from the Sanskrit word for the Indus River, "Sindu.") India's oldest devotional texts, the Vedas, reflect the blending of the native folk culture of the Indus valley and that of the invading Aryans, Sanskrit-speaking warriors who entered India after 1500 B.C.E. Transmitted orally until they were recorded around 500 B.C.E., the Vedas (the word *veda* means "sacred knowledge") are a large collection of hymns, psalms, and ritual formulas honoring nature deities similar in origin and function to those worshiped in Egypt and Mesopotamia. Among the chief Vedic deities were the sky gods Indra and Rudra (later known as Shiva), the fire god Agni, and the sun god Vishnu. Scholars of the 1990s have suggested that the Vedas are also a major fund of information concerning astronomical phenomena – the verbal equivalent of Stonehenge.

While the Vedic gods have remained an important part of popular Hinduism, the essence of Indian religious thought lies in a more abstract conception of nature known as **pantheism**. Pantheism is the belief that the divine spirit pervades all things in the universe. It is best understood through the 250 prose commentaries on the Vedas known as the *Upanishads*, which, like the Vedas themselves, were orally transmitted for centuries. The Upanishads were recorded in Sanskrit, the ancient classical language of India, during the eighth century B.C.E. While the Vedas teach worship through prayer and sacrifice, the Upanishads emphasize meditation. They affirm the existence of a single reality, the all-pervading cosmic force called **Brahman**. Unlike the nature deities of the Egyptians and Mesopotamians, and the patriarchal god of the Hebrews, Brahman is infinite, formless, impersonal, and unknowable. Brahman is the "Uncaused Cause." In every human being, there resides the individual manifestation of Brahman: the Self, or **Atman**. "Soundless, formless, intangible, undying, tasteless, odorless, without beginning, without end, eternal, immutable, beyond nature, is the Self," according to the *Upanishads*. Although housed in the material prison of the human body, Atman seeks to be one with the Absolute Spirit (Brahman), but it is able to do so only by rejecting the world of illusion and ignorance. Meditation is the technique by which the Hindu moves toward the union of Atman and Brahman.

Essentially a literature of humility, the Upanishads offer no guidelines for worship, no moral laws, and no religious dogma. They neither exalt divine power (as does "The Hymn to the Aten"), nor do they interpret it (as does the Hebrew Bible). They do, however, instruct Hindus on the subject of death and rebirth. The Hindu anticipates a succession of lives – that is, the return of the Atman in a physical form determined by the level of spiritual purity achieved at the time of death. *Karma*, the collective energy gained from accumulated spiritual experience in previous lives, determines the physical state of the reborn Atman. Reincarnation assures the continuity of the spirit until the Hindu achieves **nirvana**, that is, reabsorption of the Self into spiritual infinity and release. In this ultimate state of enlightenment Atman is liberated from mortal existence and finally merges with Brahman.

These concepts came to form the core of the most popular book in Hindu religious literature, the *Bhagavad-Gita* ("Song of God"). The *Bhagavad-Gita* belongs to a voluminous Indian epic poem called *The Mahabharata*, the source of most of the poetry, drama, and art produced throughout India's long history. *The*

Mahabharata – the world's longest poem – describes a ten-year-long struggle occurring around the year 1000 B.C.E. for control of the Ganges valley. The most famous section of the poem, the *Bhagavad-Gita*, is a devotional dialogue between Arjuna, the poem's hero, and a divine manifestation of Brahman called Krishna. Krishna's answer to Arjuna's question "How can one identify a man who is absorbed in Brahman?" represents the essence of Hindu thought as distilled from the Upanishads. Although it may have been in existence earlier, the *Bhagavad-Gita* was not recorded until sometime between the fifth and second centuries B.C.E.

READING 5

From the *Bhagavad-Gita*

He knows bliss in the Atman 1
And wants nothing else.
Cravings torment the heart:
He renounces cravings.
I call him illumined.
Not shaken by adversity,
Not hankering after happiness:
Free from fear, free from anger,
Free from the things of desire,
I call him a seer, and illumined. 10
The bonds of his flesh are broken.
He is lucky, and does not rejoice:
He is unlucky, and does not weep.
I call him illumined.

. . . .

Thinking about sense-objects
Will attach you to sense-objects;
Grow attached, and you become addicted;
Thwart your addiction, it turns to anger;
Be angry, and you confuse your mind;
Confuse your mind, you forget the lesson of experience; 20
Forget experience, you lose discrimination;
Lose discrimination, and you miss life's only purpose.
When he has no lust, no hatred,
A man walks safely among the things of lust and hatred.
To obey the Atman
Is his peaceful joy:
Sorrow melts
Into that clear peace;
His quiet mind
Is soon established in peace. 30

The uncontrolled mind
Does not guess that the Atman is present:
How can it meditate?
Without meditation, where is peace?
Without peace, where is happiness?

The wind turns a ship
From its course upon the waters:

The wandering winds of the senses
Cast man's mind adrift
And turn his better judgment from its course. 40
When a man can still the senses
I call him illumined.
The recollected mind is awake
In the knowledge of the Atman
Which is dark night to the ignorant:
The ignorant are awake in their sense-life
Which they think is daylight:
To the seer it is darkness.

Water flows continually into the ocean
But the ocean is never disturbed: 50
Desire flows into the mind of the seer
But he is never disturbed.
The seer knows peace:
The man who stirs up his own lusts
Can never know peace.
He knows peace who has forgotten desire.
He lives without craving:
Free from ego, free from pride.

This is the state of enlightenment in Brahman:
A man who does not fall back from it 60
Into delusion.
Even at the moment of death
He is alive in that enlightenment:
Brahman and he are one.

———————◆———————

The Hindu view of the relationship between people and gods differs significantly from the views of ancient Near Easterners. While Near Eastern religions regard human beings as separate from the gods, Indian religion emphasizes the oneness of all matter and spirit. Where Near Eastern religions affirm the imperishability of individual consciousness, Hinduism seeks its sublimation, or rather, its return to the cosmic matrix. Hindus anticipate the reabsorption of the individual ego into the spiritual infinite. They view the life of the individual as one with, rather than subject to, an impersonal divine force. Instead of pursuing eternal life, the Hindu tries to escape the Wheel of Rebirth.

To this day, Hinduism retains its holistic character. Hinduism tolerates an extensive mythology of Vedic gods and goddesses (see chapter 14), though it has remained relatively unaffected by the dominant ideas that arose in ancient Near Eastern civilizations and are preserved in the heritage of the West. On the other hand, since the nineteenth century, Hinduism's holistic view of nature has had increasing influence on Western thought and belief (see Book 5, chapter 27). In the last decade of the twentieth century, Hindu techniques of deep meditation are having a notable impact on the disciplines of religion, philosophy, and medical science.

Ancient China: The Harmony of Nature and the Tao

Like the ancient Egyptians, the Chinese were deeply concerned for the welfare of the dead in the life hereafter. They buried their deceased rulers in elaborate tombs filled with treasures that included bronze vessels (see Figure 1.14), ritual jades (see Figure 2.17), and ceramics (see Figures 7.26, 7.27). Also entombed were servants and animals who were expected to protect their masters in the next life. After the sixth century B.C.E. however, human and animal figures made of baked clay (see chapters 7 and 14) were used to replace living sacrifices. These surrogate figures, along with bronze and clay replicas of domestic houses, musical instruments, and household utensils, provide a detailed picture of ancient Chinese culture.

The early Chinese believed that gods and spirits, including those of their deceased ancestors, controlled the universe. As in the ancient Near East, the Chinese performed rituals to assure bountiful harvests and material well-being. The ritual vessels of ancient China, embellished with human and animal motifs, reflect a view of nature as animistic – that is, spiritually

Figure 2.15 Inscribed Oracle Bone. China. C.V. Starr. East Asian Library, Columbia University.

alive. Chinese priests looked to nature to discover divine messages. They inscribed questions to the gods on tortoise shells and on the bones of animals, which they heated to produce cracks that might be read and interpreted (Figure 2.15). The inscriptions on these ancient oracle bones, which date from between roughly 1500 and 1000 B.C.E., draw from among some five thousand characters that constitute the body of Chinese script. Chinese characters, traditionally executed with a brush in a writing style known as **calligraphy** (literally, "beautiful writing"), are both a form of art and a system of sacred sign making.

The ancient Chinese believed in the unity of nature and the interrelationship of all its particular manifestations. In the regularity of the seasonal cycle, the growth of trees and plants, and the everyday workings of nature, the Chinese perceived a harmonious order. They described that order as the product of two interacting forces, or modes of energy, *yin* and *yang*, commonly represented as an image of twin interpenetrating shapes enclosed within a circle (Figure 2.16). The interaction of *yang*, the male principle (associated with lightness, hardness, brightness, warmth, and the sun), and *yin*, the female principle (associated with darkness, softness, moisture, coolness, the earth, and the moon), was identified with creation, as well as with the order of nature, which, they believed, resided in the balance between the forces of hot and cold, day and night, heaven and earth, male and female, and so on. The circle, a figure with no beginning or end, and the ring or disc, which unifies positive form and negative space, symbolizes these complementary polarities. Circular jade discs are found in great numbers in Chinese graves as early as 2000 B.C.E. (Figure 2.17). Although their exact function is unknown, they would seem to

Figure 2.16 The Yin and Yang.

Figure 2.17 Jade Disc, Shang Dynasty, ca. 2000 B.C.E. 3/16 × 3 9/16 in. The Arthur M. Sackler Gallery, Smithsonian Institution, Washington, D.C. Accession No. 587-04.54.

represent the eternal continuity and the inherent harmony of the universe. Because jade was believed to hold protective powers, this medium was much prized by the Chinese, who used it for ritual objects, talismans for auspicious conditions, and insignias of authority.

The essence of ancient Chinese speculative thought is preserved is *Taoism*, a belief system that is as much a philosophy of nature as a religion. Taoists believe in a universal and unchanging principle known as the Tao ("way of nature"). The Tao is the source and essence of the universe, the unity behind nature's multiplicity, a cosmic energy that resists intellectual analysis. The ineffable Tao manifests itself in the harmony of things; it can be understood only by individuals who live simply and treasure life. Taoists seek to cultivate tranquility, spontaneity, compassion, and spiritual insight. Like the Hindus, they practice meditation and breath control, along with dietary and other physical means of prolonging and enriching life.

The most philosophic of all efforts to explain the spirit world, Taoism existed in China as early as 1000 B.C.E., but its basic writings, the *Tao Te Ching (The Way and Its Power)*, did not appear until the sixth century B.C.E. This modest "scripture" of some five thousand words is associated with the name Lao Tzu ("the Old One"), who may or may not have ever actually existed. The following poem, one of the eighty-one chapters of the *Tao Te Ching*, conveys the Taoist idea of nature's unity. It presents a series of simple images that illustrate the oneness of the positive and negative aspects of reality.

READING 6

From the *Tao Te Ching*

Thirty spokes will converge
In the hub of a wheel;
But the use of the cart
Will depend on the part
Of the hub that is void.   5

With a wall all around
A clay bowl is molded;
But the use of the bowl
Will depend on the part
Of the bowl that is void.   10

Cut out windows and doors
In the house as you build;
But the use of the house
Will depend on the space
In the walls that is void.   15

So advantage is had
From whatever is there;
But usefulness rises
From whatever is not.

◆

SUMMARY

Among ancient civilizations, nature and the natural environment influenced the formation of religious attitudes. Egypt's relatively secure location, regular climate, and dependable Nile River encouraged the belief in a host of essentially benevolent nature deities and the promise of life after death. In contrast with Egypt, Mesopotamia's vulnerable geographic location and unstable climatic conditions contributed to the development of a pantheon of capricious and violent gods and a generally pessimistic world view. The world's first epic, the *Epic of Gilgamesh*, describes the Mesopotamian quest for an elusive and unobtainable immortality.

Neither the Hebrews nor their Sumerian neighbors developed the deep sense of order that characterized ancient Egyptian culture; nor did these Near Eastern peoples produce a clearly defined picture of life after death such as that fashioned by the Egyptians. Among the Hebrews, a covenant with a single, personal god that stood above the forces of nature formed the basis for a religion that emphasized faith and moral conduct, concepts that have remained central to Western religious thought. The Hebrew Bible interpreted the fortunes of the Hebrews as the divinely directed history of a Chosen People.

Ancient Eastern religious beliefs were more holistic than those that emerged in the West. Ancient India developed an extensive mythology of nature deities but exalted a pantheistic worldview that formed the core of Hinduism. The Upanishads and the *Bhagavad-Gita* taught that the human spirit was part of a divine matrix to which it must ultimately return. Hinduism emphasized the sublimation of the Self by means of meditation and a stilling of the senses. The ancient Chinese also perceived universal harmony as the basic condition of nature. Their religion honored natural and ancestral spirits. Among the early Chinese there emerged a pantheistic religious philosophy that taught the "way of nature" – the Tao – the principle of cosmic unity and the all-pervading force of nature. The *yin-yang* image that symbolizes the harmonious interaction of natural forces is fundamental to Chinese speculative thought.

Common to all religions of the ancient world was the belief in forces that were greater and more powerful than those of perishable humankind. Such forces assumed positions of primary importance in the religious life of people for whom survival was a day-to-day struggle. Our ancestors' earliest efforts to explain the unknown raised questions about life's origins, the meaning of death, and the destiny and purpose of humankind – questions that remain central to the humanistic tradition.

GLOSSARY

animism the belief that the forces of nature are inhabited by spirits

Atman the Hindu name for the Self; the personal part of Brahman

Brahman the Hindu name for the Absolute Spirit; an impersonal World Soul that pervades all things

calligraphy (Greek, "beautiful writing") fine handwriting treated as a branch of art in Chinese, Japanese, and Islamic cultures

epic a long narrative poem that recounts the deeds of a legendary or historical hero in his quest for meaning or identity

fresco (Italian, "fresh") a method of painting on walls or ceilings surfaced with fresh, moist, lime plaster

hieroglyph (Greek, "sacred sign") the pictographic script of ancient Egypt

karma (Sanskrit, "deed") the law that holds that one's deeds determine one's future life in the Wheel of Rebirth

monotheism the belief in one and only one god

myth a story that explains the workings of nature, the origins of life, and other phenomena; usually associated with religious ritual or derived from the spoken part of such ritual

nirvana (Sanskrit, "extinction") the blissful reabsorption of the Self into the spiritual infinite (Brahman): release from the endless cycle of rebirth; (see also Buddhism, chapters 8, 9)

pantheism the belief that a divine spirit pervades all things in the universe

papyrus a primitive form of paper used in ancient Egypt and made from the core of plants that grow along the Nile River

polytheism the belief in many gods

relief a sculptural technique in which figures or forms are carved to stand out from the background surface; the degree of relief is designated as *high* or *low*, depending on how deeply the figures are carved

Torah (Hebrew, "law") the first five books of the Hebrew Bible: Genesis, Exodus, Leviticus, Numbers, and Deuteronomy

ziggurat a terraced tower of rubble and brick that served ancient Mesopotamians as temple-shrine

SUGGESTIONS FOR READING

Anderson, Bernhard. *Understanding the Old Testament*, 4th ed. Englewood Cliffs, N.J.: Prentice-Hall, 1986.

Basham, A.L. *The Wonder that Was India*, rev. ed. New York: Hawthorn Books, 1963.

Campbell, Joseph. *The Masks of God: Oriental Mythology*. New York: Viking, 1962.

Chaudhuri, N.C. *Hinduism*. New York: Oxford University Press, 1979.

Creel, H.G. *What is Taoism?* Chicago: University of Chicago Press, 1970.

Edwards, I.E.S. *The Pyramids of Egypt*. Baltimore: Penguin, 1986.

Frankfort, Henri, et al. *Before Philosophy*. Baltimore: Penguin, 1961.

Gabel, John B., and C.B. Wheeler. *The Bible as Literature: An Introduction*, 2nd ed. New York: Oxford University Press, 1990.

Harrelson, Walter. *From Fertility Cult to Worship*. Garden City, N.Y.: Doubleday, 1970.

Holbrook, Clyde A. *The Iconoclastic Deity: Biblical Images of God*. Lewisburg, Pa.: Bucknell University Press, 1984.

Meskill, John, ed. *An Introduction to Chinese Civilization*. Boston: Heath, 1973.

Pearlman, Moshe. *In the Footsteps of Moses: The First Days of Israel*. New York: World, 1973.

3

Ancient Civilizations:
People and the Law

If the gods had created the land, human beings inherited it. In the newly formed civilizations of the ancient world, community life demanded collective effort in matters of production, distribution, and consumption of goods. But it also required the leaders who would provide law, order, and physical protection. Families, tribes, and clans brought the land under control, and some among them established long-standing territorial claims. Those who claimed association with the local gods or who proved themselves more powerful than others assumed positions of leadership. Once such authority was established, it was almost impossible to unseat: Those who rose to power usually designated their heirs as their successors, thus establishing a **dynasty** – a sequence of rulers from the same family.

The ruling dynasty, in conjunction with a priestly caste that supervised the religious activities of the community, formed an elite group of men and women who regulated the lives of the lower classes: merchants, farmers, herders, artisans, soldiers, and servants. At the bottom of the social scale were slaves, namely unfree men and women. In the ancient world, making slaves of one's captives was a humane alternative to annihilating them. Some people fell into slavery as a result of committing certain crimes or falling deeply into debt. Slaves might be traded like property, but within some ancient cultures, they were able to acquire sufficient wealth to buy their own freedom or that of their children.

The most rigid class divisions among all early societies were those of ancient India. Following the arrival of Aryan invaders from the northwest at the beginning of the second millennium B.C.E., India developed a **caste system** based on the division between the light-skinned Aryans and the dark-skinned natives. The system eventually evolved into a hereditary division based primarily on occupation. Four castes emerged: priests and scholars, rulers and warriors, artisans and merchants, and unskilled workers. At the very bottom of the social order, or, more accurately, outside it, lay the Untouchables. These people held the most menial and degrading occupations. India's caste system was an extreme form of the kind of social stratification that existed throughout the ancient world. At the other end of the scale, in ancient Egypt the class structure was less rigid: Ambitious individuals of any class were free to rise to positions of merit, usually by way of education. The westward migration of Sudanese (black-skinned) peoples and thriving commercial activity between Egypt and Nubia – the region south of the first cataract of the Nile (see Map 2.1) – produced a multiracial and multicultural population: At all levels, light- and dark-skinned people appear to have held similar status. Indeed, in the mid-eighth century B.C.E. black Africans from the kingdom of Kush in Nubia ruled all of Egypt.

Egypt: "The Law of the Land is the Mouth of the Pharaoh"

From earliest times, political power was linked with spiritual power and superhuman might. It was believed that divine power flowed from the supreme god or goddess to a royal agent, who, as **theocratic monarch**, represented heaven's will on earth. In ancient Egypt, pharaohs ruled in the name of the sun god Amon. (In ancient Japan, by comparison, emperors claimed descent from a sun goddess known as Amaterasu.) So close was the linkage between ruler and gods that Egyptian hymns to the pharaoh address him in terms identical with those used in worshiping the gods. In the visual arts, rulers and gods alike were depicted with the attributes and physical features of powerful animals. Such is the case with the Great Sphinx, the recumbent creature that guards the entrance to the ceremonial complex at Gizeh (Figure **3.1**). This haunting figure, originally thought to have originated around 2500 B.C.E. but possibly many centuries older, unites the portrait head of the Fourth Dynasty pharaoh Khafre with the body of a lion, king of the beasts. The result is a hybrid symbol of superhuman power.

Figure 3.1 Sphinx at Gizeh, Egypt, ca. 2540—2514 B.C.E. Limestone, length 240 ft., height 65 ft. Historical Picture Service, Inc., Chicago.

Much of the art of the ancient world, even that which had a ceremonial function, served to commemorate the achievements of powerful rulers. The so-called Palette of King Narmer, for instance, records the first major event in Egypt's political history: the union of Upper and Lower Egypt by the Egyptian warrior Narmer (also known as Menes) in approximately 3100 B.C.E. (Figure **3.2**). One side of the slate palette shows Narmer seizing a fallen enemy by the hair. Below his feet are the bodies of the vanquished. To his left, a slave (represented much smaller in size than Narmer) obediently carries his master's sandals. At the upper right is the victorious falcon, symbol of the Upper Egyptian god Horus, offspring of Osiris and Isis. Horus, representing Narmer, holds by the leash the now-subdued lands of Lower Egypt, symbolized by a severed head and papyrus plants.

Narmer's victory established Egypt's first dynasty. From this point on, ancient Egypt was ruled by a succession of dynasties, as follows:

Early Dynastic Period (Dynasties I–II)	ca. 3100–2700 B.C.E.
Old Kingdom (Dynasties III–VI)	ca. 2700–2150 B.C.E.
Middle Kingdom (Dynasties XI–XII)	ca. 2050–1785 B.C.E.
New Kingdom (Dynasties XVIII–XX)	ca. 1575–1085 B.C.E.

Civil dissent marked the century prior to the Middle Kingdom, while the second intermediate period saw the invasion of warlike Hyksos tribes. Nevertheless, New Kingdom pharaohs extended Egypt's power far beyond the Nile valley to create a powerful empire.

Figure 3.2 Palette of King Narmer (front and back), ca. 3100 B.C.E. Slate, height 25 in. Egyptian Museum, Cairo. © Hirmer Fotoarchiv.

Throughout their long history, ancient Egyptians viewed the land as sacred. Owned by the gods, the land that provided sustenance for all inhabitants was ruled by pharaohs and passed on to future generations through the female line. It was necessary, therefore, that any male aspiring to the throne marry all female heiresses, including the daughters and granddaughters of the queen. This tradition, probably related to the practice of tracing parentage to the childbearer, lasted longer in Egypt than anywhere else in the ancient world. Normally, however, even the most influential Egyptian queens did not rule independent of their consorts. The fourteenth-century-B.C.E. Queen Nefertiti, who, with her mother-in-law, dominated the political affairs of her fanatical husband, Amenhotep IV (Akhenaten), bore many of the same titles as the pharaoh. The mother of six daughters, Nefertiti is often pictured in ceremonial attire as an officiating priestess — the equal of her consort. Nefertiti's confident beauty inspired numerous sculptured likenesses, some of which are striking in their blend of realism and abstraction (Figure **3.3**).

Ancient Egyptian women enjoyed economic independence, as well as civil rights and privileges. As we see in the double portrait of the Pharaoh Mycerinus and his queen, who tenderly and yet formally embraces her husband, high-ranking women might be represented equal in size and importance to men (Figure **3.4**). A manual of good conduct from the early Middle Kingdom offers the following advice to the husband concerning his wife: "Make her happy while you are alive, for she is land profitable to her lord. Neither judge her nor raise her to a position of power...her eye is a stormwind when she sees."

As chief authority in both religious and secular matters, the pharaoh appointed local priests and governors. Just as the ruler represented the gods, so his appointees represented him. Ancient Egypt was administered by a vast bureaucracy of officers who collected taxes, regulated public works, and mobilized the army. These individuals constituted the upper class. As in all societies, power was not uniformly distributed, but descended from the top rung of the hierarchy in diminishing amounts. Those closest to the pharaoh participated most fully in his authority and prestige. Other individuals might advance their positions and improve their status through service to the pharaoh, and education was the best means of rising through the ranks. At the base of the social pyramid, there were great masses of men and women who constituted the agricultural backbone of ancient Egypt. Aided by slaves, peasants farmed the land owned by the gods, and shared in its bounty. With this socialistic economy, Egypt enjoyed for many centuries an abundance of food supplies and widespread trade, conditions well illustrated on the walls of the tomb of Sennudjem, who is pictured with his wife reaping wheat in "the fields of the blessed" (Figure 3.5). In the lower registers of the

Figure 3.4 Pair Statue of Mycerinus and His Queen, from Gizeh Dynasty IV, 2599–1571 B.C.E. Slate schist, height 4ft. 6½ in. (complete statue). Courtesy, Museum of Fine Arts, Boston. Harvard MFA Expedition.

Figure 3.3 (left) Portrait head of Queen Nefertiti, ca. 1355 B.C.E. New Kingdom, Eighteenth Dynasty. Painted limestone, height 20 in. State Museums, Berlin.

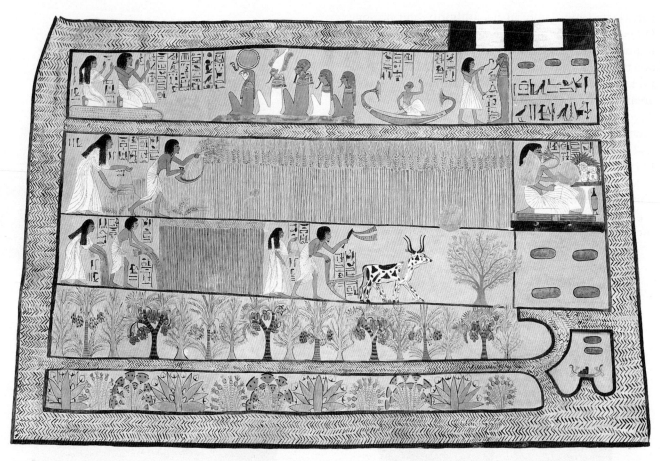

Figure 3.5 The fields of the blessed. Deceased and wife in fields of Iaru, adoring deities, Tomb of Sennudjem, Egypt, ca. 1200 B.C.E. Length 33 in., height 21 in.; scale 1:2. Copyist: Charles K. Wilkinson, 1922. The Metropolitan Museum of Art, New York.

fresco, fruit trees flourish, while the borders bear markings that may symbolize life-giving water. (Compare similar markings in the fowling scene pictured in Figure 2.8.)

Long-standing customs and unwritten rules preceded the codification and transcription of civil laws. In ancient Egypt, the law consisted of the unwritten decrees of the pharaoh. An inscription on an Old Kingdom tomb wall reads, "the law of the land is the mouth of the pharaoh." In Egypt no written laws have been preserved from any period before the fourth century B.C.E. When one considers that toward the end of the thirteenth century B.C.E., the pharaoh Rameses II ruled approximately three million people, it is clear that the oral tradition – the verbal transmission of rules and customs – played a vital part in establishing political continuity. At the same time, written documents, such as contracts, court decisions, and royal edicts, provided strong precedents for legal action.

The importance of law and order to the well-being of the ancient Egyptian community is reflected in a document that describes the activities of the pharaoh's most important administrator, his vizier. As chief tax collector and director of public services and public

works, the fifteenth-century-B.C.E. vizier Rekh-mi-Re was a secular officer who also served as priest of justice, a title that indicates the close association between spiritual and secular power common to ancient society. Rekh-mi-Re was second only to the pharaoh, to whom he reported daily. The text that appears on the walls of Rekh-mi-Re's tomb indicates that although the pharaoh was a god "by whose guidance men live," the vizier was essential to the operations of state. The vizier was in charge of appointing members of the royal bureaucracy and dispatching the local bailiffs, who reported their affairs to him regularly. He oversaw the mobilization of troops, the irrigation of canals, and the taking of inventories. Paying scrupulous attention to matters of hygiene, he inspected the water supply on the first day of every ten-day period. And, with the assistance of official scribes, he handled all litigation for the Egyptian state. The fact that the text makes much of the vizier's impartiality and tolerance suggests that graft and corruption were widespread in ancient Egypt. Indeed, thirteenth-century-B.C.E. royal edicts attempted to correct bureaucratic corruption with very harsh penalties, a fact that indicates not all officials were as scrupulous or as dedicated as Rekh-mi-Re.

READING 7

From *The Autobiography of Rekh-mi-Re*

I was the heart of the Lord, the ears and eyes of the   1
Sovereign. Yea, I was his own skipper, and knew not
slumber night or day. Whether I stood or sat, my heart
was set upon prow rope and stern rope, and the
sounding-pole(?) never was idle in my hands. I was
watchful for any chance of stranding. Every king of
Upper and Lower Egypt is a god by whose guidance
men live. He is the father and mother [of all men], alone
by himself, without an equal. I did not suffer evil to
overtake me. No neglect of mine led to misfortune.   10
. . . I judged [poor and] rich (alike). I rescued the
weak from the strong. I opposed the rage of the
ill-disposed and quelled the covetous in his hour.
I [checked] the (passionate) moment of the infuriated.
I restrained weeping by replacing (it with) an avenger(?).
I defended the husbandless widow. I established the
son and heir on the seat of his father. I gave [bread to
the hungry], water to the thirsty, meat and ointment and
clothes to him who had nothing. I relieved the old man,
giving [him] my staff, and causing the old women to   20
say, "What a good action!" I [hated] iniquity, and
wrought it not, causing false men to be fastened head
downwards. I was innocent before God. No one who
knew said concerning me, "What has he done?"
I judged great matter(s?). . . . [I caused] both parties
to go forth at peace. I did not per[vert justice] for
reward. I was not deaf to the empty-handed, nay more, I
never accepted anyone's bribe. . . .
. . . I was clever in all undertakings, deliberate in
counsel, ready to listen. I was skilled in past matters(?),   30
and the [condition?] of yesterday caused me to know
tomorrow.
I judged the suppliant. I did not incline to one side.
I paid no attention to rewards. I was not angry [with him
who came?] as a suppliant. I did not rebuff(?) him.
I tolerated him in his moment of passion. I rescued the
timid man from the violent. . . . .

———————————◆———————————

Figure 3.6 Bronze head from Nineveh, Akkadian, ca. 2415–2290
B.C.E. Height 14⅛ in. Iraq Museum, Baghdad. © Hirmer
Fotoarchiv.

Mesopotamia: Babylon's Written Law

Unlike ancient Egypt, whose political traditions remained relatively unchanged for more than two thousand years, Mesopotamia was the scene of constant upheaval. Mesopotamia's first political units, located at the southeast tip of the Fertile Crescent (see Map 2.1), were the Sumerian city-states, urban centers that governed the neighboring countryside. Ruled by kings or priest-kings who led the army, regulated the economy, and acted as deputies of the gods, the city-states of Sumer were rivalrous and disunited. Sumer's geographic vulnerability to attacks from fierce tribal warriors from the mountainous regions to the north

caused further political instability and invited the intrusion of local warlords. Around 2350 B.C.E., a warrior named Sargon (Figure 3.6) united the city-states of Sumer. By bringing together different peoples and language groups under a single administrator, Sargon created the world's first empire. Sargon's empire eventually fell to the attacks of nomadic tribes that entered Mesopotamia around 2000 B.C.E. Thereafter, the Fertile Crescent was the scene of a rapid turnover of civilizations, each building on the accomplishments of former states.

Shortly after 2000 B.C.E., the rulers of the city-state of Babylon took over the neighboring territories, establishing the First Babylonian Empire. In an effort to consolidate his authority and unify the Empire, Babylon's sixth ruler, Hammurabi, called for a systematic codification of local legal practices. Hammurabi's Code — a collection of 282 clauses engraved on an eight-foot-high **stele** (an upright stone slab) — is our most valuable index to life in ancient Mesopotamia (Figure 3.7). The Code is not the first example of recorded law — Babylonian kings had issued local laws regularly for many generations. It is, however, the most extensive and com-

Figure 3.7 Stele of Hammurabi, ca. 1760 B.C.E. Babylonian. Basalt, entire stele height approx. 7 ft. 4 in. Louvre, Paris. © Hirmer Fotoarchiv.

prehensive set of laws to survive from ancient times.

Written law represented an advance in the development of human rights in that it protected the individual from the decisions of the capricious monarchs. On the other hand, written law provided a less personal kind of justice than oral law. It replaced the flexibility of the spoken word with the rigidity of the written word. It did not usually recognize exceptions and was not easily or quickly changed. Ultimately, recording the law shifted the burden of judgment away from the individual ruler to rest with a set of impartial and objective standards.

Hammurabi's Code is a compilation of civil and criminal statutes that provide penalties for murder, theft, incest, adultery, kidnapping, assault and battery, and many other crimes. It covers a broad spectrum of moral, social, and commercial obligations. But even more important for our understanding of the humanistic tradition, it contains a storehouse of details concerning the nature of class divisions, family relations, and human rights. The Code informs us, for instance, on matters of inheritance (clauses 162 and 168), professional obligations (clauses 218, 219, 229, and 232), and the individual's responsibilities to the community (clauses 109 and 152). Hammurabi's Code documents the fact that under Babylonian law, individuals were not regarded as equals. Human worth was defined in terms of one's wealth and status in society. Violence committed by one free person upon another was punished reciprocally (clause 196), but the same violence committed upon a lower-class individual drew considerably less punishment (clause 198), and penalties were reduced even further if the victim was a slave (clause 199). Similarly, a principle of "pay according to your status" was applied in punishing thieves (clause 8), the upper-class thief being more heavily penalized than the lower-class one. One who could not pay at all fell into slavery or was put to death. Slaves, whether captives of war or victims of debt, had no civil rights under law and enjoyed only the protection of the household to which they belonged.

In Mesopotamian society, women were considered intellectually and physically inferior to men and – much like slaves – were regarded as the chattel property of the male head of the household. A woman went from her father's house to that of her husband, where she was expected to bear children (clause 138). Nevertheless, as indicated by the Code, women enjoyed commercial freedom (clause 109) and considerable legal protection (clauses 134, 138, 209, and 210) that acknowledged their value as childbearers and housekeepers. Clause 142 is an astonishingly early example of no-fault divorce: Since a husband's neglect of his spouse was not punishable, neither party to the marriage was legally "at fault."

Figure 3.8 Stele of Hammurabi (detail, upper portion showing Hammurabi and Shamash, sungod and lawgiver), ca. 1760 B.C.E. Basalt. Louvre, Paris. Cliché des Musées Nationaux, Paris.

READING 8

From the Code of Hammurabi

Clause 8 If a man has stolen an ox, or sheep or an ass, or a pig or a goat, either from a god or a palace, he shall pay thirty-fold. If he is a plebeian,[1] he shall render ten-fold. If the thief has nothing to pay, he shall be slain.

14 If a man has stolen a man's son under age, he shall be slain.

109 If rebels meet in the house of a wine-seller and she does not seize them and take them to the palace, that wine-seller shall be slain.

129 If the wife of a man is found lying with another male, they shall be bound and thrown into the water; unless the husband lets his wife live, and the king lets his servant live.

134 If a man has been taken prisoner, and there is no food in his house, and his wife enters the house of another; then that woman bears no blame.

138 If a man divorces his spouse who has not borne him children, he shall give to her all the sliver of the bride-price, and restore to her the dowry which she brought from the house of her father; and so he shall divorce her.

141 If a man's wife, dwelling in a man's house, has set her face to leave, has been guilty of dissipation, has wasted her house, and has neglected her husband; then she shall be prosecuted. If her husband says she is divorced, he shall let go her way; he shall give her nothing for divorce. If her husband says she is not divorced, her husband may espouse another woman, and that woman shall remain a slave in the house of her husband.

142 If a woman hate her husband, and says "Thou shalt not possess me," the reason for her dislike shall be inquired into. If she is careful and has no fault, but her husband takes himself away and neglects her; then that woman is not to blame. She shall take her dowry and go back to her father's house.

143 If she has not been careful, but runs out, wastes her house and neglects her husband; then that woman shall be thrown into the water.

152 If, after that woman has entered the man's house, they incur debt, both of them must satisfy the trader.

154 If a man has known his daughter, that man shall be banished from his city.

157 If a man after his father has lain in the breasts of his mother, both of them shall be burned.

162 If a man has married a wife, and she has borne children, and that woman has gone to her fate; then her father has no claim upon her dowry. The dowry is her children's.

168 If a man has set his face to disown his son, and has said to the judge, "I disown my son," then the judge shall look into his reasons. If the son has not borne a heavy crime which would justify his being disowned from filiation, then the father shall not disown his son from filiation.

195 If a son has struck his father, his hand shall be cut off.

196 If a man has destroyed the eye of a free man,[2] his own eye shall be destroyed.

198 If he has destroyed the eye of a plebeian, or broken the bone of a plebeian, he shall pay one mina[3] of silver.

199 If he has destroyed the eye of a man's slave, or broken the bone of a man's slave, he shall pay half his value.

209 If a man strike the daughter of a free man, and causes her foetus to fall; he shall pay ten shekels[4] of silver for her foetus.

210 If that woman die, his daughter shall be slain.

213 If he has struck the slave of a man, and made her foetus fall; he shall pay two shekels of silver.

214 If that slave die, he shall pay a third of a mina of silver.

218 If a doctor has treated a man with a metal knife for a severe wound, and has caused the man to die, or has opened a man's tumor with a metal knife, and destroyed the man's eye; his hands shall be cut off.

219 If a doctor has treated a slave of a plebeian with a metal knife for a severe wound, and caused him to die he shall render slave for slave.

229 If a builder has built a house for a man, and his work is not strong, and if the house he has built falls in and kills the householder, that builder shall be slain.

232 If goods have been destroyed, he shall replace all that has been destroyed; and because the house that he built was not made strong, and it has fallen in, he shall restore the fallen house out of his own personal property.

282 If a slave shall say to his master, "Thou are not my master," he shall be prosecuted as a slave, and his owner shall cut off his ear.

———————————◆———————————

Hammurabi's Code reveals a wide range of provisions for the administration of law and order in ancient Mesopotamia. And although the Code dealt primarily with secular matters, its provisions bore the force of divine decree. This fact is indicated by the low-relief carving at the top of the stele on which the laws are inscribed, where Hammurabi is seen receiving the law (symbolized by a staff) from the sun god Shamash (Figure 3.8). Wearing a zigguratlike crown topped with bull's horns, and discharging flames from his shoulders, the god sits enthroned atop a sacred mountain, symbolized by triangular markings beneath his feet.

The Hebrews: The Laws

The laws of ancient Babylon guided Hammurabi's empire some five hundred years before Moses received the Ten Commandments from Yahweh (see chapter 2). The latter differed dramatically from Hammurabi's Code. Not only were the Ten Commandments unconditional and absolute, but the penalties for violation remained unspecified, hence more potentially terrible. As the prophets of Israel made clear, if the Hebrews

---

[1] A member of the lower class, probably a peasant who worked the land for the ruling class.
[2] Above the lower-class peasant, the free man who rented land owed only a percentage of the produce to the ruling class.

[3] A monetary unit equal to approximately one pound of silver.
[4] 60 shekels = 1 mina.

violated the covenant, their children would suffer "to the third and fourth generation." Throughout Hebrew history, the patriarchal bond – protection in exchange for loyalty – characterized the relationship between Hebrew kings and their people, and between Jewish fathers and their families. The covenant between God and the Hebrew people, as expressed in the laws, established a model for secular authority.

The Ten Commandments answered the needs of a relatively unstructured tribal society. They were not, however, the only laws that governed Hebrew life. The Torah (Hebrew for "Law") contains a wide variety of laws pertaining to almost every aspect of daily life. Many of the laws recorded in Exodus and Deuteronomy resemble Hammurabi's: They deal with explicit social and commercial obligations and prescribe specific consequences for their violation. Some of these laws so closely parallel those of the First Babylonian Empire that scholars think a common source may have existed. However, among the Hebrew laws, punishment is not graded according to social class. This is not to say that class distinctions did not exist in Hebrew society, but rather, that the law was meant to apply equally to all classes, with the exception of slaves. The humanitarian bias of the Hebrew laws is best reflected in Jehovah's frequent admonition to the Hebrews that they were once slaves whom God had freed. If the emphasis in Babylonian law is on economic prosperity and political stability, it is the unity of religious and moral life and the personal relationship between God and the individual that lie at the heart of the Hebrew laws.

READING 9

The Book of the Covenant

(Hebrew Bible   Exodus 21: 1–2, 18–27, 37; 23: 1–9)

Chapter 21: Laws Concerning Slaves

[1]"These are the laws you must give them: [2]When you buy a Hebrew slave, his service will last for six years. In the seventh year he will leave a free man without paying compensation."

Blows and Wounds

[18]"If people quarrel and one strikes the other a blow with stone or fist so that the injured party, though not dead, is confined to bed, [19] but later recovers and can go about, even with a stick, the one who struck the blow will have no liability, other than to compensate the injured party for the enforced inactivity and to take care of the injured party until the cure is complete.
[20]"If someone beats his slave, male or female, and the slave dies at his hands, he must pay the penalty. [21]But should the slave survive for one or two days, he will pay no penalty because the slave is his by right of purchase.
[22]"If people, when brawling, hurt a pregnant woman and she suffers a miscarriage but no further harm is done, the person responsible will pay compensation as fixed by the woman's master, paying as much as the judges decide. [23]If further harm is done, however, you will award life for life, [24]eye for eye, tooth for tooth, hand for hand, foot for foot, [25]burn for burn, wound for wound, stroke for stroke.
[26]"If anyone strikes the eye of his slave, male or female, and destroys the use of it, he will give the slave his freedom to compensate for the eye. [27]If he knocks out the tooth of his slave, male or female, he will give the slave his freedom to compensate for the tooth."

Theft of Animals

[37]"If anyone steals an ox or a sheep and slaughters or sells it, he will pay back five beasts from the herd for the ox, and four animals from the flock for the sheep."

Chapter 23: Justice. Duties towards Enemies

[1]"You will not spread false rumours. You will not lend support to the wicked by giving untrue evidence. [2]You will not be led into wrong-doing by the majority nor, when giving evidence in a lawsuit, side with the majority to pervert the course of justice; [3]nor will you show partiality to the poor in a lawsuit.
[4]"If you come on your enemy's ox or donkey straying, you will take it back to him. [5]If you see the donkey of someone who hates you fallen under its load, do not stand back; you must go and help him with it.
[6]"You will not cheat the poor among you of their rights at law. [7]Keep clear of fraud. Do not cause the death of the innocent or upright, and do not acquit the guilty. [8]You will accept no bribes, for a bribe blinds the clear-sighted and is the ruin of the cause of the upright.
[9]"You will not oppress the alien; you know how an alien feels, for you yourselves were once aliens in Egypt."

———————————◆———————————

Empires of the Near East: Assyrian Power

While the first kings of Israel administered the laws of the young Hebrew nation, all of Mesopotamia was feeling the effects of the new iron technology. The manufacture of iron tools and weapons in combination with improved methods of transportation and communication encouraged the growth of large and powerful political units. In the first millennium B.C.E., three consecutive empires – Assyrian, neo-Babylonian, and Persian – succeeded in bringing under their control most of the ancient Near East. Building on traditions that had dominated earlier Mesopotamian civilizations, these empires grew in size and in military might. In 722 B.C.E., the Assyrians – perhaps the cruelest people of the ancient Near East – overthrew Israel and dispersed its population. By the middle of the seventh century B.C.E. they had swallowed up the lands between the Persian Gulf and the Nile valley.

The imposing power of the ambitious eighth-century-B.C.E. Assyrian ruler Sargon II is reflected in his walled citadel located some ten miles from Nineveh

Figure 3.9 Reconstruction drawing of the citadel of Sargon II. Khorsabad, Iraq, ca. 720 B.C.E. (By Charles Altman.) Institute of Archeology Library, University of London.

(see Map 2.1). Covering twenty-five acres, this magnificent complex, protected by turreted walls, featured a ziggurat and an elaborate palace with more than two hundred rooms and courtyards (Figure **3.9**). Accompanied by cuneiform inscriptions, scenes of war and pillage carved in low relief on the palace walls at Nineveh and at the seventh-century-B.C.E. citadel at Nimrud illustrate the conquests of the mighty Assyrian army (Figure **3.10**). In the relief showing the sack of Hamanu, the Elamite stronghold, Assyrian soldiers with pickaxes demolish the enemy fortification and set fire to the town. Such advertisements of Assyrian military superiority represent some of the earliest large-scale efforts to use pictorial narrative as political propaganda.

At Nineveh and Nimrud, scenes of hunting flank those of war, for these two closely related activities graphically portrayed the virtues of courage and physi-

Figure 3.10 The Sack of the City of Hamanu by Ashurbanipal from Nineveh (Kuyunjik), ca. 650 B.C.E. Limestone relief, 36 × 24½ in. Reproduced by courtesy of the Trustees of the British Museum, London.

Figure 3.11 King Ashurnasirpal II Killing Lions, from Palace of King Ashurnasirpal II, Nimrud, ca. 883–859 B.C.E. Alabaster relief, 3 ft. 3 in. × 8 ft. 4 in. Reproduced by courtesy of the Trustees of the British Museum, London.

Figure 3.12 Winged human-headed bull from Khorsabad, Iraq, ca. 720 B.C.E. Limestone, approx. height 13 ft. 10 in. Louvre, Paris.

cal might. Ceremonial lion hunts celebrated the invincibility of the monarch, who in earlier times might have proved his prowess by combating wild animals in the field – even as the legendary Gilgamesh had done. In the contest between the rulers of men and the rulers of beasts, the Assyrians were the undisputed victors. One dramatic scene from Nimrud shows a wounded lion attacking the royal chariot as it speeds away (Figure **3.11**). The artist describes the musculature of the animals' bodies realistically but stylizes other features, such as the warriors' beards and the lions' manes. Spatial depth is indicated by superimposing the chariot wheels over the rear lion's legs, but clarity of design dictates that the second lion fit precisely within the space between front and rear legs of the prancing steeds. The sensitive balance of figures (positive shapes) with unadorned areas of ground (negative space) results in an enormously powerful formal design. The Assyrian reliefs – housed in large numbers at the British Museum in London – are dramatic examples of the ancient artist's ability to infuse violent subject matter with grandeur.

If the lion hunt reliefs made implicit reference to the ruler's invincibility, colossal sculpture clearly manifested the ruler's superhuman magnitude. Similar in spirit to the sphinxes of ancient Egypt (see Figure 3.1), the hybrid beasts that guarded the gateways of Assyrian palaces (Figure **3.12**) combine the physical attributes of the bull (symbol of fertility and strength), the lion (king of the beasts), and the eagle (mighty, winged predator) with the facial features of the monarch. The winged, human-headed creatures from the citadel at Khorsabad must have inspired awe and fear among those who passed beneath their impassive gaze.

China: The Natural Hierarchy and the Mandate of Heaven

As in Egypt and Mesopotamia, the rulers of ancient China were thought to receive their authority to rule from the gods. That authority, known as the Mandate of Heaven, demanded obedience to a divine and self-existing moral law. From the earliest years of the Shang Dynasty (1766–1111 B.C.E.), China's rulers, the so-called "Sons of Heaven," were charged with maintaining the will of heaven on earth. The Chinese placed great emphasis on the idea that nature, which determined human intelligence and ability, dictated a person's proper place in society. Within the natural hierarchy, argued the Chinese, those with greater intellectual abilities should govern, and those with lesser abilities should fulfill the physical needs of the state.

Exactly how those with greater abilities were distinguished from those with lesser abilities is difficult to discern. Nevertheless, between the twelfth and eighth centuries B.C.E., when the Chou emperors controlled most of civilized China, the principle of the natural order (*li*) already provided the basis for the political hierarchy within Chinese society. Since the Chou rulers delegated local authority to aristocrats of their choosing, it is probable that the assumptions of superiority and inferiority among people came after the fact of a division of labor among the members of society. On the other hand, well before the second century B.C.E., the Chinese put into practice the first system in world history in which individuals were selected for government service on the basis of merit and education. Exams tested the competence and skill of those who sought government office. Such a system persisted for centuries and became the basis for the aristocracy of merit that has characterized Chinese culture well into modern times.

Throughout their early history, the Chinese maintained that in an orderly society social positions were distinct and fixed. To know one's place within the order and to act according to *li* were considered essential to the harmony of society as a whole. These views are best transmitted in the accumulated teachings of the sixth-century-B.C.E. thinker named K'ung-futzu, better known as Confucius, a Latinization of his Chinese name. Confucius himself wrote nothing, but conversations compiled by his students offer an idea of that body of unwritten laws that dominated ancient Chinese life. Emphasizing the importance of social tradition, a respect for elders, and the exercise of propriety and manners, Confucius outlined the proper relationship between ruler and ruled. Confucian precepts were basic to Chinese life and thought for well over two thousand years.

READING 10

From *The Teachings of Confucius*

Tsze-kung asked about government. The Master [Confucius] said, *"The requisites of government* are that there be sufficiency of food, sufficiency of military equipment, and the confidence of the people in their ruler." Tsze-kung said, "If it cannot be helped, and one of these must be dispensed with, which of the three should be foregone first?" "The military equipment," said the Master. Tsze-kung *again* asked, "If it cannot be helped, and one of the remaining two must be dispensed with, which of them should be foregone first?" The Master answered, "Part with the food. From of old, death has been the lot of all men; but if the people have no faith *in their rulers*, there is no standing *for the state."*

Ke K'ang asked Confucius about government. Confucius replied, "To govern means to rectify. If you lead on the people with correctness, who will dare not to be correct?"

Ke K'ang asked Confucius about government, saying, "What do you say to killing the unprincipled [bad citizens] for the good of the principled [good citizens]?" Confucius replied, "Sir, in carrying on your government, why should you use killing at all? Let your evinced desires to be for what is good, and the people will be good. The relation between superiors and inferiors is like that between the wind and the grass. The grass must bend, when the wind blows across it."

The ancients who wished to illustrate illustrious virtue throughout the empire first ordered well their own States. Wishing to order well their States, they first regulated their families. Wishing to regulate their families, they first cultivated their persons. Wishing to cultivate their persons, they first rectified their hearts. Wishing to rectify their hearts, they first sought to be sincere in their thoughts. Wishing to be sincere in their thoughts, they first extended to the utmost their knowledge. Such extension of knowledge lay in the investigation of things.

Things being investigated, knowledge became complete. Their knowledge being complete, their thoughts were sincere. Their thoughts being sincere, their hearts were then rectified. Their hearts being rectified, their persons were cultivated. Their persons being cultivated, their families were regulated. Their families being regulated, their States were rightly governed. Their States being rightly governed, the whole empire was made tranquil and happy.

From the emperor down to the mass of the people, all must consider the cultivation of the person the root of *every thing besides*.

It cannot be, when the root is neglected, that what should spring from it will be well ordered.

What is meant by "In order rightly to govern his State, it is necessary first to regulate his family," is this: — It is not possible for one to teach others, while he cannot teach his own family. Therefore, the ruler, without going beyond his family, completes the lessons for the State. There is filial piety: — therewith the sovereign should be served. There is fraternal submission: — therewith elders and superiors should be served. There is kindness: — therewith the multitude should be treated.

From the loving *example* of one family, a whole State becomes loving, and from its courtesies, the whole State becomes courteous, while, from the ambition and perverseness of the one man, the whole State may be led to rebellious disorder; — such is the nature of the influence. This verifies the saying, "Affairs may be ruined by a single sentence; a kingdom may be settled by its one man." 60

By the ruler's cultivation of his own character, the duties of *universal obligation* are set forth. By honoring men of virtue and talents, his is preserved from errors of judgment. By showing affection to his relatives, there is no grumbling or resentment among his uncles and brethren. 70 By respecting the great ministers, he is kept from errors in the practice of government. By kind and considerate treatment of the whole body of officers, they are led to make the most grateful return for his courtesies. By dealing with the mass of people as his children, they are led to exhort one another to what is good. . . .

————————◆————————

The teachings of Confucius preserved the ideas set forth in the imperial edicts of the Shang and Chou dynasties. Confucius stated that the ruler was the parent of the people, an idea that closely parallels the patriarchal view of the Hebrews, as well as the Egyptian assertion that the pharaoh "is the father and mother of all men." In accordance with Chinese moral law, however, the cultivation of character and the regulation of the family preceded the ruler's ability to govern. Good influence was of greater political value than physical force or the threat of punishment. Without setting moral examples in their own conduct, rulers could not expect to inspire virtue among their subjects. For Confucius, moral and political life were one. Moral harmony was the root of political harmony, and moral rectitude made government itself all but unnecessary.

SUMMARY

Within the civilizations of the ancient world, powerful rulers identified themselves with the gods in bringing law and order to human society. The close association between secular authority and spiritual power fostered the concept of law as a form of divine justice. It also inspired the creation of art that advertised the omnipotence of the ruler. Although laws necessarily restricted individual freedom, they safe-guarded the basic religious and secular values of the community. Egyptian laws remained unwritten until the end of the first millennium B.C.E., but the Egyptian bureaucracy, controlled by viziers, served to regulate the activities of the state.

Under the Babylonian ruler Hammurabi, laws were codified and recorded. Hammurabi's Code governed a complex society by way of strict rules that varied according to one's class. Among the Hebrews,

specific and conditional laws similar to Hammurabi's complemented the unconditional Ten Commandments. Such laws showed a lack of class bias and a strong personal bond between God and the Hebrew people. The first millennium B.C.E. proved to be an age of ruthless imperialism in which empires like that of Assyria used pictorial propaganda to broadcast the majesty and invincibility of the state.

Ancient Chinese concepts of political harmony were rooted in the idea of universal moral order, the doctrine of natural equality, and a system of advancement based on merit. Confucius confirmed the ancient Chinese concept of the Mandate of Heaven, which held that the ruler must carry out the will of heaven on earth. Throughout the ancient world, the establishment of authority, law, and order enabled early civilizations to function efficiently, if not aggressively, and to grow in size and cultural complexity.

GLOSSARY

caste system   a system of rigid social stratification based on differences in wealth, rank, or occupation

dynasty   a sequence of rulers from the same family

li   (Chinese, "arrangement") the natural and universal order, which governs all of the laws and usages of Chinese social and political life

stele   an upright stone slab or pillar carved or inscribed for commemorative purposes

theocratic monarch   one who rules as the representative of the gods

SUGGESTIONS FOR READING

Creel, H.G. *Confucius and the Chinese Way*. New York: Harper, 1960.

Dawson, Raymond. *Confucius*. Oxford: Oxford University Press, 1981.

Kramer, S.N. *History Begins at Sumer*, 3rd ed. Philadelphia: University of Pennsylvania Press, 1981.

Lloyd, Seton. *The Art of the Ancient Near East*. New York: Praeger, 1965.

Loewe, Michael. *Everyday Life in Early Imperial China*. New York: Putnam, 1968.

Munro, Donald J. *The Concept of Man in Early China*. Stanford, Calif.: Stanford University Press, 1969.

Murray, M.S. *The Splendor That Was Egypt*. New York: Praeger, 1972.

Romer, John. *Ancient Lives: Daily Life in Egypt of the Pharaohs*. New York: Holt, 1984.

Saggs, W.F. *The Might That Was Assyria*. Salem, N.H.: Merrimack, 1984.

Sewell, Barbara. *Egypt Under the Pharaohs*. New York: Putnam, 1968.

Watterson, Barbara. *Women in Ancient Egypt*. New York: St. Martin's Press, 1992.

White, J.M. *Everyday Life in Ancient Egypt*. New York: Capricorn, 1967.

PART

II

THE CLASSICAL LEGACY

Between 500 B.C.E. and 500 C.E., the great civilizations of Greece and Rome came to flower in the Mediterranean world. Their influence upon the humanistic tradition was both profound and long lasting and far exceeded that of any culture that preceded them. To the civilizations of Greece and Rome we owe almost all of the basic forms of literary expression (including drama, the epistle, lyric poetry, satire, and historical narrative), the beginnings of philosophic and scientific inquiry, the development of civil and judicial law, and the formulation of aesthetic norms in art and music that persisted for well over a thousand years.

The civilizations of Greece and Rome are called "classical." *Classic* and *classical* generally mean "first-ranking," "enduring," or "the best of its kind." However, these terms are used variously in the study of culture. First, we may use the word classic to mean the most characteristic phase or form of expression, or the best of its kind. So, "classic" Chinese literature refers to the teachings of Confucius and the early poets, and "classic" cars refer to the finest vintage automobiles. Second, because the civilizations of Greece and Rome provided enduring and authoritative models in both art and life, we use the adjectives "classic" or "classical" as an historical designation for those civilizations and the period in which they flourished (ca. 500 B.C.E. to 500 C.E.). Finally, we use "classical" as a stylistic term

embracing the principles of clarity, harmony, and order that dominated all phases of Greek and Roman expression. A standard of beauty and excellence, the classical style became the object of frequent revival in the West.

The Greek and Roman civilizations both emerged north and west of Africa and the Near East where the ancient civilizations of Egypt and Mesopotamia had flourished (see Maps 2.1, 4.1). Between 1200 and 750 B.C.E., the earliest Greek city-states appeared on islands and peninsulas in the Aegean Sea, on the coast of Asia Minor, at the southern tip of Italy, and in Sicily. This ancient civilization called itself "Hellas" and its people "Hellenes." During the fifth century B.C.E., a period known as the Golden Age of Greece, the Hellenic city-states produced some of the finest minds in the history of culture, including Socrates, Sophocles, Pericles, and Plato. After the fall of Greece in 338 B.C.E. and under the leadership of Alexander the Great, Hellenic culture spread throughout Asia into the Far East. And well into the period of Roman dominance in the Mediterranean, the legacy of Greece continued to mold and shape the culture of the West.

While Greece was enjoying a Golden Age of culture, Rome established itself as the leading city-state of the Italian peninsula. Rome's history is often divided into two phases: the Republic (509–31 B.C.E.) and the Empire (31 B.C.E.–476 C.E.). The Romans created the largest and most powerful empire in the ancient world. Their achievements in engineering, architecture, literature, and law would be imitated in the West long after the collapse of Rome itself. They also absorbed and

(opposite) Figure 6.3 Exekias, Black Amphora with Achilles and Ajax Playing Dice, ca. 530 B.C.E. Height 24 in. Vatican Museums, Rome.

transmitted to the West the heritage of classical Greek culture and the fundamentals of a young religious faith called Christianity.

Chapter 4 of this unit gives attention to the development of humanism and individualism – the hallmarks of the classical legacy. It explores these qualities as they first appeared in the Homeric epics and as they come to be identified with the Greek community, especially the city-state of Athens. The democratic leadership of Pericles, the heroic idealism of Socrates, and the conflict between the individual and the state as revealed in Sophocles' *Antigone* are the principal themes of this chapter. The Greek contribution to philosophy and speculative thought is the subject of chapter 5, which surveys the contributions of the pre-Socratics, the Stoics, and the philosophers Plato and Aristotle. Plato's *Republic* and Aristotle's *Ethics* are the central texts in this chapter. Chapter 6 describes the classical style in the arts of painting, sculpture, architecture, music, literature, and dance. The chapter also considers the diffusion of the classical style eastward during the Hellenistic Age, the era ushered in by Alexander the Great. The final chapter in this unit treats the Roman cultural achievement. It gives special attention to the ways in which Roman imperialism influenced and shaped the various forms of cultural expression. The chapter closes with a brief look at the extraordinary achievements of the Han dynasty, whose role in preserving the classical culture of China parallels that of Rome in the West.

4

Humanism, Individualism, and the Greek Community

Few civilizations have been as deeply concerned with the quality of human life as that of the ancient Greeks. Their art, their literature, and even their religion emphasized human interests and concerns. For this reason, we call the ancient Greeks *humanists*. The ancient Greeks were also *individualists* – that is, they asserted the distinctness of the individual over the group. They challenged fortune and made every effort to control their own destinies. These attitudes fostered a sense of optimism and pride that is apparent even in the formative stages of Greek civilization.

The Bronze Age Civilizations of the Aegean *(ca. 2500–1200 B.C.E.)*

The Bronze Age culture of Mycenae was not known to the world until the late nineteenth century, when an amateur German archeologist named Heinrich Schliemann uncovered the first artifacts of ancient Troy (Map 4.1). Schliemann's excavations also revealed the civilization of an adventuresome tribal people, the Mycenaeans, who had established themselves on the

Map 4.1 Ancient Greece.

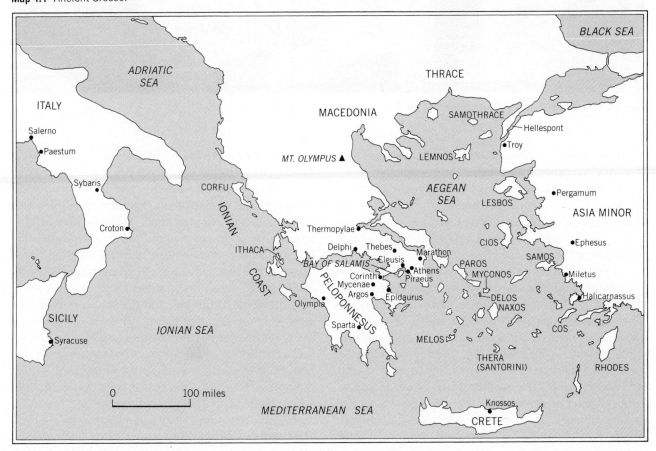

Figure 4.1 Palace of Minos, Knossos, Crete, ca. 1500 B.C.E. Photo: Gloria K. Fiero.

Greek mainland around 1600 B.C.E. Subsequent discoveries by other archeologists uncovered an even earlier pre-Greek civilization located on the island of Crete in the Aegean Sea. Named Minoan, after the legendary King Minos, this maritime civilization flourished between 2000 and 1400 B.C.E, when it was absorbed by the Mycenaeans.

Centered at the palace in Knossos on Crete (Figure 4.1), Minoan culture was prosperous and peace-loving. So much so, that Minoan cities lacked protective walls. The three-story palace at Knossos was a labyrinthian masonry structure with dozens of rooms and corridors built around a courtyard. The interior walls of the palace were decorated with frescoes illustrating natural and marine motifs (Figure 4.2), ritual processions, and other aspects of Cretan life. The most famous of the palace frescoes, the so-called "Bull-leaping" fresco, shows two women and a man, the latter vigorously

somersaulting over the back of a bull (Figure 4.3). A ritual game probably associated with the cult of the bull – ancient symbol of virility – the scene is an early version of the modern bullfight, the "rules" of which were codified in Roman times by Julius Caesar. The significance of the representation lies in the dimension it gives to the human beings, who are pictured not as pawns in a divine game, but rather, as contestants who challenge or interact with divine forces. Minoan fertility cults honored the bull and the snake, both associated with regenerative power. The small statue of a bare-breasted female brandishing snakes may represent a fertility goddess, or it may depict a priestess in the performance of cult rites (Figure 4.4). Minoan writing (known as "Linear A") has not yet been deciphered, but a later version of the script ("Linear B") found on mainland Greece appears to be an early form of Greek. The Greeks recalled Minoan society through myths and

Figure 4.2 The Queen's Quarters, Palace of Minos, Knossos, Crete, ca. 1450 B.C.E. Ancient Art and Architecture Collection, Middlesex.

Figure 4.3 Bull-leaping fresco from the Palace of Minos, Knossos, Crete, ca. 1500 B.C.E. Height 32 in. Archaeological Museum, Heraklion, Crete. Scala, Florence.

legends such as that describing the Minotaur – a monstrous half-man, half-bull hybrid born of the union of Minos' wife and a sacred white bull. According to the story, the Athenian hero Theseus killed the Minotaur, thus releasing Athens from its ancient bondage to the Minoans.

In contrast to the Minoans, the Mycenaeans were a militant and aggressive people. They built heavily fortified citadels at Tiryns and Mycenae (Figure 4.5), and used warships to challenge other east Mediterranean traders. Sometime after 1200 B.C.E., the Mycenaeans attacked Troy ("Ilion," in Greek), a commercial stronghold on the coast of Asia Minor. The ten-year-long war between Mycenae and Troy provided the context for two great epics, the *Iliad* and the *Odyssey*.

Figure 4.4 Priestess with Snakes, Minoan, ca. 1600 B.C.E. Faience, height 13½ in. Archaeological Museum, Heraklion, Crete. © Hirmer Fotoarchiv.

Figure 4.5 Lion gate, Citadel at Mycenae, 1500–1300 B.C.E. Limestone, ght of relief 9 ft. 6 in. © Hirmer Fotoarchiv.

The Heroic Age (ca. 1200–750 B.C.E.)

Soon after 1200 B.C.E., more powerful, iron-bearing tribes of Dorians, a Greek-speaking people from the north, destroyed Mycenaean civilization. During the long period of darkness that followed, the adventures and beliefs of the Mycenaeans were transmitted orally, in the form of stories about the Trojan War. It was not until at least the ninth century B.C.E that these stories, in the form of the epic poems known as the *Iliad* and the *Odyssey*, were transcribed, and it was another three hundred years before they reached their present form. These two great epics became the "national" poems of ancient Greece, uniting the Greeks and establishing the basis for a common heritage. Indeed, much of what is known about the early history of the Greeks comes from these two poems. Little is known, however, about Homer, the blind poet to whom the epic poems are traditionally attributed. We are not sure when or where he lived, or indeed, if he existed at all. The only fact of which we can be fairly certain is that Homer represents the culmination of a long and vigorous oral tradition in which tale-telling – possibly to instrumental accompaniment – was a major source of entertainment.

The *Iliad* takes place in the last days of the Trojan War. It is the story of the hero Achilles (or Achilleus), who, moved to anger by an affront to his honor, refuses to fight against Troy alongside his Achaean comrades. When his dearest friend, Patroclos, is killed by Hector, the leader of the Trojan forces, Achilles finally and

Figure 4.6 Contest of Two Warriors. Attic Black Figure Amphora. 11½ × 9½ in. Courtesy, Museum of Fine Arts, Boston. H.L. Pierce Fund.

fiercely goes to war. The *Odyssey*, the second of the two Greek epics, is the story of the long, adventure-packed sea journey undertaken by Odysseus, the resourceful hero of the Trojan War, in his effort to return to his home and family in Ithaca. Both the *Iliad* and the *Odyssey* follow the oral tradition of the *Epic of Gilgamesh*, but while the *Epic of Gilgamesh* deals with the hero's pursuit of everlasting life, the Greek epics examine the hero's quest for honor and glory.

Although the *Iliad* is a tale of adventure, its true subject is the personality of Achilles. Like Gilgamesh, Achilles is part god and part man: He is the son of Peleus, King of Thessaly, and the sea nymph Thetis, who dipped her infant son in the river Styx and made him invulnerable except for the heel by which she held him. But Achilles is a far more complex character than Gilgamesh: The emotions he exhibits, his anger, love, rage, and grief, are wholly human. The story of the *Iliad* turns on Achilles' decision to take action that will bring glory to his tribe and to himself. The importance of heroic action in proving virtue, or excellence (the Greek word *arete* connotes both), is central to the *Iliad*, as it is to Hellenic culture as a whole. To the ancient Greeks, moral value lay in proper action, even if the consequence of that action meant death (Figure **4.6**). The excerpts from the *Iliad* in Reading 11 illustrate these values.

The language of the *Iliad* is embellished with vivid **similes** (anger "swarms like smoke inside a man's heart"), **epithets** ("the bronze-armored Achaeans"), and colorful **catalogs** of people and things. Both for its majestic poetry and for its heroic personalities, the *Iliad* has inspired generations of Western writers, including Virgil and Milton, who will be discussed later.

READING 11

From the *Iliad*

(Books 18, 19, 24)

So these fought on in the likeness of blazing fire. Meanwhile, 1
Antilochos came, a swift-footed messenger, to Achilles,
and found him sitting in front of the steep-horned ships,
    thinking
over in his heart of things which had now been accomplished.
Disturbed, Achilles spoke to the spirit in his own great heart:
"Ah me, how is it that once again the flowing-haired Achaeans[1]
are driven out of the plain on their ships in fear and confusion?
May the gods not accomplish vile sorrows upon the heart in me
in the way my mother once made it clear to me, when she told
    me

how while I yet lived the bravest of all the Myrmidons[2] 10
must leave the light of the sun beneath the hands of the
    Trojans.
Surely, then, the strong son of Menoitios[3] has perished.
Unhappy! and yet I told him, once he had beaten the fierce fire
off, to come back to the ships, not fight in strength against
    Hector."
Now as he was pondering this in his heart and his spirit,
meanwhile the son of stately Nestor was drawing near him
and wept warm tears, and gave Achilles his sorrowful message:
"Ah me, son of valiant Peleus; you must hear from me
the ghastly message of a thing I wish never had happened.
Patroclos has fallen, and now they are fighting over his body 20
which is naked. Hector of the shining helm has taken his
    armor."
He spoke, and the black cloud of sorrow closed on Achilles.
In both hands he caught up the grimy dust, and poured it
over his head and face, and fouled his handsome countenance,
and the black ashes were scattered over his immortal tunic.
And he himself, mightily in his might, in the dust lay
at length, and took and tore at his hair with his hands, and
    defiled it.
And the handmaidens Achilles and Patroclos had taken
captive, stricken at heart cried out aloud, and came running
out of doors about valiant Achilles, and all of them 30
beat their breasts with their hands, and the limbs went slack
    in each of them.
On the other side Antilochos mourned with him, letting the
    tears fall,
and held the hands of Achilles as he grieved in his proud heart,
fearing Achilles might cut his throat with the iron. He cried out
terribly, aloud, and the lady his mother heard him
as she sat in the depths of the sea at the side of her aged father,
and she cried shrill in turn, and the goddesses gathered about
    her,
all who along the depth of the sea were daughters of Nereus.[4]

. . . .

There as he sighed heavily the lady his mother stood by him
and cried out shrill and aloud, and took her son's head in
    her arms, then 40
sorrowing for him she spoke to him in winged words: "Why
    then,
child, do you lament? What sorrow has come to your heart
    now?
Speak out, do not hide it. These things are brought to
    accomplishment
through Zeus: in the way that you lifted your hands and
    prayed for,
that all the sons of the Achaeans be pinned on their
    grounded vessels
by reason of your loss, and suffer things that are shameful."
Then sighing heavily Achilles of the swift feet answered her:
"My mother, all these things the Olympian brought to
    accomplishment.

---

[1] The Mycenaeans, who inhabited the kingdom near Thessaly, and, more broadly, the Greek army that besieged Troy.

[2] The name by which the subjects of Peleus and Achilles are known in Homer. It derives from the Greek word for *ants*, the creatures out of which Zeus was said to have created the inhabitants of the island of Aegina, ruled by Peleus.

[3] Patroclos, Achilles' favorite companion and friend.

[4] A sea-god, the "Old Man" of the sea and father of some fifty to one hundred daughters, including Thetis, mother of Achilles.

But what pleasure is this to me, since my dear companion
    has perished,
Patroclos, whom I loved beyond all other companions,   50
as well as my own life. I have lost him, and Hector, who
    killed him,
has stripped away that gigantic armor, a wonder to look on
and splendid, which the gods gave Peleus, a glorious present,
on that day they drove you to the marriage bed of a mortal.
I wish you had gone on living then with the other goddesses
of the sea, and that Peleus had married some mortal woman.
As it is, there must be on your heart a numberless sorrow
for your son's death, since you can never again receive him
won home again to his country; since the spirit within does
    not drive me
to go on living and be among men, except on condition   60
that Hector first be beaten down under my spear, lose his
    life
and pay the price for stripping Patroclos, the son of
    Menoitios."
    Then in turn Thetis spoke to him, letting the tears fall:
"Then I must lose you soon, my child, by what you are saying,
since it is decreed your death must come soon after Hector's."
    Then deeply disturbed Achilles of the swift feet
    answered her:
"I must die soon, then; since I was not to stand by my
    companion
when he was killed. And now, far away from the land of his
    fathers,
he has perished, and lacked my fighting strength to defend
    him.
Now, since I am not going back to the beloved land of my
    fathers,   70
since I was no light of safety to Patroclos, nor to my other
companions, who in their numbers went down before
    glorious Hector,
but sit here beside by ships, a useless weight on the good land,
I, who am such as no other of the bronze-armored Achaeans
in battle, though there are others also better in council —
why, I wish that strife would vanish away from among gods
    and mortals,
and gall, which makes a man grow angry for all his great mind,
that gall of anger that swarms like smoke inside of a man's
    heart
and becomes a thing sweeter to him by far than the
    dripping of honey.
So it was here that the lord of men Agamemnon[5] angered
    me.   80
Still, we will let all this be a thing of the past, and for all our
sorrow beat down by force the anger deeply within us.
Now I shall go, to overtake that killer of a dear life,
Hector; then I will accept my own death, at whatever
time Zeus wishes to bring it about, and the other immortals.

[Hephaestus (Hephaistos), god of fire and of metalworking, has
forged a special set of arms for Achilles. In the following lines
from Book 19, Achilles prepares to lead the Achaeans into
battle.]

As when in their thickness the snowflakes of Zeus come
    fluttering
cold beneath the blast of the north wind born in the bright sky,
so now in their thickness the pride of the helms bright shining
were carried out from the ships, and shields massive in the
    middle
and the corselets strongly hollowed and the ash spears
    were worn forth.   90
The shining swept to the sky and all earth was laughing
    about them
under the glitter of bronze and beneath their feet stirred
    the thunder
of men, within whose midst brilliant Achilles helmed him.
A clash went from the grinding of his teeth, and his eyes
    glowed
as if they were the stare of a fire, and the heart inside him
was entered with sorrow beyond endurance. Raging at the
    Trojans
he put on the gifts of the god, that Hephaestus wrought
    him with much toil.
    First he placed along his legs the fair greaves linked with
silver fastenings to hold the greaves at the ankles.
Afterward he girt on about his chest the corselet,   100
and across his shoulders slung the sword with the nails of
    silver,
a bronze sword, and caught up the great shield, huge and
    heavy
next, and from it the light glimmered far, as from the moon.
And as when from across water a light shines to mariners
from a blazing fire, when the fire is burning high in the
    mountains
in a desolate steading, as the mariners are carried unwilling
by storm winds over the fish-swarming sea, far away from
    their loved ones;
so the light from the fair elaborate shield of Achilles
shot into the high air. And lifting the helm he set it
massive upon his head, and the helmet crested with
    horsehair   110
shone like a star, the golden fringes were shaken about it
which Hephaestus had driven close along the horn of the
    helmet.
And brilliant Achilles tried himself in his armor, to see
if it fitted close, and how his glorious limbs ran within it,
and the armor became as wings and upheld the shepherd
    of the people.
Next he pulled out from its standing place the spear of his
    father,
huge, heavy, thick, which no one else of all the Achaeans
could handle, but Achilles alone knew how to wield it,
the Pelian ash spear which Cheiron[6] had brought to his
    father
from high on Pelion, to be death for fighters in battle.   120
Automedon and Alkimos, in charge of the horses,
yoked them, and put the fair breast straps about them, and
    forced the bits home
between their jaws, and pulled the reins back against the
    compacted

---

[5]King of Mycenae, who led the Greek forces in the Trojan War.

[6]Or Chiron, a centaur (half-man, half-horse), one of the creatures driven
from Mount Pelion by the Lapiths (see Figure 6.24).

chariot seat, and one, Automedon, took up the shining
whip caught close in his hand and vaulted up to the chariot,
while behind him Achilles helmed for battle took his stance
shining in all his armor like the sun when he crosses
     above us,
and cried in a terrible voice on the horses of his father:
"Xanthos, Balios, Bay and Dapple, famed sons of Podarge,
take care to bring in another way your charioteer back   130
to the company of the Danaans, when we give over fighting,
not leave him to lie fallen there, as you did to Patroclos."

[After Achilles defeats Hector, Priam, Hector's father and king
of Troy, comes to the Achaean camp. In the following lines from
Book 24, Priam begs for the return of his son's body.]

. . . The old man made straight for the dwelling
where Achilles the beloved of Zeus was sitting. He found him
inside, and his companions were sitting apart, as two only,
Automedon the hero and Alkimos, scion of Ares,
were busy beside him. He had just now got through with his
    dinner,
with eating and drinking, and the table still stood by. Tall
    Priam
came in unseen by the other men and stood close beside him
and caught the knees of Achilles in his arms, and kissed
    the hands   140
that were dangerous and manslaughtering and had killed
    so many
of his sons. As when dense disaster closes on one who has
    murdered
a man in his own land, and he comes to the country of
    others,
to a man of substance, and wonder seizes on those who
    behold him,
so Achilles wondered as he looked on Priam, a godlike
man, and the rest of them wondered also, and looked at
    each other.
But now Priam spoke to him in the words of a suppliant:
"Achilles like the gods, remember your father, one who
is of years like mine, and on the door-sill of sorrowful old age.
And they who dwell nearby encompass him and afflict
    him,   150
nor is there any to defend him against the wrath, the
    destruction.
Yet surely he, when he hears of you and that you are still
    living,
is gladdened within his heart and all his days he is hopeful
that he will see his beloved son come home from the Troad.[7]
But for me, my destiny was evil. I have had the noblest
of sons in Troy, but I say not one of them is left to me.
Fifty were my sons, when the sons of the Achaeans came
    here.
Nineteen were born to me from the womb of a single mother,
and other women bore the rest in my palace; and of these
violent Ares broke the strength in the knees of most of
    them,   160
but one was left me who guarded my city and people, that
    one

you killed a few days since as he fought in defence of his
    country,
Hector; for whose sake I come now to the ships of the
    Achaeans
to win him back from you, and I bring you gifts beyond
    number.
Honor then the gods, Achilles, and take pity upon me
remembering your father, yet I am still more pitiful;
I have gone through what no other mortal on earth has gone
    through;
I put my lips to the hands of the man who has killed my
    children."
    So he spoke, and stirred in the other a passion of grieving
for his own father. He took the old man's hand and pushed
    him   170
gently away, and the two remembered, as Priam sat
    huddled
at the feet of Achilles and wept close for manslaughtering
    Hector
and Achilles wept now for his own father, now again
for Patroclos. The sound of their mourning moved in the
    house. Then
when great Achilles had taken full satisfaction in sorrow
and the passion for it had gone from his mind and body,
    thereafter
he rose from his chair, and took the old man by the hand,
    and set him
on his feet again, in pity for the grey head and the grey
    beard,
and spoke to him and addressed him in winged words: "Ah,
    unlucky,
surely you have had much evil to endure in your spirit.   180
How could you dare to come alone to the ships of the
    Achaeans
and before my eyes, when I am one who have killed in such
    numbers
such brave sons of yours? The heart in you is iron. Come, then,
and sit down upon this chair, and you and I will even let
our sorrows lie still in the heart for all our grieving. There is not
any advantage to be won from grim lamentation.
Such is the way the gods spun life for unfortunate mortals,
that we live in unhappiness, but the gods themselves have
    no sorrows.
There are two urns that stand on the door-sill of Zeus. They
    are unlike
for the gifts they bestow: an urn of evils, an urn of
    blessings.   190
If Zeus who delights in thunder mingles these and bestows
    them
on man, he shifts, and moves now in evil, again in good
    fortune.
But when Zeus bestows from the urn of sorrows, he makes
    a failure
of man, and the evil hunger drives him over the shining
earth, and he wanders respected neither of gods nor mortals.
Such were the shining gifts given by the gods to Peleus
from his birth, who outshone all men beside for his riches
and pride of possession, and was lord over the Myrmidons.
    Thereto

---

[7] The coastal region of Asia Minor south of Troy.

the gods bestowed an immortal wife on him, who was mortal.
But even on him the god piled evil also. There was not   200
any generation of strong sons born to him in his great house
but a single all-untimely child he had, and I give him
no care as he grows old, since far from the land of my
    fathers
I sit here in Troy, and bring nothing but sorrow to you and
    your children.
And you, old sir, we are told you prospered once; for as much
as Lesbos, Makar's hold, confines to the north above it
and Phrygia from the north confines, and enormous
    Hellespont,
of these, old sir, you were lord once in your wealth and your
    children.
But now the Uranian gods brought us, an affliction upon you,
forever there is fighting about your city, and men killed.   210
But bear up, nor mourn endlessly in your heart, for there is
    not
anything to be gained from grief for your son; you will never
bring him back; sooner you must go through yet another
    sorrow."
    In answer to him again spoke aged Priam the godlike:
"Do not, beloved of Zeus, make me sit on a chair while
    Hector
lies yet forlorn among the shelters; rather with all speed
give him back, so my eyes may behold him, and accept the
    ransom
we bring you, which is great. You may have joy of it, and go
    back
to the land of your own fathers, since once you have
    permitted me
to go on living myself and continue to look on the
    sunlight."   220
    . . . .

Then when the serving-maids had washed the corpse and
    anointed it
with olive oil, they threw a fair great cloak and a tunic
about him, and Achilles himself lifted him and laid him
on a litter, and his friends helped him lift it to the smooth-
    polished
mule wagon. He groaned then, and called by name on his
    beloved companion:
"Be not angry with me, Patroclos, if you discover,
though you be in the house of Hades, that I gave back great
    Hector
to his loved father, for the ransom he gave me was not
    unworthy.
I will give you your share of the spoils, as much as is fitting."
    So spoke great Achilles and went back into the shelter   230
and sat down on the elaborate couch from which he had
    risen,
against the inward wall, and now spoke his word to Priam:
"Your son is given back to you, aged sir, as you asked it.
He lies on a bier. When dawn shows you yourself shall see him
as you take him away. Now you and I must remember our
    supper."
    . . . .

———————————◆———————————

The Greek Gods

The ancient Greeks saw their gods as a family of immortals who intervened in the lives of human beings. Originating in the combined cultures of Crete and Mycenae, their gods included: the powerful sky god Zeus; Poseidon, god of the sea; Hera, queen of heaven; Apollo, god of light, medicine, and music; Dionysus, god of wine and vegetation; Athena, goddess of wisdom and war; and Aphrodite, goddess of love and procreation. Around these deities and others there emerged an elaborate mythology. Although immortal, the Greek gods were much like the human beings who worshiped them – fun loving, capricious, and quarrelsome. They lived not in heaven, but, conveniently enough, atop a mountain in northern Greece, among the Greeks themselves. From their home on Mount Olympus, the gods might intervene in combat (as they do in the *Iliad*), seduce mortal women, and meddle in the lives of ordinary human beings. The gods were not always benevolent, nor did they hold out the promise of a better life in the hereafter. And unlike the Hebrew God, they established no clear principles of moral conduct and no guidelines for religious worship. Popular Greek religion produced no sacred scripture and no dogma. This circumstance may have contributed to the freedom of intellectual inquiry for which the Greeks were noted. It also may have contributed to the development of a culture whose focus was this-worldly rather than otherworldly. For despite the interference of the gods in the actions of such epic heroes as Achilles and Odysseus, it is the men, not the gods, who dominate the Homeric world.

The Greek City-State and the Persian Wars (ca. 750–480 B.C.E.)

Toward the end of the Homeric Age, the Greeks formed small rural colonies that grew into urban communities mainly through maritime trade. Geographic conditions – a rocky terrain interrupted by mountains, valleys, and narrow rivers – encouraged the evolution of the independent city-state (in Greek, *polis*). Ancient Greece consisted of some two hundred city-states, some as large as four hundred square miles and others as tiny as two square miles. Many, like Athens, were small enough that a person might walk around their walls in only a few hours. Although all of the Greek city-states shared the same language, traditions, and religion, each *polis* established its own government, issued its own coinage, and provided its own military defenses. The autonomy of the Greek city-states led to fierce competition and commercial rivalry. However, when menaced by outside enemies such as the expanding Persian Empire, they united in self-defense.

By the sixth century B.C.E., the Persian Empire stretched from the frontiers of India westward to Asia Minor. Persia's annexation of Ionia, the coastal cities of Asia Minor (see Map 4.1), threatened mainland Greece, and when, in 499 B.C.E., in the Ionian cities revolted against Persian rule, the other Greek city-states came to their aid. In retaliation, the Persians sent military expeditions to punish the rebel cities of the Greek mainland. In 490 B.C.E., on the plain of Marathon, twenty-five miles from Athens, a Greek force of eleven thousand men met a Persian army twice its size and defeated them, losing only 192 men to Persian casualties of more than six thousand. But the Greeks soon realized that without a strong navy even the combined land forces of the city-states could not hope to oust the Persians. They thus proceeded to build a fleet of warships, which, in 480 B.C.E., defeated the Persian armada at Salamis, one of the final battles of the Persian Wars.

The story of the Persian Wars was told by the Greek historian, Herodotus (ca. 485–425 B.C.E), who is often called "the father of history." Writing not as an eye-witness, Herodotus nevertheless produced a systematic and critical assessment of his sources. *The Persian Wars*, which followed the Homeric poems by some three hundred years, is also important as the first major classical work in prose. Herodotus' sprawling history is filled with fascinating anecdotes and colorful digressions, including a "travelogue" of his visits to Egypt and Asia, an account that remains one of our most detailed sources of information about ancient Near Eastern social and political customs.

Athens and the Golden Age of Greece *(ca. 480–430 B.C.E.)*

Although all of the city-states had contributed to expelling the Persians, it was Athens that claimed the crown of victory; indeed in the wake of the Persian Wars, Athens assumed political dominance among the city-states, as well as commercial supremacy in the Aegean Sea. The defeat of Persia inspired a mood of confidence and a spirit of vigorous chauvinism. This spirit ushered in a Golden Age of drama, philosophy, music, art, and architecture. In fact the period between 480 and 430 B.C.E. was one of the most creative in the history of the world. At that time, too, the heroic idealism of the *Iliad* was transformed into civic patriotism.

Athens, the most cosmopolitan of the city-states, was unique among the Greek communities, for its democratic government that came to prevail was the exception rather than the rule in ancient Greece. In its early history, Athens – like most of the other Greek city-states – was an **oligarchy** – that is, a government controlled by an elite minority. But a series of enlightened rulers who governed Athens between roughly 600 and 500 B.C.E. introduced reforms that placed increasing authority in the hands of its citizens. The Athenian statesman and legislator Solon (sixth century B.C.E.) abolished the custom of debt slavery and encouraged members of the lower classes to serve in public office, thus broadening the civic responsibilities of Athenian citizens and educating all classes in the activities of government. By 550 B.C.E., the Popular Assembly of Citizens was operating alongside the Council of Five Hundred (made up of aristocrats who handled routine state business) and the Board of Ten Generals (an annually elected executive body). When, in the year 508 B.C.E., the Popular Assembly acquired the right to make laws, Athens became the first and only direct democracy in world history.

Democracy is a Greek word describing a government in which the people (*demos*) hold power (*kratos*). In the democracy of ancient Athens, Athenian citizens exercised political power directly, thus, unlike the United States, where power rests in the hands of representatives of the people, the citizens of Athens themselves held the authority to make the laws and approve state policy. Athenian democracy was, however, highly exclusive. Its citizens included only landowning males over the age of eighteen. Of an estimated population of 250,000, this probably constituted some forty thousand people. Women, children, resident aliens, and slaves – approximately 150,000 people – did not qualify as citizens. Clearly, in the mind of the Athenian, Hellenes were superior to non-Greeks (or outsiders), Athenians were superior to non-Athenians, Athenian males were superior to Athenian females, and all classes of free men and women were superior to slaves.

Nevertheless, Athenian government stands in vivid contrast to that of the Near East and Asia, where rulers – the incarnate representatives of the gods – held absolute power. Fundamental to Athenian democracy was a commitment to the legal equality of its participants; one citizen's vote weighed as heavily as the next. Equally important to that democracy was the hypothesis that individuals were willing and able to take responsible action in the interest of the common good. The small size of Athens probably contributed to the success of the world's first and only direct democracy. Although probably no more than five thousand citizens attended the Assembly that met to make laws in the open-air marketplace (the Agora) located at the foot of the Acropolis, these men were the heroes of a brave new enterprise in governing.

Pericles' Glorification of Athens

The leading proponent of Athenian democracy was the statesman Pericles (Figure 4.7), who dominated the Board of Ten Generals for more than thirty years until his death in 429 B.C.E. An aristocrat by birth, Pericles was a democrat at heart. He initiated some of Athens' most sweeping domestic reforms, such as payment for holding public office and a system of public audit in which the finances of outgoing magistrates were subject to scrutiny. Pericles' foreign policy was even more ambitious than his domestic policies. In the wake of the Persian Wars, he encouraged the Greek city-states to form a defensive alliance against future invaders. At the outset, the league's collective funds were kept in a treasury on the sacred island of Delos (hence the name "Delian League"). But, in a bold display of chauvinism, Pericles moved the fund to Athens and expropriated its monies to rebuild the Athenian temples that had been burned by the Persians.

Pericles' high-handed actions, along with his imperialistic efforts to dominate the commercial policies of league members, led to antagonism and armed dispute. The ensuing Peloponnesian Wars (431–404 B.C.E.), which culminated in the defeat of Athens and its allies by a federation of rival city-states led by Sparta, brought an end to the Greek Golden Age. Our knowledge of the Peloponnesian Wars is based mainly on the account made by the great historian Thucydides (ca. 460–400 B.C.E.), himself a general in the combat. Thucydides went beyond merely recording the events of the war to provide insights into its causes and a first-hand assessment of its political and moral consequences. Thucydides' terse, graphic descriptions and his detached analyses of events distinguish his style from that of Herodotus.

The following speech by Pericles, excerpted from Thucydides' *History of the Peloponnesian Wars*, was presented on the occasion of a mass funeral held outside the walls of Athens to honor those who had died in the first battles of the war. Nowhere are the concepts of humanism and individualism more closely linked to civic patriotism than in this speech. Pericles reviews the "principles of action" by which Athens rose to power. He describes Athens as the best living example of political, cultural, and social life – a model for other Greek communities – and hence, "the school of Hellas." The greatness of Athens, according to Pericles, lies not merely in its military might and in the superiority of its political institutions, but in the quality of its citizens, their nobility of spirit, and their love of beauty and wisdom. Pericles' views, which were shared by most Athenians as primary articles of faith, reflect the spirit of civic pride that characterized Hellenic culture at its peak.

Figure 4.7 Marble bust from Tivoli inscribed with the name of Pericles. Roman copy after a bronze original of 450–425 B.C.E. Reproduced by courtesy of the Trustees of the British Museum, London.

READING 12

From Thucydides' *Peloponnesian Wars: Pericles' Funeral Speech*

"I will speak first of our ancestors, for it is right and becoming that now, when we are lamenting the dead, a tribute should be paid to their memory. There has never been a time when they did not inhabit this land, which by their valor they have handed down from generation to generation, and we have received from them a free state. But if they were worthy of praise, still more were our fathers, who added to their inheritance, and after many a struggle transmitted to us their sons this great empire. And we ourselves assembled here to-day, who are still most of us in the vigor of life, have chiefly done the work of improvement, and have richly endowed our city with all things, so that she is sufficient for herself both in peace and war. Of the military exploits by which our various possessions were acquired, or of the energy with which we or our fathers drove back the tide of war, Hellenic or barbarian, I will not speak; for the tale would be long and is familiar to you. But before I praise the dead, I should like to point out by what principles of action we rose to power, and under what institutions and through what manner of life our empire became great. For I conceive that such thoughts are not unsuited to the occasion, and that this numerous assembly of citizens and strangers may   1

10

20

profitably listen to them.

"Our form of government does not enter into rivalry with the institutions of others. We do not copy our neighbors, but are an example to them. It is true that we are called a democracy, for the administration is in the hands of the many and not of the few. But while the law secures equal justice to all alike in their private disputes, the claim of excellence is also recognized; and when a citizen is in any way distinguished, he is preferred to the public service, not as a matter of privilege, but as the reward of merit. Neither is poverty a bar, but a man may benefit his country whatever be the obscurity of his condition. There is no exclusiveness in our public life, and in our private intercourse we are not suspicious of one another, nor angry with our neighbor if he does what he likes; we do not put on sour looks at him which, though harmless, are not pleasant. While we are thus unconstrained in our private intercourse, a spirit of reverence pervades our public acts; we are prevented from doing wrong by respect for authority and for the laws, having an especial regard to those which are ordained for the protection of the injured as well as to those unwritten laws which bring upon the transgressor of them the reprobation of the general sentiment.

"And we have not forgotten to provide for our weary spirits many relaxations from toil; we have regular games[1] and sacrifices throughout the year; at home the style of our life is refined; and the delight which we daily feel in all these things helps to banish melancholy. Because of the greatness of our city the fruits of the whole earth flow in upon us; so that we enjoy the goods of other countries as freely as of our own.

"Then, again, our military training is in many respects superior to that of our adversaries. Our city is thrown open to the world, and we never expel a foreigner or prevent him from seeing or learning anything of which the secret if revealed to an enemy might profit him. We rely not upon management or trickery, but upon our own hearts and hands. And in the matter of education, whereas they from early youth are always undergoing laborious exercises which are to make them brave, we live at ease, and yet are equally ready to face the perils which they face. And here is the proof. The Lacedaemonians[2] come into Attica not by themselves, but with their whole confederacy following; we go alone into a neighbor's country; and although our opponents are fighting for their homes and we on a foreign soil, we have seldom any difficulty in overcoming them. Our enemies have never yet felt our united strength; the care of a navy divides our attention, and on land we are obliged to send our own citizens everywhere. But they, if they meet and defeat a part of our army, are as proud as if they had routed us all, and when defeated they pretend to have been vanquished by us all.

"If then we prefer to meet danger with a light heart but without laborious training, and with a courage which is gained by habit and not enforced by law, are we not greatly the gainers? Since we do not anticipate the pain, although, when the hour comes, we can be as brave as those who never allow themselves to rest; and thus too our city is equally admirable in peace and in war.

"For we are lovers of the beautiful, yet with economy, and we cultivate the mind without loss of manliness. Wealth we employ, not for talk and ostentation, but when there is a real use for it. To avow poverty with us is no disgrace; the true disgrace is in doing nothing to avoid it. An Athenian citizen does not neglect the state because he takes care of his own household; and even those of us who are engaged in business have a very fair idea of politics. We alone regard a man who takes no interest in public affairs, not as a harmless, but as a useless character; and if few of us are originators, we are all sound judges of a policy. The great impediment to action is, in our opinion, not discussion, but the want of that knowledge which is gained by discussion preparatory to action. For we have a peculiar power of thinking before we act and of acting too, whereas other men are courageous from ignorance but hesitate upon reflection. And they are surely to be esteemed the bravest spirits who, having the clearest sense both of the pains and pleasures of life, do not on that account shrink from danger. In doing good, again, we are unlike others; we make our friends by conferring, not by receiving favors . . . . We alone do good to our neighbors not upon a calculation of interest, but in the confidence of freedom and in a frank and fearless spirit.

"To sum up: I say that Athens is the school of Hellas, and that the individual Athenian in his own person seems to have the power of adapting himself to the most varied forms of action with the utmost versatility and grace. This is no passing and idle word, but truth and fact; and the assertion is verified by the position to which these qualities have raised the state. For in the hour of trial Athens alone among her contemporaries is superior to the report of her. No enemy who comes against her is indignant at the reverses which he sustains at the hands of such a city; no subject complains that his masters are unworthy of him. And we shall assuredly not be without witnesses; there are mighty monuments of our power which will make us the wonder of this and of succeeding ages; we shall not need the praises of Homer or of any other panegyrist whose poetry may please for the moment, although his representation of the facts will not bear the light of day. For we have compelled every land and every sea to open a path for our valor, and have everywhere planted eternal memorials of our friendship and of our enmity. Such is the city for whose sake these men nobly fought and died; they could not bear the thought that she might be taken from them; and every one of us who survive should gladly toil on her behalf.

"I have dwelt upon the greatness of Athens because I want to show you that we are contending for a higher prize than those who enjoy none of these privileges, and to establish by manifest proof the merit of these men whom I am now commemorating. Their loftiest praise has been already spoken. For in magnifying the city I have magnified them, and men like them whose virtues made her glorious."

---

[1]Athletic games were part of many Greek festivals, the most famous of which was the Panhellenic festival, in which all the city-states participated. During the latter, held every four years, a sacred truce was proclaimed. The games usually included footraces, boxing, chariot races, discus throwing, wrestling, and long jumps. The victors, who were awarded wreaths of wild olive (laurel) also might be honored in literature and art (see chapter 6).
[2]Citizens of the city-state of Sparta, ideologically opposed to Athens.

The Individual and the Community in Greek Drama

The ancient Greeks were the first masters of the art of drama, a literary genre that tells a story through the imitation of action. Both drama and dance originated in religious rituals that – like the Pygmy hunting ceremony described in chapter 1 – were performed in order to bring about favorable results in farming and in the survival of the community. Greek drama grew out of imitative actions associated with the worship of Dionysus, god of wine and vegetation, associated with seasonal regeneration. Religious rites performed in his honor featured a dialogue between two choruses or between a leader and a chorus. With the sixth-century-B.C.E. poet Thespis, chorus and actors – the performers – seem to have become separate from those who witnessed the action – the audience. At the same time, the drama itself assumed two principal forms: tragedy and comedy. Tragedy and comedy probably evolved from fertility rituals similar to those that prevailed in all ancient cultures. Tragedy has its roots in rituals surrounding the death and decay of the crops, while comedy may have developed out of village revels celebrating seasonal rebirth. Two annual festivals dedicated to Dionysus were the occasion for the performances of tragedies and comedies, and, on each occasion, the author of the best play in its category received a prize.

Three great playwrights emerged in the Golden Age of Athens – Aeschylus (ca. 525–456 B.C.E.), Sophocles (496–406 B.C.E.), and Euripides (480–406 B.C.E.). Their plays were staged in the open-air theaters built into the hillsides at sacred sites throughout Greece (Figure 4.8). These acoustically superb structures, which seated thirteen to twenty-seven thousand people, featured a *proscenium* (the "stage"), an *orchestra* (the semi-circular "dancing space" in front of the proscenium), and an *altar* dedicated to the god Dionysus. Music and dance were essential to dramatic performances, and action was continuous. Actors wore elaborate costumes and masks that served to amplify their voices.

The tragedies of Aeschylus, Sophocles, and Euripides deal with human conflicts as revealed in Greek history, myth, and legend. They focus on issues involving a specific moment of friction between the individual and fate, the gods, or the community. The events of the

Figure 4.8 Theater at Epidaurus, Greece, ca. 350 B.C.E. Designed by Polycleitus the Younger. This view shows the great size (13,000 capacity) typical of Greek theaters. Nevertheless, actors and chorus could be heard even from the top row.

play are developed in dialogue spoken by individual characters but also through the commentary of the chorus. Aeschylus, the author of the oldest surviving Western tragedy, gave the chorus a principal role in the drama. He brought deep religious feeling to his plays, the most famous of which is the three-part composition, or trilogy, known as the *Oresteia*. Sophocles (Figure 4.9) developed his plots primarily through the actions of the characters. He abandoned the ritual nature of earlier Greek tragedies by individualizing the characters and introducing moments of great psychological intimacy. Euripides, the last of the great tragedians, painted a strikingly realistic portrait of the human soul in its experience of grief. In the genre of comedy, the only writer whose plays survive is Aristophanes (ca. 450–385 B.C.E.). His inventive wit, sharply directed at Athenian policies and current affairs, is best revealed in *Lysistrata*, the oldest of his eleven surviving comedies.

The drama that is most relevant to the theme of this chapter is Sophocles' *Antigone*, the third of a trilogy of plays that includes *Oedipus the King* and *Oedipus at Colonus*. The story of *Antigone* proceeds from the last phase of the history of Thebes, a history with which most Athenians would have been familiar, since it recalled the ancient ascendancy of Athens over Thebes: Following the death of Oedipus, King of Thebes, his sons Polynices and Eteocles kill each other in a dispute over the throne, thus leaving the crown to Creon, the brother-in-law of Oedipus and the only surviving male member of the ill-fated royal family. Upon becoming king, Creon forbids the burial of Polynices, contending that Eteocles had been the rightful ruler of Thebes. Driven by familial duty and the wish to fulfill the divine laws requiring burial of the dead, Oedipus' daughter Antigone violates Creon's decree and buries her brother Polynices. These circumstances provoke further violence and tragic death.

Antigone deals with conflicts between personal and communal obligations, between individual choice and social conformity, and, on a more universal plane, between divine and human law. It reflects Sophocles' concern for reconciliation of human passions, the will of the gods, and the laws of the state. Heroic idealism is a major motif in *Antigone*. It drives the action of the play, and it is contemplated in a magnificent choral passage (lines 284–291) that weighs the grandeur of human beings against their frailties.

Figure 4.9 Sophocles. Marble. Lateran, Rome. Alinari/Art Resource, New York.

READING 13

Sophocles' *Antigone*

Characters

Antigone and Ismene, daughters of Oedipus
Creon, king of Thebes, brother of Jocasta
Haemon, son of Creon
Teiresias, a blind prophet
A Sentry
A Messenger
Eurydice, wife of Creon
Chorus of Theban elders
Attendants of the king and queen
Soldiers
A Boy who leads Teiresias

Scene

An open space before the house of Creon. The house is at the back, with gates opening from it. On the right, the city is to be supposed; to the left and in the distance, the Theban plain and the hills rising beyond it. Antigone and Ismene come from the middle door of three in the King's house.

ANTIGONE: Ismene, O my dear, my little sister, of all the griefs bequeathed us by our father Oedipus, is there any that Zeus will share us while we live? There is no sorrow and no shame we have not known. And now what is this new edict they tell about, that our Captain has published all through Thebes? Do you know? Have you heard? Or is it kept from you that our friends are threatened with the punishment due to foes? 1

ISMENE: I have heard no news, Antigone, glad or sad, about our friends, since we two sisters lost two brothers at a single blow; and since the Argive army fled last night, I do not know whether my fortune is better or worse. 10

ANTIGONE: I know, I know it well. That is why I sent for you to come outside the gates, to speak to you alone.

ISMENE: What is it? I can see that you are troubled.

ANTIGONE: Should I not be? — when Creon gives honors to one of our brothers, but condemns the other to shame? Eteocles, they say, he has laid in the earth with due observance of right and custom, that all may be well with him among the shades below. But the poor corpse of Polynices — it has been published to the city that none shall bury him, none shall mourn him; but he shall be left unwept and unsepulchred, and the birds are welcome to feast upon him! 20

Such, they say, are the orders the good Creon has given for you and me — yes, for me! He is coming now to make his wishes clear; and it is no light matter, for whoever disobeys him is condemned to death by stoning before all the people. Now you know! — and now you will show whether you are nobly bred, or the unworthy daughter of a noble line. 30

ISMENE: Sister, sister! — if we are caught in this web, what could I do to loose or tighten the knot?

ANTIGONE: Decide if you will share the work and the danger.

ISMENE: What are you planning? — what are you thinking of?

ANTIGONE: Will you help this hand to lift the dead?

ISMENE: Oh, you would bury him! — when it is forbidden to anyone in Thebes? 40

ANTIGONE: He is still my brother, if he is not yours. No one shall say I failed in my duty to him.

ISMENE: But how can you dare, when Creon has forbidden it?

ANTIGONE: He has no right to keep me from my own.

ISMENE: Alas, sister, remember how our father perished hated and scorned, when he had struck out his eyes in horror of the sins his own persistency had brought to light. Remember how she who was both his mother and his wife hung herself with a twisted cord. And only yesterday our two brothers came to their terrible end, each by the other's hand. Now only we two are left, and we are all alone. Think how we shall perish, more miserably than all the rest, if in defiance of the law we brave the King's decree and the King's power. No, no, we must remember we were born women, not meant to strive with men. We are in the grip of those stronger than ourselves, and must obey them in this and in things still more cruel. Therefore I will ask forgiveness of the gods and spirits who dwell below, for they will see that I yield to force, and I will hearken to our rulers. It is foolish to be too zealous even in a good cause. 50 60

ANTIGONE: I will not urge you. No, if you wished to join me now I would not let you. Do as you think best. As for me, I will bury him; and if I die for that, I am content. I shall rest like a loved one with him whom I have loved, innocent in my guilt. For I owe a longer allegiance to the dead than to the living; I must dwell with them forever. You, if you wish, may dishonor the laws which the gods have established.

ISMENE: I would not dishonor them, but to defy the State — I am not strong enough for that! 70

ANTIGONE: Well, make your excuses — I am going now to heap the earth above the brother whom I love.

ISMENE: Oh, I fear something terrible will happen to you!

ANTIGONE: Fear not for me; but look to your own fate.

ISMENE: At least, then, tell no one what you intend, but hide it closely — and so too will I.

ANTIGONE: No, but cry it aloud! I will condemn you more if you are silent than if you proclaim my deed to all.

ISMENE: You have so hot a heart for deeds that make the blood run cold! 80

ANTIGONE: My deeds will please those they are meant to please.

ISMENE: Ah yes, if you can do what you plan — but you cannot.

ANTIGONE: When my strength fails, I shall confess my failure.

ISMENE: The impossible should not be tried at all.

ANTIGONE: If you say such things I will hate you, and the dead will haunt you! — But leave me, and the folly that is mine alone, to suffer what I must; for I shall not suffer anything so dreadful as an ignoble death. 90

ISMENE: Go then, if you must, though your errand is mad; and be sure of this, my love goes with you!

(Antigone *goes toward the plain.* Ismene *retires into the King's house. The* Chorus, *being the elders of Thebes, comes into the place before the house.*)

CHORUS: Over the waters, see! — over the stream of Dirke, the golden eye of the dawn opens on the seven gates;

Terror crouched in the night, how welcome to Thebes is
the morning, when the warriors of the white shields
flee from the spears of the sun.

From Argos mailed they came, swords drawn for   100
Polynices; like eagles that scream in the air these
plumed ones fell on our land.
They ravened around our towers, and burst the doors of
our dwellings; their spears sniffed at our blood — but
they fled without quenching that thirst.

They heaped the eager pine-boughs, flaming, against
our bastions, calling upon Hephaestos; but he the
fire-god failed them.
The clash of battle was loud, the clamor beloved of the
war-god; but a thing they found too hard was   110
to conquer the dragon's brood.

And a thing abhorred by Zeus is the boastful tongue of
the haughty: one proud chief, armored in gold, with
triumph in his throat,
The stormy wave of the foe flung to the crest of our
rampart — the god, with a crooked bolt, smites him
crashing to earth.

At the seven gates of the city, seven of the host's grim
captains yielded to Zeus who turns the tide of battle,
their arms of bronze;   120
And woe to those two sons of the same father and
mother, they crossed their angry spears, and brought
each other low.

But now since Victory, most desired of all men, to
Thebes of the many chariots has come scattering joy,
Let us forget the wars, and dance before the temples;
and Bacchus be our leader, loved by the land of
Thebes!

But see, the King of this land comes yonder — Creon, son
of Menoekeus, our new ruler by virtue of the new turn the   130
gods have given things. What counsel is he pondering, that
he has called by special summons this gathering of the
elders?

CREON: Sirs, our State has been like a ship tossed by
stormy waves; but thanks to the gods, it sails once more
upon a steady keel. You I have summoned here apart from
all the people because I remember that of old you had great
reverence for the royal power of Laius; and I know how you
upheld Oedipus when he ruled this land, and, when he
died, you loyally supported his two sons. Those sons have   140
fallen, both in one moment, each smitten by the other,
each stained with a brother's blood; now I possess the
throne and all its powers, since I am nearest kindred of the
dead.

No man's worthiness to rule can be known until his mind
and soul have been tested by the duties of government and
lawgiving. For my part, I have always held that any man
who is the supreme guardian of the State, and who fails in
his duty through fear, remaining silent when evil is done, is
base and contemptible; nor have I any regard for him who   150
puts friendship above the common welfare. Zeus, who sees
all things, be my witness that I will not be silent when
danger threatens the people; nor will I ever call my
country's foe my friend. For our country is the ship that
bears us all, and he only is our friend who helps us sail a

prosperous course.

Such are the rules by which I will guard this city's
greatness; and in keeping with them is the edict I have
published touching the sons of Oedipus. For Eteocles, who
fell like a true soldier defending his native land, there shall   160
be such funeral as we give the noblest dead. But as to his
brother Polynices — he who came out of exile and sought to
destroy with fire the city of his fathers and the shrines of his
fathers' gods — he who thirsted for the blood of his kin, and
would have led into slavery all who escaped death — as to
this man, it has been proclaimed that none shall honor
him, none shall lament over him, but he shall lie unburied,
a corpse mangled by birds and dogs, a gruesome thing to
see. Such is my way with traitors.

CHORUS: Such is your way, Creon, son of Menoekeus, with   170
the false and with the faithful; and you have power, I know,
to give such orders as you please, both for the dead and for
all of us who live.
CREON: Then look to it that my mandate is observed.
CHORUS: Call on some younger man for this hard task.
CREON: No, watchers of the corpse have been appointed.
CHORUS: What is this duty, then, you lay on us?
CREON: To side with no one breaking this command.
CHORUS: No man is foolish enough to go courting death.
CREON: That indeed shall be the penalty; but men have   180
been lured even to death by the hope of gain.

(A Guard, *coming from the direction of the plain,
approaches* Creon.*)*

GUARD: Sire, I will not say that I am out of breath from
hurrying, nor that I have come here on the run; for in fact
my thoughts made me pause more than once, and even
turn in my path, to go back. My mind was telling me two
different things. "Fool," it said to me, "why do you go
where you are sure to be condemned?" And then on the
other hand, "Wretch, tarrying again? If Creon hears of this
from another, you'll smart for it." Torn between these
fears, I came on slowly and unwillingly, making a short   190
road long. But at last I got up courage to come to you, and
though there is little to my story, I will tell it; for I have got
a good grip on one thought — that I can suffer nothing but
what is my fate.
CREON: Well, and what is it that makes you so upset?
GUARD: First let me tell you that I did not do the deed and
I did not see it done, so it would not be just to make me
suffer for it.
CREON: You have a good care for your own skin, and armor
yourself well against blame. I take it that you have news to   200
tell?
GUARD: Yes, that I have, but bad news is nothing to be in
a hurry about.
CREON: Tell it, man, will you? — tell it and be off.
GUARD: Well, this is it. The corpse — someone has done it
funeral honors — sprinkled dust upon it, and other pious
rites.
CREON: What — what do you say? What man has dared this
deed?
GUARD: That I cannot tell you. There was no sign of a pick   210
being used, no earth torn up the way it is by a mattock. The
ground was hard and dry, there was no track of wheels.
Whoever did it left no trace; when the first day-watchman
showed it to us, we were struck dumb. You couldn't see the

dead man at all; not that he was in any grave, but dry dust was strewn that thick all over him. It was the hand of someone warding off a curse did that. There was no sign that any dog or wild beast had been at the body.

Then there were loud words, and hard words, among us of the guard, everyone accusing someone else, 'til we 220 nearly came to blows, and it's a wonder we didn't. Everyone was accused and no one was convicted, and each man stuck to it that he knew nothing about it. We were ready to take red-hot iron in our hands — to walk through fire — to swear by the gods that we did not do the deed and were not in the secret of whoever did it.

At last, when all our disputing got us nowhere, one of the men spoke up in a way that made us look down at the ground in silence and fear; for we could not see how to gainsay him, nor how to escape trouble if we heeded him. 230 What he said was, that this must be reported to you, it was no use hiding it. There was no doubt of it, he was right; so we cast lots, and it was my bad luck to win the prize. Here I am, then, as unwelcome as unwilling, I know; for no man likes the bearer of bad news.

CHORUS: O King, my thoughts have been whispering, could this deed perhaps have been the work of gods?

CREON: Silence, before your words fill me with anger, and you prove yourself as foolish as you are old! You say what is not to be borne, that the gods would concern themselves 240 with this corpse. What! — did they cover his nakedness to reward the reverence he paid them, coming to burn their pillared shrines and sacred treasures, to harry their land, to put scorn upon their laws? Do you think it is the way of the gods to honor the wicked? No! From the first there were some in this city who muttered against me, chafing at this edict, wagging their heads in secret; they would not bow to the yoke, not they, like men contented with my rule.

I know well enough, it is such malcontents who have bribed and beguiled these guards to do this deed or let it be 250 done. Nothing so evil as money ever arose among men. It lays cities low, drive peoples from their homes, warps honest souls 'til they give themselves to works of shame; it teaches men to practise villainies and grow familiar with impious deeds.

But the men who did this thing for hire, sooner or later they shall pay the price. Now, as Zeus still has my reverence, know this — I tell you on my oath: Unless you find the very man whose hand strewed dust upon that body, and bring him here before mine eyes, death alone 260 shall not be enough for you, but you shall first be hung up alive until you reveal the truth about this outrage; that henceforth you may have a better idea about how to get money, and learn that it is not wise to grasp at it from any source. I will teach you that ill-gotten gains bring more men to ruin than to prosperity.

GUARD: May I speak? Or shall I turn and go?
CREON: Can you not see that your voice offends me?
GUARD: Are your ears troubled, or your soul?
CREON: And why should you try to fix the seat of my pain? 270
GUARD: The doer of the deed inflames your mind, but I, only your ears.
CREON: Bah, you are a babbler born!
GUARD: I may be that, but I never did this deed.
CREON: You did, for silver; but you shall pay with your life.
GUARD: It is bad when a judge misjudges.

CREON: Prate about "judgment" all you like; but unless you show me the culprit in this crime, you will admit before long that guilty wages were better never earned.

(Creon *goes into his house.*)

GUARD: Well, may the guilty man be found, that's all I ask. 280 But whether he's found or not — fate will decide that — you will not see me here again. I have escaped better than I ever hoped or thought — I owe the gods much thanks.

(*The* Guard *departs, going toward the plain.*)

CHORUS: Wonders are many in the world, and the
    wonder of all is man.
With his bit in the teeth of the storm and his faith in a
        fragile prow,
Far he sails, where the waves leap white-fanged, wroth
    at his plan.
And he has his will of the earth by the strength of his 290
    hand on the plough.

The birds, the clan of the light heart, he snares with his
    woven cord,
And the beasts with wary eyes, and the stealthy fish in
    the sea;
That shaggy freedom-lover, the horse, obeys his word,
And the sullen bull must serve him, for cunning of wit is
    he.

Against all ills providing, he tempers the dark and the
    light,   300
The creeping siege of the frost and the arrows of sleet
    and rain,
The grievous wounds of the daytime and the fever that
    steals in the night;
Only against Death man arms himself in vain.

With speech and wind-swift thought he builds the State
    to his mood,
Prospering while he honors the gods and the laws of the
    land.
Yet in his rashness often he scorns the ways that are 310
    good —
May such as walk with evil be far from my hearth and
    hand!

(*The* Guard *reappears leading* Antigone.)

CHORUS: But what is this? — what portent from the gods is this? I am bewildered, for surely this maiden is Antigone; I know her well. O luckless daughter of a luckless father, child of Oedipus, what does this mean? Why have they made you prisoner? Surely they did not take you in the folly of breaking the King's laws?

GUARD: Here she is, the doer of the deed! We caught this 320 girl burying him. But where is Creon?

CHORUS: Look, he is coming from the house now.

(Creon *comes from the house.*)

CREON: What is it? What has happened that makes my coming timely?

GUARD: Sire, a man should never say positively "I will do this" or "I won't do that," for things happen to change the mind. I vowed I would not soon come here again, after the way you scared me, lashing me with your threats. But there's nothing so pleasant as a happy turn when we've given up hope, so I have broken my sworn oath to hurry 330 back here with this girl, who was taken showing grace to the dead. This time there was no casting of lots; no, this is my good luck, no one else's. And now, Sire, take her yourself, question her, examine her, all you please; but I have a right to free and final quittance of this trouble.

CREON: Stay! — this prisoner — how and where did you take her?

GUARD: She was burying the man; that's all there is to tell you.

CREON: Do you mean what you say? Are you telling the 340 truth?

GUARD: I saw her burying the corpse that you had forbidden to bury. Is that plain and clear?

CREON: What did you see? Did you take her in the act?

GUARD: It happened this way. When we came to the place where he lay, worrying over your threats, we swept away all the dirt, leaving the rotting corpse bare. Then we sat us down on the brow of the hill to windward, so that the smell from him would not strike us. We kept wide awake 350 frightening each other with what you would do to us if we didn't carry out your command. So it went until the sun was bright in the top of the sky, and the heat began to burn. Then suddenly a whirlwind came roaring down, making the sky all black, hiding the plain under clouds of choking dust and leaves torn from the trees. We closed our eyes and bore this plague from the gods.

And when, after a long while, the storm had passed, we saw this girl, and she crying aloud with the sharp cry of a bird in its grief; the way a bird will cry when it sees the nest bare and the nestlings gone, it was that way she lifted up 360 her voice when she saw the corpse uncovered; and she called down dreadful curses on those that did it. Then straightway she scooped up dust in her hands, and she had a shapely ewer of bronze, and she held that high while she honored the dead with three drink-offerings.

We rushed forward at this and closed on our quarry, who was not at all frightened at us. Then we charged her with the past and present offences, and she denied nothing — I was both happy and sorry for that. It is good to escape danger one's self, but hard to bring trouble to one's 370 friends. However, nothing counts with me so much as my own safety.

CREON: You, then — you whose face is bent to the earth — do you confess or do you deny the deed?

ANTIGONE: I did it; I make no denial.

CREON (to Guard): You may go your way, wherever you will, free and clear of a grave charge.

(To Antigone): Now tell me — not in many words, but briefly — did you know of the edict that forbade what you did? 380

ANTIGONE: I knew it. How could I help knowing? — it was public.

CREON: And you had the boldness to transgress that law?

ANTIGONE: Yes, for it was not Zeus made such a law; such is not the Justice of the gods. Nor did I think that your decrees had so much force, that a mortal could override the unwritten and unchanging statutes of heaven. For their authority is not of today nor yesterday, but from all time, and no man knows when they were first put forth.

Not through dread or any human power could I answer to 390 the gods for breaking these. That I must die I knew without your edict. But if I am to die before my time, I count that a gain; for who, living as I do in the midst of many woes, would not call death a friend?

It saddens me little, therefore, to come to my end. If I had let my mother's son lie in death an unburied corpse, that would have saddened me, but for myself I do not grieve. And if my acts are foolish in your eyes, it may be that a foolish judge condemns my folly.

CHORUS: The maiden shows herself the passionate 400 daughter of a passionate father, she does not know how to bend the neck.

CREON: Let me remind you that those who are too stiff and stubborn are most often humbled; it is the iron baked too hard in the furnace you will oftenest see snapped and splintered. But I have seen horses that show temper brought to order by a little curb. Too much pride is out of place in one who lives subject to another. This girl was already versed in insolence when she transgressed the law that had been published; and now, behold, a second insult 410 — to boast about it, to exult in her misdeed!

But I am no man, she is the man, if she can carry this off unpunished. No! She is my sister's child, but if she were nearer to me in blood than any who worships Zeus at the altar of my house, she should not escape a dreadful doom — nor her sister either, for indeed I charge her too with plotting this burial.

And summon that sister — for I saw her just now within, raving and out of her wits. That is the way minds plotting evil in the dark give away their secret and convict 420 themselves even before they are found out. But the most intolerable thing is that one who has been caught in wickedness should glory in the crime.

ANTIGONE: Would you do more than slay me?

CREON: No more than that — no, and nothing less.

ANTIGONE: Then why do you delay? Your speeches give me no pleasure, and never will; and my words, I suppose, buzz hatefully in your ear. I am ready; for there is no better way I could prepare for death than by giving burial to my brother. Everyone would say so if their lips were not sealed by fear. 430 But a king has many advantages, he can do and say what he pleases.

CREON: You slander the race of Cadmus;[1] not one of them shares your view of this deed.

ANTIGONE: They see it as I do, but their tails are between their legs.

CREON: They are loyal to their king; are you not ashamed to be otherwise?

ANTIGONE: No; there is nothing shameful in piety to a brother. 440

CREON: Was it not a brother also who died in the good cause?

ANTIGONE: Born of the same mother and sired by the same father.

CREON: Why then do you dishonor him by honoring that other?

ANTIGONE: The dead will not look upon it that way.

CREON: Yes, if you honor the wicked equally with the virtuous.

---

[1] The ancestor of the noble families of Thebes.

ANTIGONE: It was his brother, not his slave, that died.   450

CREON: One perished ravaging his fatherland, the other defending it.

ANTIGONE: Nevertheless, Hades desires these rites.

CREON: Surely the good are not pleased to be made equal with the evil!

ANTIGONE: Who knows how the gods see good and evil?

CREON: A foe is never a friend — even in death.

ANTIGONE: It is not my nature to join in hating, but in loving.

CREON: Your place, then, is with the dead. If you must   460 love, love them. While I live, no woman shall overbear me.

(Ismene is led from the King's house by two attendants.)

CHORUS: See, Ismene come through the gate shedding such tears as loving sisters weep. It seems as if a cloud gathers about her brow and breaks in rain upon her cheek.

CREON: And you, who lurked like a viper in my house, sucking the blood of my honor, while I knew not that I was nursing two reptiles ready to strike at my throne — come, tell me now, will you confess your part in this guilty burial, or will you swear you knew nothing of it?

ISMENE: I am guilty if she is, and share the blame.   470

ANTIGONE: No, no! Justice will not permit this. You did not consent to the deed, nor would I let you have part in it.

ISMENE: But now that danger threatens you, I am not ashamed to come to your side.

ANTIGONE: Who did the deed, the gods and the dead know; a friend in words is not the friend I love.

ISMENE: Sister, do not reject me, but let me die with you, and duly honor the dead.

ANTIGONE: Do not court death, nor claim a deed to which you did not put your hand. My death will suffice.   480

ISMENE: How could life be dear to me without you?

ANTIGONE: Ask Creon, you think highly of his word.

ISMENE: Why taunt me so, when it does you no good?

ANTIGONE: Ah, if I mock you, it is with pain I do it.

ISMENE: Oh tell me, how can I serve you, even now?

ANTIGONE: Save yourself; I do not grudge your escape.

ISMENE: Oh, my grief! Can I not share your fate?

ANTIGONE: You chose to live, and I to die.

ISMENE: At least I begged you not to make that choice.

ANTIGONE: This world approved your caution, but the gods   490 my courage.

ISMENE: But now I approve, and so I am guilty too.

ANTIGONE: Ah little sister, be of good cheer, and live. My life has long been given to death, that I might serve the dead.

CREON: Behold, one of these girls turns to folly now, as the other one has ever since she was born.

ISMENE: Yes, Sire, such reason as nature gives us may break under misfortune, and go astray.

CREON: Yours did, when you chose to share evil deeds   500 with the evil.

ISMENE: But I cannot live without her.

CREON: You mistake; she lives no more.

ISMENE: Surely you will not slay your own son's betrothed?

CREON: He can plough other fields.

ISMENE: But he cannot find such love again.

CREON: I will not have an evil wife for my son.

ANTIGONE: Ah, Haemon, my beloved! Dishonored by your father!

CREON: Enough! I'll hear no more of you and your   510 marriage!

CHORUS: Will you indeed rob your son of his bride?

CREON: Death will do that for me.

CHORUS: It seems determined then, that she shall die.

CREON: Determined, yes — for me and for you. No more delay — servants, take them within. Let them know that they are women, not meant to roam abroad. For even the boldest seek to fly when they see Death stretching his hand their way.

(Attendants lead Antigone and Ismene into the house.)

CHORUS: Blest are they whose days have not tasted   520 of sorrow:
For if a house has dared the anger of heaven,
Evil strikes at it down the generations,
Wave after wave, like seas that batter a headland.

I see how fate has harried the seed of Labdakos;
Son cannot fly the curse that was laid on the sire,
The doom incurred by the dead must fall on the living:
When gods pursue, no race can find deliverance.

And even these, the last of the children of Oedipus —
Because of the frenzy that rose in a passionate heart,   530
Because of a handful of blood-stained dust that was
    sprinkled —
The last of the roots is cut, and the light extinguished.

O Zeus, how vain is the mortal will that opposes
The Will Immortal that neither sleeps nor ages,
The Imperturbable Power that on Olympus
Dwells in unclouded glory, the All-Beholding!
Wise was he who said that ancient saying:
Whom the gods bewilder, at last takes evil for virtue;
And let no man lament if his lot is humble —   540
No great things come to mortals without a curse.

But look, Sire: Haemon, the last of your sons, approaches. I wonder if he comes grieving over the doom of his promised bride, Antigone, and bitter that his marriage-hopes are baffled?

(Haemon comes before his father.)

CREON: We shall know soon, better than seers could tell us. My son, you have heard the irrevocable doom decreed for your betrothed. Do you come to rage against your father, or do you remember the duty of filial love, no matter what I do.   550

HAEMON: Father, I am yours; and knowing you are wise, I follow the paths you trace for me. No marriage could be more to me than your good guidance.

CREON: Yes, my son, this should be your heart's first law, in all things to obey your father's will. Men pray for dutiful children growing up about them in their homes, that such may pay their father's foe with evil, and honor as their father does, his friend. But if a man begets undutiful children, what shall we say that he has sown, only sorrow for himself and triumph for his enemies? Do not then, my   560 son, thinking of pleasures, put aside reason for a woman's sake. If you brought an evil woman to your bed and home, you would find that such embraces soon grow hateful; and nothing can wound so deeply as to find a loved one false. No, but with loathing, and as if she were your enemy, let this girl go to find a husband in the house of Hades. For she alone in all the city defied and disobeyed me; I have taken her in the act, and I will not be a liar to my people — I will slay her.

Let her appeal all she pleases to the claims of kindred blood. If I am to rear my own kin to evil deeds, certainly I must expect evil among the people. Only a man who rules his own household justly can do justice in the State. If anyone transgresses, and does violence to the laws, or thinks to dictate to the ruler, I will not tolerate it. No! — whoever the city shall appoint to rule, that man must be obeyed, in little things and great things, in just things and unjust; for the man who is a good subject is the one who would be a good ruler, and it is he who in time of war will stand his ground where he is placed, loyal to his comrades and without fear, though the spears fall around him like rain in a storm. 580

But disobedience is the worst of evils. It desolates households; it ruins cities; it throws the ranks of allies into confusion and rout. On the other hand, note those whose lives are prosperous: they owe it, you will generally find, to obedience. Therefore we must uphold the cause of order; and certainly we must not let a woman defy us. It would be better to fall from power by a man's hand, than to be called weaker than a woman. 590

CHORUS: Unless the years have stolen our wits, all that you say seems wise.

HAEMON: Father, the gods implant reason in men, the highest of all things that we call our own. I have no skill to prove, and I would not wish to show, that you speak unwisely; and yet another man, too, might have some useful thought. I count it a duty to keep my ears alert for what men say about you, noting especially when they find fault. The people dare not say to your face what would displease you; but I can hear the things murmured in the 600 dark, and the whole city weeps for this maiden. "No woman ever," they say, "so little merited a cruel fate. None was ever doomed to a shameful death for deeds so noble as hers; who, when her brother lay dead from bloody wounds, would not leave him unburied for the birds and dogs to mangle. Does not so pious an act deserve golden praise?"

Such is the way the people speak in secret. To me, father, nothing is so precious as your welfare. What is there father or son can so rejoice in as the other's fair repute? I pray you therefore do not wear one mood too stubbornly, as 610 if no one else could possibly be right. For the man who thinks he is the only wise man always proves hollow when we sound him. No, though a man be wise, it is no shame for him to learn many things, and to yield at the right time. When the streams rage and overflow in Winter, you know how those trees that yield come safely through the flood; but the stubborn are torn up and perish, root and branch. Consider too, the sailor who keeps his sheet always taut, and never slackens it; presently his boat overturns and his keel floats uppermost. 620

So, though you are angry, permit reason to move you. If I, young as I am, may offer a thought, I would say it were best if men were by nature always wise; but that being seldom so, it is prudent to listen to those who offer honest counsel.

CHORUS: Sire, it is fitting that you should weigh his words, if he speaks in season; and you, Haemon, should mark your father's words; for on both parts there has been wise speech.

CREON: What! Shall men of our age be schooled by youths 630 like this?

HAEMON: In nothing that does not go with reason; but as to my youth, you should weigh my merits, not my years.

CREON: Is it your merit that you honor the lawless?

HAEMON: I could wish no one to respect evil-doers.

CREON: This girl — is she not tainted with that plague?

HAEMON: Our Theban folk deny it, with one voice.

CREON: Shall Thebes, then, tell me how to rule?

HAEMON: Now who speaks like a boy?

CREON: Tell me — am I to rule by my own judgment or the 640 views of others?

HAEMON: That is no city which belongs to one man.

CREON: Is not the city held to be the ruler's?

HAEMON: That kind of monarchy would do well in a desert.

CREON: Ho, this boy, it seems, is the woman's champion!

HAEMON: Yes, if you are a woman, for my concern is for you.

CREON: Shameless, to bandy arguments with your father!

HAEMON: Only because I see you flouting Justice.

CREON: Is it wrong for me to respect my royal position? 650

HAEMON: It is a poor way to respect it, trampling on the laws of the gods.

CREON: This is depravity, putting a woman foremost!

HAEMON: At least you will not find me so depraved that I fear to plead for justice.

CREON: Every word you speak is a plea for that girl.

HAEMON: And for you, and for me, and for the gods below.

CREON: Marry her you shall not, this side the grave.

HAEMON: She must die then, and in dying destroy others?

CREON: Ha, you go so far as open threats? 660

HAEMON: I speak no threats, but grieve for your fatal stubbornness.

CREON: You shall rue your unwise teaching of wisdom.

HAEMON: If you were not my father, I would call you unwise.

CREON: Slave of a woman, do not think you can cajole me.

HAEMON: Then no one but yourself may speak, you will hear no reason?

CREON: Enough of this — now, by Olympus, you shall smart for baiting me this way! Bring her here, that hateful 670 rebel, that she may die forthwith before his eyes — yes, at her bridegroom's side!

HAEMON: No, no, never think it, I shall not witness her death; but my face your eyes shall never see again. Give your passion its way before those who can endure you!

(Haemon rushes away.)

CHORUS: He has gone, O King, in angry haste; a youthful mind, when stung, is impetuous.

CREON: Let him do what he will, let him dream himself more than a common man, but he shall not save those girls from their doom. 680

CHORUS: Are you indeed determined to slay them both?

CREON: Not the one whose hands are clean of the crime — you do well to remind me of that.

CHORUS: But how will you put the other one to death?

CREON: I will take her where the path is loneliest, and hide her, living, in a rocky vault, with only so much food as the pious laws require, that the city may avoid reproach. There she can pray to Hades, whose gods alone she worships; perhaps they will bargain with death for her escape. And if they do not, she will learn, too late, that it is lost labor to 690 revere the dead.

[Antigone *engages in an impassioned lament over her destiny*. Creon will not relent, and the guards lead Antigone *to the tomb*.]

TEIRESIAS: Princes of Thebes, it is a hard journey for me to come here, for the blind must walk by another's steps and see with another's eyes; yet I have come.

CREON: And what, Teiresias, are your tidings?

TEIRESIAS: I shall tell you; and listen well to the seer.

CREON: I have never slighted your counsel.

TEIRESIAS: It is that way you have steered the city well.

CREON: I know, and bear witness, to the worth of your words. 700

TEIRESIAS: Then mark them now: for I tell you, you stand on fate's thin edge.

CREON: What do you mean? I shudder at your message.

TEIRESIAS: You will know, when you hear the signs my art has disclosed. For lately, as I took my place in my ancient seat of augury, where all the birds of the air gather about me, I heard strange things. They were screaming with feverish rage, their usual clear notes were a frightful jargon; and I knew they were rending each other murderously with their talons: the whir of their wings told 710 an angry tale.

Straightway, these things filling me with fear, I kindled fire upon an altar, with due ceremony, and laid a sacrifice among the faggots; but Hephaestus would not consume my offering with flame. A moisture oozing out from the bones and flesh trickled upon the embers, making them smoke and sputter. Then the gall burst and scattered on the air, and the steaming thighs lay bared of the fat that had wrapped them.

Such was the failure of the rites by which I vainly asked 720 a sign, as this boy reported them; for his eyes serve me, as I serve others. And I tell you, it is your deeds that have brought a sickness on the State. For the altars of our city and the altars of our hearths have been polluted, one and all, by birds and dogs who have fed on that outraged corpse that was the son of Oedipus. It is for this reason the gods refuse prayer and sacrifice at our hands, and will not consume the meat-offering with flame; nor does any bird give a clear sign by its shrill cry, for they have tasted the fatness of a slain man's blood. 730

Think then on these things, my son. All men are liable to err; but he shows wisdom and earns blessings who heals the ills his errors caused, being not too stubborn; too stiff a will is folly. Yield to the dead, I counsel you, and do not stab the fallen; what prowess is it to slay the slain anew? I have sought your welfare, it is for your good I speak; and it should be a pleasant thing to hear a good counsellor when he counsels for your own gain.

CREON: Old man, you all shoot your shafts at me, like archers at a butt — you must practise your prophecies on 740 me! Indeed, the tribe of augurs has long trafficked in me and made me their merchandise! Go, seek your price, drive your trade, if you will, in the precious ore of Sardis and the gold of India; but you shall not buy that corpse a grave! No, though the eagles of Zeus should bear their carrion

dainties to their Master's throne — no, not even for dread of that will I permit this burial! — for I know that no mortal can pollute the gods. So, hoary prophet, the wisest come to a shameful fall when they clothe shameful counsels in fair words to earn a bribe. 750

TEIRESIAS: Alas! Does no man know, does none consider . . . .

CREON: What pompous precept now?

TEIRESIAS: . . . . that honest counsel is the most priceless gift?

CREON: Yes, and folly the most worthless.

TEIRESIAS: True, and you are infected with that disease.

CREON: This wise man's taunts I shall not answer in kind.

TEIRESIAS: Yet you slander me, saying I augur falsely.

CREON: Well, the tribe of seers always liked money.

TEIRESIAS: And the race of tyrants was ever proud and 760 covetous.

CREON: Do you know you are speaking to your king?

TEIRESIAS: I know it: you saved the city when you followed my advice.

CREON: You have your gifts, but you love evil deeds.

TEIRESIAS: Ah, you will sting me to utter the dread secret I have kept hidden in my soul.

CREON: Out with it! — but if you hope to earn a fee by shaking my purpose, you babble in vain.

TEIRESIAS: Indeed I think I shall earn no reward from you. 770

CREON: Be sure you shall not trade on my resolve.

TEIRESIAS: Know then — aye, know it well! — you will not live through many days, seeing the sun's swift chariot coursing heaven, 'til one whose blood comes from your own heart shall be a corpse, matching two other corpses; because you have given to the shadows one who belongs to the sun, you have lodged a living soul in the grave; yet in this world you detain one who belongs to the world below, a corpse unburied, unhonored and unblest. These things outrage the gods; therefore those dread Erinyes, who serve 780 the fury of the gods, lie now in wait for you, preparing a vengeance equal to your guilt.

And mark well if I speak these things as a hireling. A time not long delayed will waken the wailing of men and women in your house. But after these cries I hear a more dreadful tumult. For wrath and hatred will stir to arms against you every city whose mangled sons had the burial-rite from dogs and wild beasts, or from birds that will bear the taint of this crime even to the startled hearths of the unburied dead. 790

Such arrows I do indeed aim at your heart, since you provoke me — they will find their mark, and you shall not escape the sting. — Boy, lead me home, that he may spend his rage on younger men, or learn to curb his bitter tongue and temper his violent mind.

(Teiresias *is led away*.)

CHORUS: The seer has gone, O King, predicting terrible things. And since the days when my white hair was dark, I know that he has never spoken false auguries for our city.

CREON: I know that too, I know it well, and I am troubled in soul. It is hard to yield; but if by stubbornness I bring my 800 pride to ruin — that too would be hard.

CHORUS: Son of Menoekeus, it is time to heed good counsel.

CREON: What shall I do, then? Speak, and I will obey.

CHORUS: Go free the living maiden from her grave, and

make a grave for the unburied dead.

CREON: Is this indeed your counsel? Do you bid me yield?

CHORUS: Yes, and without delay; for the swift judgments of the gods cut short the folly of men.

CREON: It is hard to do – to retreat from a firm stand – but 810 I yield, I will obey you. We must not wage a vain war with Fate.

CHORUS: Go then, let your own hand do these things; do not leave them to others.

CREON: Even as I am I will go: come, servants, all of you, bring tools to raise one grave and open another. Since our judgment has taken this turn, I who buried the girl will free her myself. – My heart misgives me, it is best to keep the established laws, even to life's end.

(Creon *and his servants go toward the plain.*)

[*The* Chorus sings a hymn in praise of Dionysus.]

(*A* Messenger *appears, from the direction of the plain.*)

MESSENGER: Neighbors of the house of Cadmus, dwellers 820 within Amphion's[2] walls, there is no state of mortal life that I would praise or pity, for none is beyond swift change. Fortune raises men up and fortune casts them down from day to day, and no man can foretell the fate of things established. For Creon was blest in all that I count happiness; he had honor as our savior; power as our king; pride as the father of princely children. Now all is ended. For when a man is stripped of happiness, I count him not with the living – he is but a breathing corpse. Let a man have riches heaped in his house, and live in royal splendor; 830 yet I would not give the shadow of a breath for all, if they bring no gladness.

CHORUS: What fearful news have you about our princes?

MESSENGER: Death; and the living are guilty of the dead.

CHORUS: Who is the slayer – who is slain?

MESSENGER: Haemon has perished, and it was no stranger shed his blood.

CHORUS: His father's hand, or his own?

MESSENGER: His own, maddened by his father's crime.

CHORUS: O prophet, how true your word has proved! 840

MESSENGER: This is the way things are: consider then, how to act.

CHORUS: Look! – the unhappy Eurydice, Creon's consort, comes from the house; is it by chance, or has she heard these tidings of her son?

(Eurydice *comes from the house.*)

EURYDICE: I heard your words, citizens, as I was going to the shrine of Pallas with my prayers. As I loosed the bolts of the gate, the message of woe to my household smote my ear. I sank back, stricken with horror, into the arms of my handmaids, and my senses left me. Yet say again these 850 tidings. I shall hear them as one who is no stranger to grief.

MESSENGER: Dear lady, I will tell you what I saw, I will hide nothing of the truth. I would gladly tell you a happier tale, but it would soon be found out false. Truth is the only way. – I guided your lord the King to the furthest part of the plain, where the body of Polynices, torn by dogs, still lay unpitied. There we prayed to the goddess of the roads, and to Pluto,[3] in mercy to restrain their wrath. We washed the dead with holy rites, and all that was left of the mortal man we burned with fresh-plucked branches; and over the 860 ashes at last we raised a mound of his native earth.

That done, we turned our steps toward those fearsome caves where in a cold nuptial chamber, with couch of stone, that maiden had been given as a bride of Death. But from afar off, one of us heard a voice wailing aloud, and turned to tell our master Creon.

And as the King drew nearer, the sharp anguish of broken cries came to his ears. Then he groaned and said like one in pain, "Can my sudden fear be true? Am I on the saddest road I ever went? That voice is my son's! Hurry, my 870 servants, to the tomb, and through the gap where the stones have been torn out, look into the cell – tell me if it is Haemon's voice I hear, or if my wits are tortured by the gods."

At these words from our stricken master, we went to make that search; and in the dim furthest part of the tomb we saw Antigone hanging by the neck, her scarf of fine linen twisted into a cruel noose. And there too we saw Haemon – his arms about her waist, while he cried out upon the loss of his bride, and his father's deed, and his ill- 880 starred love.

But now the King approached, and saw him, and cried out with horror, and went in and called with piteous voice, "Unhappy boy, what a deed have you done, breaking into this tomb! What purpose have you? Has grief stolen your reason? Come forth, my son! I pray you – I implore!" The boy answered no word, but glared at him with fierce eyes, spat in his face, and drew his cross-hilted sword. His father turned and fled, and the blow missed its mark. Then that maddened boy, torn between grief and rage and penitence, 890 straightway leaned upon his sword, and drove it half its length into his side; and in the little moment before death, he clasped the maiden in his arms, and her pale cheek was red where his blood gushed forth.

Corpse enfolding corpse they lie; he has won his bride, poor lad, not here but in the halls of Death; to all of us he has left a terrible witness that man's worst error is to reject good counsel.

(Eurydice *goes into the house.*)

CHORUS: What does this mean? The lady turns and goes without a word. 900

MESSENGER: I too am startled; but I think it means she is too proud to cry out before the people. Within the house, with her hand-maids about her, the tears will flow. Life has taught her prudence.

CHORUS: It may be; yet I fear. To me such silence seems more ominous than many lamentations.

MESSENGER: Then I will go into the house, and learn if some tragic purpose has formed in her tortured heart. Yes, you speak wisely; too much silence may hide terrible meanings. 910

---

[2]Son of Zeus and Antiope; with his twin brother Zethus, he built the walls of Thebes.

[3]Another name for Hades, the Greek god of the netherworld, the shadowy realm where the souls of dead were thought to rest.

(The Messenger *enters the house. As he goes, Creon comes into the open place before the house with attendants carrying the shrouded body of* Haemon *on a bier.)*

CHORUS: See, the King himself draws near, with the sad proof of his folly; this tells a tale of no violence by strangers, but — if I may say it — of his own misdeeds.

CREON: Woe for the sins of a darkened soul, the sins of a stubborn pride that played with death! Behold me, the father who has slain, behold the son who has perished! I am punished for the blindness of my counsels. Alas my son, cut down in youth untimely, woe is me! — your spirit fled — not yours the fault and folly, but my own!

CHORUS: Too late, too late your eyes are opened!   920

CREON: I have learned that bitter lesson. But it was some god, I think, darkened my mind and turned me into ways of cruelty. Now my days are overthrown and my joys trampled. Alas, man's labors come but to foolish ends!

(The Messenger *comes from the house.)*

MESSENGER: Sire, one sees your hands are not empty, but there is more laid up in store for you. Woeful is the burden you bear, and you must look on further woes within your house.

CREON: Why, how can there be more?

MESSENGER: Your queen is dead, the mother of that lad —   930 unhappy lady! This is Fate's latest blow.

CREON: Death, Death, how many deaths will stay your hunger? For me is there no mercy? O messenger of evil, bearer of bitter tidings, what is this you tell me? I was already dead, but you smite me anew. What do you say? — what is this news you bring of slaughter heaped on slaughter?

(The doors of the King's house are opened, and the corpse of Eurydice *is disclosed.)*

CHORUS: Behold with your own eyes!

CREON: Oh, horror! — woe upon woe! Can any further dreadful thing await me? I have but now raised my son in   940 these arms — and here again I see a corpse before me. Alas, unhappy mother — alas, alas my child!

MESSENGER: At the altar of your house, self-stabbed with a keen knife, she suffered her darkening eyes to close, while she lamented that other son, Megareus, who died so nobly but a while ago, and then this boy whose corpse is here beside you. But with her last breath and with a bitter cry she invoked evil upon you, the slayer of your sons.

CREON: Will no one strike me to the heart with the two-edged sword? — miserable that I am, and plunged in   950 misery!

MESSENGER: Yes, both this son's death and that other son's, were charged to you by her whose corpse you see.

CREON: But how did she do this violence upon herself?

MESSENGER: Her own hand struck her to the heart, when she had heard how this boy died.

CREON: I cannot escape the guilt of these things, it rests on no other of mortal kind. I, only I, am the slayer, wretched that I am — I own the truth. Lead me away, my servants, lead me quickly hence, for my life is but death.   960

CHORUS: You speak well, if any speech is good amid so much evil. When all is trouble, the briefest way is best.

CREON: Oh let it come now, the fate most merciful for me, my last day — that will be the best fate of all. Oh let it come

swiftly, that I may not look upon tomorrow's light!

CHORUS: That is hidden in the future. Present tasks claim our care. The ordering of the future does not rest with mortals.

CREON: Yet all my desire is summed up in that prayer.

CHORUS: Pray no more: no man evades his destiny.   970

CREON: Lead me away, I pray you; a rash, foolish man, who has slain you, O my son, unwittingly, and you too, my wife — unhappy that I am! Where can I find comfort, where can I turn my gaze? — for where I have turned my hand, all has gone wrong; and this last blow breaks me and bows my head.

(Creon is led into his house as the Chorus *speaks.)*

CHORUS: If any man would be happy, and not broken by Fate, Wisdom is the thing he should seek, for happiness hides there. Let him revere the gods and keep their words inviolate, for proud men who speak great words come in   980 the end to despair. And learn wisdom in sorrow, when it is too late.

◆

The tragedy of *Antigone* springs from the irreconcilability of Antigone's personal idealism and Creon's hardheaded political realism. Creon means well by the state; he is committed to the exercise of justice under the law. As a king newly come to power, he perceives his duty in terms of his authority: "whoever the city shall appoint to rule," says Creon, "that man must be obeyed, in little things and in great things, in just things and unjust; for the man who is a good subject is the one who would be a good ruler..." But Creon ignores the ancient imperatives of divine law and familial duty. His blind devotion to the state and his unwillingness to compromise trap him into making a decision whose consequences are disastrous.

In most Greek tragedies, the weakness or "tragic flaw" of the **protagonist** (the leading character) brings that character into conflict with fate or with an **antagonist** (one who opposes the protagonist), and ultimately to his or her fall. Creon's excessive pride (in Greek, *hubris*) results in the loss of those who are dearest to him. But Antigone, the real protagonist of the play, is also a victim of self-righteous inflexibility. In an age that confined women to the domestic household and expected them to conform to male opinion, Antigone was unique. By challenging male authority, she threatened the status quo: "*She* is the man," Creon angrily objects, "if she can carry this off unpunished." Antigone's sister, Ismene, argues "We must remember we were born women, not meant to strive with men." But Antigone persists: Her heroism derives from her unswerving dedication to the ideals of divine justice and to the right of the individual to challenge the laws of the state. Sophocles perceived the difficulties involved in reconciling public good and private conscience, and in achieving harmony between the individual and the state. In *Antigone*, he offered a moving plea for sound judgment and rational action, a plea that rings with the unbounded optimism of the choral chant: "Wonders are many in the world, and the wonder of all is man.... With speech and windswift thought he builds the State to his mood" (lines 284–285, 306–307).

The Individual and the Community: The Case of Socrates

The question of right conduct was central to the life and teachings of Socrates (469–399 B.C.E.), a contemporary of Sophocles and Athens' most notorious philosopher. Socrates, who had fought bravely for his *polis* in the Peloponnesian War, opposed the moral chaos of post-war Athens. A self-appointed teacher, he roamed the streets of Athens, engaging his fellow-citizens in conversation and debate. Arguing that the unexamined life is not worth living, he challenged his peers on matters of public and private virtue, constantly posing the question, "What is the greatest good?" In this pursuit, he employed a rigorous question-and-answer technique known as the **dialectical method**. Such tactics won Socrates as many enemies as friends. Outspoken in his commitment to free inquiry, he fell into disfavor with the reactionary regime that governed Athens after its defeat in the Peloponnesian War. And in the year 399 B.C.E., when he was over seventy years of age, he was brought to trial for subversive behavior, impiety, and atheism. Found guilty by a narrow margin of votes and offering no serious alternative to the proposed death penalty, Socrates went to prison to await death by drinking hemlock, a poisonous herb.

Socrates wrote no books: What we know of him comes mainly from the writings of his students. The dialogue called *Crito*, written by Socrates' student, Plato, narrates the last events of Socrates' life: Socrates' friend and pupil Crito urges him to escape from prison, but the old philosopher refuses. He explains that to run away would be to subvert the laws by which he had lived and to criticize implicitly the system and the city-state that he had defended throughout his life. For Socrates, the loyalty of the citizen to the *polis*, like that of the child to its parents, was a primary obligation. Like Achilles and Antigone, he prefers death to dishonor. He defends right action as crucial to the destiny of both the individual and the community. Here, we encounter once more the Hellenic view that immortality is achieved through human deeds, the effects of which outlast human lives.

READING 14
From Plato's *Crito*

CRITO: . . . O my good Socrates, I beg you for the last time to listen to me and save yourself. For to me your death will be more than a single disaster: not only shall I lose a friend the like of whom I shall never find again, but many persons who do not know you and me well will think that I might have saved you if I had been willing to spend money, but that I neglected to do so. And what reputation could be more disgraceful than the reputation of caring more for money than for one's friends? The public will never believe that we were anxious to save you, but that you yourself refused to escape. [1] [10]

SOCRATES: But, my dear Crito, why should we care so much about public opinion? Reasonable men, of whose opinion it is worth our while to think, will believe that we acted as we really did.

CRITO: But you see, Socrates, that it is necessary to care about public opinion, too. This very thing that has happened to you proves that the multitude can do a man not the least, but almost the greatest harm, if he is falsely accused to them. [20]

SOCRATES: I wish that the multitude were able to do a man the greatest harm, Crito, for then they would be able to do him the greatest good, too. That would have been fine. But, as it is, they can do neither. They cannot make a man either wise or foolish: they act wholly at random. . . . Consider it in this way. Suppose the laws and the commonwealth were to come and appear to me as I was preparing to run away (if that is the right phrase to describe my escape) and were to ask, "Tell us, Socrates, what have you in your mind to do? What do you mean by trying to [30] escape but to destroy us, the laws, and the whole state, so far as you are able? Do you think that a state can exist and not be overthrown, in which the decisions of law are of no force, and are disregarded and undermined by private individuals?" How shall we answer questions like that, Crito? Much might be said, especially by an orator, in defense of the law which makes judicial decisions supreme. Shall I reply, "But the state has injured me by judging my case unjustly." Shall we say that?

CRITO: Certainly we will, Socrates. [40]

SOCRATES: And suppose the laws were to reply, "Was that our agreement? Or was it that you would abide by whatever judgments the state should pronounce?" And if we were surprised by their words, perhaps they would say, "Socrates, don't be surprised by our words, but answer us; you yourself are accustomed to ask questions and to answer them. What complaint have you against us and the state, that you are trying to destroy us? Are we not, first of all, your parents? Through us your father took your mother and brought you into the world. Tell us, have you any fault [50] to find with those of us that are the laws of marriage?" "I have none," I should reply. "Or have you any fault to find with those of us that regulate the raising of the child and the education which you, like others, received? Did we not do well in telling your father to educate you in music and athletics?" "You did," I should say. "Well, then, since you were brought into the world and raised and educated by us, how, in the first place, can you deny that you are our child and our slave, as your fathers were before you? And if this be so, do you think that your rights are on a level with ours? Do you think that you have a right to retaliate if we should try to do anything to you? You had not the same rights that your father had, or that your master would have had if you had been a slave. You had no right to retaliate if they ill-treated you, or to answer them if they scolded you, or to strike them back if they struck you, or to repay them evil with evil in any way. And do you think that you may retaliate in the case of your country and its laws? If we try to destroy you, because we think it just, will you in return do all that you can to destroy us, the laws, and your country, and say that in so doing you are acting justly — you, the man who really thinks so much of excellence? Or are you too wise to see that your country is worthier, more to be revered, more sacred, and held in higher honor both by the gods and by all men of understanding, than your father and your mother and all your ancestors; and that you ought to reverence it, and to submit to it, and to approach it more humbly when it is angry with you than you would approach your father; and either to do whatever it tells you to do or to persuade it to excuse you; and to obey in silence if it orders you to endure flogging or imprisonment, or if it sends you to battle to be wounded or die? That is just. You must not give way, nor retreat, nor desert your station. In war, and in the court of justice, and everywhere, you must do whatever your state and your country tell you to do, or you must persuade them that their commands are unjust. But it is impious to use violence against your father or your mother; and much more impious to use violence against your country." What answer shall we make, Crito? Shall we say that the laws speak the truth, or not?

CRITO: I think that they do.

SOCRATES: "Then consider, Socrates," perhaps they would say, "if we are right in saying that by attempting to escape you are attempting an injustice. We brought you into the world, we raised you, we educated you, we gave you and every other citizen a share of all the good things we could. Yet we proclaim that if any man of the Athenians is dissatisfied with us, he may take his goods and go away wherever he pleases; we give that privilege to every man who chooses to avail himself of it, so soon as he has reached manhood, and sees us, the laws, and the administration of our state. No one of us stands in his way or forbids him to take his goods and go wherever he likes, whether it be to an Athenian colony, or to any foreign country, if he is dissatisfied with us and with the state. But we say that every man of you who remains here, seeing how we administer justice, and how we govern the state in other matters, has agreed, by the very fact of remaining here, to do whatsoever we tell him. And, we say, he who disobeys us acts unjustly on three counts: he disobeys us who are his parents, and he disobeys us who reared him, and he disobeys us after he has agreed to obey us, without persuading us that we are wrong. Yet we did not tell him sternly to do whatever we told him. We offered him an alternative; we gave him his choice either to obey us or to convince us that we were wrong; but he does neither.

"These are the charges, Socrates, to which we say that you will expose yourself if you do what you intend; and you are more exposed to these charges than other Athenians." And if I were to ask, "Why?" they might retort with justice

that I have bound myself by the agreement with them more than other Athenians. They would say, "Socrates, we have very strong evidence that you were satisfied with us and with the state. You would not have been content to stay at home in it more than other Athenians unless you had been satisfied with it more than they. You never went away from Athens to the festivals, nor elsewhere except on military service; you never made other journeys like other men; you had no desire to see other states or other laws; you were contented with us and our state; so strongly did you prefer us, and agree to be governed by us. And what is more, you had children in this city, you found it so satisfactory. Besides, if you had wished, you might at your trial have offered to go into exile. At that time you could have done with the state's consent what you are trying now to do without it. But then you gloried in being willing to die. You said that you preferred death to exile. And now you do not honor those words: you do not respect us, the laws, for you are trying to destroy us; and you are acting just as a miserable slave would act, trying to run away, and breaking the contracts and agreement which you made to live as our citizen. First, therefore, answer this question. Are we right, or are we wrong, in saying that you have agreed not in mere words, but in your actions, to live under our government?" What are we to say, Crito? Must we not admit that it is true?

CRITO: We must, Socrates . . . .

———————◆———————

The Political Views of the Greek Philosophers

The dialogue between Crito and Socrates illustrates the tough-minded idealism of a man whose faith in the democratic process remained unshakable, even when that process contributed to his own demise. Socrates was a victim of the very democracy he helped to shape. Athenian democracy operated more or less successfully for more than two hundred years, but it drew criticism from the philosophers Plato (ca. 427–347 B.C.E.) and Aristotle (384–322 B.C.E.), whose philosophic contributions will be discussed in chapter 5.

Neither Plato nor Aristotle believed that all human beings were capable of ruling themselves. Plato held that all people were born equal, but that each would rise to an appropriate place in society according to his or her abilities. (Plato's theories have much in common with the ancient Chinese doctrine of natural or biological equality and the Confucian "aristocracy of merit," discussed in chapter 3.) Plato staunchly defended the idea that the state must be ruled by those who are the most intellectually fit. Aristotle, on the other hand, held that political privilege was the logical result of the fact that some human beings were naturally superior to others. Contending that from the hour of their birth, some human beings were marked out for subjection and others for rule, he argued that governments must function in the interest of the state, not in the interest of any single individual or group. Aristotle rejected democracy as the ideal form of government because, at least in theory, it put power in the hands of great masses of poor people who might rule in their own interests. He also observed that Athenian demogogues occasionally had persuaded the Assembly to pass less-than-worthy laws. In his *Politics*, the first treatise on political theory produced in the West, Aristotle concluded that the best type of government was a constitutional one ruled by the middle class. He insisted that humankind could reach its full potential only within the political framework of the state. Aristotle defined the human being as a *polis*-person (from which term we derive the word *political*), that is, as a community animal. Only beasts and gods, he observed, have no need for the state. He resolved the relationship between the individual and the state as follows:

> [The] state is by nature clearly prior to the family and to the individual, since the whole is of necessity prior to the part . . . . The proof that the state is a creation of nature and prior to the individual is that the individual, when isolated, is not self-sufficing; and therefore he is like a part in relation to the whole. But he who is unable to live in society, or who has no need because he is sufficient for himself, must be either a beast or a god: he is no part of a state. A social instinct is implanted in all men by nature, and yet he who first founded the state was the greatest of benefactors.
>
> For man, when perfected, is the best of animals, but, when separated from law and justice, he is the worst of all; since armed injustice is the more dangerous, and he is equipped at birth with arms, meant to be used by intelligence and virtue, he is the most unholy and the most savage of animals, and the most full of lust and gluttony. But justice is the bond of men in states, for the administration of justice, which is the determination of what is just, is the principle of order in political society.

SUMMARY

The rise of Greek civilization marks a shift in attention to the quality of human life in the secular world, and more particularly, in the community. Indebted to the pre-Greek civilizations of Crete and Mycenae, the Homeric epics describe an aggressive and warlike people who balance vigorous individualism against a deep devotion to their tribal community. The heroes of the *Iliad*, unlike those of other ancient civilizations, are not at the mercy of the gods; rather, they determine their own destinies.

The spirit of individualism that characterized the Homeric epics shaped the values of the emerging Greek city-states. That spirit contributed to the creation of the world's first and only direct democracy, established in the city-state of Athens, and to the Golden Age in

cultural productivity that followed the Persian Wars. In Pericles' Funeral Speech, the heroic ideal assumes a civic context. In Sophocles' *Antigone*, individualism comes into conflict with the inflexible demands of the state. And in the *Crito*, Socrates chooses death over civil disobedience. These literary works are memorable for the majesty of their language and the profundity of their insights into the human condition. At issue here is not the unchanging covenant between people and the gods, but rather, the dynamic relationship between the individual and the community.

The Greeks realized that freedom of expression and action was no gift of heaven, and that the exercise of such freedom might be perilous. Nevertheless, they insisted that individual engagement in the life of the *polis* was essential and that the good life was within the grasp of mortals.

GLOSSARY

antagonist the character that directly opposes the protagonist in drama or fiction

catalog a list of people, things, or attributes, characteristic of biblical and Homeric literature

democracy a government in which supreme power is vested in the people

dialectical method a question-and-answer style of inquiry made famous by Socrates

epithet a characterizing word or phrase; in Homeric verse, a compound adjective used to identify a person or thing

oligarchy a government in which power lies in the hands of an elite minority

protagonist the leading character in a play or story

simile a figure of speech comparing two essentially unlike things, often introduced by "like" or "as"

SUGGESTIONS FOR READING

Bowra, C. M. *The Greek Experience*. New York: New American Library, 1957.

Cartledge, Paul. *The Greeks: A Portrait of Self and Others*. New York: Oxford University Press, 1993.

Finley, M. I., ed. *The Legacy of Greece: A New Appraisal*. Oxford: Oxford University Press, 1981.

Hamilton, Edith. *The Greek Way*. New York: Norton, 1960.

Hooper, Finley. *Greek Realities: Life and Thought in Ancient Greece*. New York: Scribner's, 1967.

Kitto, H. D. F. *The Greeks*. Baltimore: Penguin, 1951.

Lefkowitz, M. R., and M. B. Fant. *Women in Greece and Rome*, rev. ed. Baltimore: Johns Hopkins, 1982.

Loraux, Nicole. *The Children of Athena: Athenian Ideas about Citizenship and the Division Between the Sexes*, trans. C. Levine. Princeton, N. J.: Princeton University Press, 1993.

Pomeroy, S. B. *Goddesses, Whores, Wives and Slaves*. New York: Schocken, 1975.

Robinson, Cyril. *Everyday Life in Ancient Greece*. Westport, Conn.: Greenwood, 1978.

Stone, I. F. *The Trial of Socrates*. New York: Doubleday, 1989.

5

Greek Philosophy: The Speculative Leap

In the ancient world, where most people saw themselves at the mercy of forces they could not comprehend, a small group of Greek thinkers emerged as masters of intellectual perception. These men, whom we call philosophers (literally, "lovers of wisdom"), laid the foundations for Western scientific and philosophic inquiry. Instead of making nature the object of worship, they made it the object of study. Taking issue with those who explained devastating natural events (such as earthquakes and lightning) as expressions of the anger of the gods, the Greek philosophers argued that such events had natural, not supernatural, causes. Challenging all prevailing myths, they made the speculative leap from supernatural to natural explanations of the unknown.

The Greeks were not the first to believe in a natural order. The ancient Chinese, for instance, had viewed the universe as the interaction of two forces, the *yin* and the *yang*. The Hindus of ancient India had stressed the oneness of all aspects of the universe. But while Taoists and Hindus embraced the wholeness of nature, the Greeks subjected it to close analysis, a process that separates the whole into its component parts. They defended rationalism and objectivity as alternatives to the intuitive and holistic modes of understanding that characterize most non-Western cultures. Ancient Greek claims to intellectual detachment and objectivity – the fundamentals of the scientific method – also stand in clear contrast to the Hebrew call for fervent commitment and unswerving belief in God. Indeed, the Greek glorification of reason provides a notable contrast to the Hebrew emphasis on faith. These two modes of experience – reason (based in the Greco-Roman tradition) and faith (rooted in the Judeo-Christian tradition) – have competed for primacy in shaping Western culture from earliest times to the present. At the same time, the bipolar realms of reason and intuition (rooted in Asian and African traditions) may be said to have divided the West and the East, despite their mutual influence over the centuries.

Naturalist Philosophy: The Pre-Socratics

The earliest Greek philosopher-scientists, who lived just prior to the time of Socrates, were the first of the great philosophers. These sixth-century-B.C.E. thinkers, many of whom came from the city of Miletus on the Ionian coast of Asia Minor, were the first to insist that the workings of nature could be explained by natural causes. They asked, "What is everything made of?" "How do things come into existence?" and "What permanent substance lies behind appearances?" Observing a world of constant change, they tried to identify a single, unifying substance that formed the basic "stuff" of nature. Thales (ca. 620–555 B.C.E.), the "father of philosophy," held that water was the fundamental substance and source from which all things proceeded. Water's potential for change – from solid to liquid to gas – and its pervasiveness on earth convinced him that water formed the material basis of the universe.

Whereas the Egyptians and the Mesopotamians deified water, sun, and other natural elements, the pre-Socratics stripped these elements of all supernatural associations. They made accurate predictions of solar and lunar eclipses, plotted astronomical charts, and discovered the processes of respiration in plants and animals. Thales' followers challenged his view of the universe by suggesting that air, earth, or fire, or a mixture of these primordial elements might constitute the basic stuff of nature. Around 500 B.C.E., Leucippus of Miletus arrived at the theory that physical reality consisted of minute, invisible particles that moved ceaselessly in the void. These he called *atoms*, the Greek word meaning "indivisible." Democritus (ca. 460–370 B.C.E.), a follower of Leucippus and the best known of the Greek materialists, developed the atomic theory of matter. For Democritus, the *psyche* (the mind or soul) was made of the same indivisible material substances as everything else in nature. According to Democritus, atoms moved constantly and eternally, compounding by chance in time and space. The atomic theory survived into Roman times, and although forgotten for two thousand years thereafter it was validated by physicists of the early twentieth century.

The concept that a single, unifying substance underlay reality drew opposition from some of the pre-Socratics. The universe, argued Heraclitus of Ephesus (?–460 B.C.E.), has no permanence, but rather, is in constant process or flux. Heraclitus defended the idea that change itself was the basis of reality. "You cannot step twice into the same river," he wrote, "for fresh waters are ever flowing in upon you." Yet, Heraclitus believed that an underlying Form or Guiding Force (in Greek, *logos*) permeates nature – an idea that resembles Hindu pantheism and anticipated the Christian concept (found in the Gospel of John) that a Great Intelligence stands at the beginning of time. For Heraclitus this Force was impersonal, universal, and eternal.

Around 500 B.C.E., one of the most remarkable of the pre-Socratics, Pythagoras, advanced an idea that departed from both the material and immaterial views of the universe. Pythagoras believed that proportion, discovered through number, was the true basis of reality. According to Pythagoras, all universal relationships could be expressed through numbers, the truths of which were eternal and unchanging. The formula in plane geometry that equates the square of the hypotenuse in right angle triangles to the sum of the square of the other two sides – a theorem associated with Pythagoras – is an example of such an unchanging and eternal truth, as is the simplest of mathematical equations: $2 + 2 = 4$. Pythagoras was the founding father of pure mathematics and the first to demonstrate the relationship between musical harmonics and numbers. His view that number gives order and harmony to the universe is basic to the principles of balance and proportion that dominate classical art and music (see chapter 6). The speculative systems of Pythagoras, Heraclitus, and other pre-Socratics may have been influenced by philosophic and religious theories originating in China and India – theories that filtered westward along the overland trade routes that linked East Asia with Near Eastern civilizations. The Pythagorean proscription against eating animal flesh and certain plants, for example, suggests some familiarity with the Hindu belief in reincarnation and the transmigration of souls (see chapter 2).

The separation of the natural from the supernatural was essential to the birth of medical science among the early Greeks. Hippocrates (ca. 460–377 B.C.E.), the most famous of Greek physicians and so-called "father of medicine," insisted on the necessary relationship of cause and effect in matters of illness. He investigated the influence of diet and environment on general health and initiated the idea that an imbalance among bodily "humours" – blood, phlegm, black bile, and yellow bile – was the cause of disease. To this day, all graduating physicians take the Hippocratic Oath (probably not written by Hippocrates himself), which binds them to heal the sick and abstain from unprofessional medical practices.

Although no agreement as to the nature of reality was ever reached among the pre-Socratics, they laid the groundwork for a rational investigation of the cosmos. Their efforts represent the beginnings of both science and philosophy.

Humanist Philosophy
Socrates and the Search for Virtue

Pre-Socratic philosophers were concerned with describing physical reality and with identifying the unity that lay behind the chaos of human perceptions. The philosophers who followed them turned their attention from the world of nature to the world of the mind, from physical matters to moral concerns, and from the gathering of information to the cultivation of wisdom. They fathered the field of inquiry known as metaphysics (literally, "beyond physics"), the branch of philosophy concerned with abstract thought. The transition from the examination of matter to the exploration of mind established the humanistic direction of Greek philosophy for the next two centuries.

The first humanist philosophers were a group of traveling scholars called Sophists. Masters of formal debate, the Sophists were concerned with defining the limits of human knowledge. The famous Sophist Protagoras (ca. 490–421 B.C.E.) believed that knowledge could not exceed human opinion, a position summed up in his famous dictum "Man is the measure of all things." His contemporary Gorgias (ca. 485–380 B.C.E.) tried to prove that reality is incomprehensible and that even if one could comprehend it, it could not be communicated to others. Such skepticism was common to the Sophists, who argued that truth and justice were relative: What might be considered just and true for one individual or situation might not be just and true for another.

Athens' foremost philosopher, Socrates, whom we met in chapter 4, vigorously opposed these views (Figure 5.1). Insisting on the absolute nature of truth and justice, he described the ethical life as part of a larger set of universal truths and an unchanging moral order. For Socrates, virtue was not a matter of cleverly argued opinions, nor was it relative to individual circumstance. Rather, virtue was a condition of the *psyche*. Since, according to Socrates, the *psyche* was the seat of both intelligence and character, knowing the

Figure 5.1 Portrait bust of Socrates. Roman marble copy of an original bronze supposedly created by Lysippos in ca. 350 B.C.E. © Hirmer Fotoarchiv.

meaning of virtue was identical with acting virtuously. To know good was to do good.

Trained as a stonemason, Socrates preferred to spend his time engaging his fellow Athenians in intellectual debate. Unlike the Sophists, he refused to charge fees for educating others. He argued that wealth did not produce excellence, but rather, derived from it. He defined his role in Athenian society by comparing himself to a large horsefly and Athens to "a horse that is large and well-bred but rather sluggish because of its size." Socrates saw himself as the horsefly "constantly alighting" upon Athenian citizens to "arouse, persuade, and reproach" them and, most important, to demand that they give rational justification for their beliefs and actions. He used the dialectical method of inquiry to reason from specific examples to general principles and from particular to universal truths. His style of intellectual cross-examination proceeded from his first principle of inquiry: "Know thyself." Philosophers were, as Socrates observed, "different from the multitude." The great masses of Greek citizens found comfort in supernatural explanations for the workings of nature: They paid homage to the traditional Greek gods and goddesses and set faith above reason in their everyday

existence. Socrates' religious skepticism and his insistence on coaxing truth from stringent self-examination drew mounting criticism from his enemies, whose hostile accusations of impiety and subversion brought him to trial and, ultimately, to his death (see Reading 14).

Plato and the Theory of Forms

Socrates' teachings were an inspiration to his pupil Plato (427–347 B.C.E.). Born in Athens during the Peloponnesian wars, Plato lived during the late phase of Hellenic culture. In 387 B.C.E., more than a decade after the death of his master, he founded the first school of philosophy, called the Academy. Plato wrote some two dozen treatises, most of which were cast in a dialogue format that exposed multiple points of view. Some of the dialogues may be precise transcriptions of actual conversations, while others are clearly fictional, but the major philosophical arguments in almost all of Plato's treatises are put in the mouth of Socrates. And since Socrates himself wrote nothing, it is impossible to distinguish between his teachings and those of Plato.

Plato's most famous treatise, the *Republic*, asks the questions "What is the meaning of justice?" and "What is the nature of a just society?" In trying to answer these questions, Plato introduces a theory of knowledge that is both visionary and dogmatic. It asserts the existence of a two-level reality, one consisting of constantly changing particulars available to our senses, the other consisting of eternal truths understood by way of the intellect. According to Plato, the higher reality of eternal truths, which he calls Forms, is distinct from the imperfect and transient objects of sensory experience, which are mere copies of the Forms. Plato's Theory of Forms proposes that things in the world of our senses are only imitations of the imperishable and unchanging Forms. Consider: The circle and its three-dimensional counterpart, the sphere, exist quite apart from any particular circle and sphere. They have always existed and will always exist. But the beach ball I toss in the air, an imperfect copy of the sphere, is transitory. Indeed, if all of the particular beach balls in the world were destroyed, the Universal Form of Sphere would still exist. Similarly, individual instances of justice, love, and beauty are imitations of the Forms of Justice, Love, and Beauty, which stand as unchanging and eternal models.

According to Plato, the Forms descend from an ultimate Form, the Form of the Good. Plato never located or defined the Ultimate Good, except by analogy with the sun. Like the sun, the Form of the Good illuminates all that is intelligible and makes possible the mind's perception of the Forms, as objects of thought. The Ultimate Good, knowledge of which is the goal of dialectical inquiry, is the most difficult to reach.

In the *Republic,* Plato uses a literary device known as **allegory** to illustrate the dilemma facing the *psyche* or mind in its ascent to knowledge of the imperishable and unchanging Forms. By way of allegory, the device by which the literal meaning of the text implies a figurative or "hidden" meaning, Plato describes a group of ordinary mortals chained within an underground chamber (the *psyche* imprisoned within the human body); their woeful position permits them to see only the shadows on the walls of the cave (the imperfect and perishable imitations of the Forms, that is, the world of our senses), which the prisoners, in their ignorance, believe to be real (Figure **5.2**). Only when one of the prisoners (the philosopher-hero) ascends to the "upper" world of light (true knowledge, or knowledge of the Forms) does it become clear that what the cave-dwellers perceive as truth is nothing more than shadows of Reality. This intriguing parable is presented as a dialogue between Socrates and Plato's older brother, Glaucon.

READING 15

The "Allegory of the Cave" from Plato's *Republic*

Next, said [Socrates], here is a parable to illustrate the degrees in which our nature may be enlightened or unenlightened. Imagine the condition of men living in a sort of cavernous chamber underground, with an entrance open to the light and a long passage all down the cave. Here they have been from childhood, chained by the leg and also by the neck, so that they cannot move and can see only what is in front of them, because the chains will not let them turn their heads. At some distance higher up is the light of a fire burning behind them; and between the prisoners and the fire is a track[1] with a parapet built along it, like the screen at a puppet-show, which hides the performers while they show their puppets over the top. 1

I see, said he.

Now behind this parapet imagine persons carrying along various artificial objects, including figures of men and animals in wood or stone or other materials, which project above the parapet. Naturally, some of these persons will be talking, others silent.[2]

It is a strange picture, he said, and a strange sort of prisoners. 20

---

[1]The track crosses the passage into the cave at right angles and is above the parapet built along it.

[2]A modern Plato would compare his Cave to an underground cinema, where the audience watch the play of shadows thrown by the film passing before a light at their backs. The film itself is only an image of "real" things and events in the world outside the cinema. For the film Plato has to substitute the clumsier apparatus of a procession of artificial objects carried on their heads by persons who are merely part of the machinery, providing for the movement of the objects and the sound whose echo the prisoners hear. The parapet prevents these persons' shadows from being cast on the wall of the Cave.

Like ourselves, I replied; for in the first place prisoners so confined would have seen nothing of themselves or of one another, except the shadows thrown by the fire-light on the wall of the Cave facing them, would they?

Not if all their lives they had been prevented from moving their heads.

And they would have seen as little of the objects carried past.

Of course. 30

Now, if they could talk to one another, would they not suppose that their words referred only to those passing shadows which they saw?

Necessarily.

And suppose their prison had an echo from the wall facing them? When one of the people crossing behind them spoke, they could only suppose that the sound came from the shadow passing before their eyes.

No doubt.

In every way, then, such prisoners would recognize as reality nothing but the shadows of those artificial objects. 40

Inevitably.

Now consider what would happen if their release from the chains and the healing of their unwisdom should come about in this way. Suppose one of them set free and forced suddenly to stand up, turn his head, and walk with eyes lifted to the light; all these movements would be painful, and he would be too dazzled to make out the objects whose shadows he had been used to see. What do you think he would say, if someone told him that what he had formerly seen was meaningless illusion, but now, being somewhat nearer to reality and turned towards more real objects, he was getting a truer view? Suppose further that he were shown the various objects being carried by and were made to say, in reply to questions, what each of them was. Would he not be perplexed and believe the objects now shown him to be not so real as what he formerly saw? 50

Yes, not nearly so real.

And if he were forced to look at the fire-light itself, would not his eyes ache, so that he would try to escape and turn back to the things which he could see distinctly, convinced that they really were clearer than these other objects now being shown to him? 60

Yes.

And suppose someone were to drag him away forcibly up the steep and rugged ascent and not let him go until he had hauled him out into the sunlight, would he not suffer pain and vexation at such treatment, and, when he had come out into the light, find his eyes so full of its radiance that he could not see a single one of the things that he was now told were real? 70

Certainly he would not see them all at once.

He would need, then, to grow accustomed before he could see things in that upper world. At first it would be easiest to make out shadows, and then the images of men and things reflected in water, and later on the things themselves. After that, it would be easier to watch the heavenly bodies and the sky itself by night, looking at the light of the moon and stars rather than the Sun and the Sun's light in the day-time. 80

Yes, surely.

Last of all, he would be able to look at the Sun and contemplate its nature, not as it appears when reflected in

Figure 5.2 "Allegory of the Cave." From *The Great Dialogues of Plato*, translated by W.H.D. Rouse, translation copyright © 1956, renewed 1984 by J.C.G. Rouse. Used by permission of Dutton Signet, a division of Penguin Books USA Inc.

water or any alien medium, but as it is in itself in its own domain.

No doubt.

And now he would begin to draw the conclusion that it is the Sun that produces the seasons and the course of the year and controls everything in the visible world, and moreover is in a way the cause of all that he and his companions used to see. 90

Clearly he would come at last to that conclusion.

Then if he called to mind his fellow prisoners and what passed for wisdom in his former dwelling-place, he would surely think himself happy in the change and be sorry for them. They may have had a practice of honoring and commending one another, with prizes for the man who had the keenest eye for the passing shadows and the best memory for the order in which they followed or accompanied one another, so that he could make a good 100 guess as to which was going to come next. Would our released prisoner be likely to covet those prizes or to envy the men exalted to honor and power in the Cave? Would he not feel like Homer's Achilles, that he would far sooner "be on earth as a hired servant in the house of a landless man"[3] or endure anything rather than go back to his old beliefs and live in the old way?

Yes, he would prefer any fate to such a life.

Now imagine what would happen if he went down again to take his former seat in the Cave. Coming suddenly out of 110 the sunlight, his eyes would be filled with darkness. He might be required once more to deliver his opinion on those shadows, in competition with the prisoners who had never been released, while his eyesight was still dim and unsteady; and it might take some time to become used to the darkness. They would laugh at him and say that he had gone up only to come back with his sight ruined; it was worth no one's while even to attempt the ascent. If they

could lay hands on the man who was trying to set them free and lead them up, they would kill him.[4] 120

Yes, they would.

Every feature in this parable, my dear Glaucon, is meant to fit our earlier analysis. The prison dwelling corresponds to the region revealed to us through the sense of sight, and the fire-light within it to the power of the Sun. The ascent to see the things in the upper world you may take as standing for the upward journey of the soul into the region of the intelligible; then you will be in possession of what I surmise, since that is what you wish to be told. Heaven knows whether it is true; but this, at any rate, is how it 130 appears to me. In the world of knowledge, the last thing to be perceived and only with great difficulty is the essential Form of Goodness. Once it is perceived, the conclusion must follow that, for all things, this is the cause of whatever is right and good; in the visible world it gives birth to light and to the lord of light, while it is itself sovereign in the intelligible world and the parent of intelligence and truth. Without having had a vision of this Form no one can act with wisdom, either in his own life or in matters of state. 140

So far as I can understand, I share your belief.

Then you may also agree that it is no wonder if those who have reached this height are reluctant to manage the affairs of men. Their souls long to spend all their time in that upper world — naturally enough, if here once more our parable holds true. Nor, again, is it at all strange that one who comes from the contemplation of divine things to the miseries of human life should appear awkward and ridiculous when, with eyes still dazed and not yet accustomed to the darkness, he is compelled, in a low- 150 court or elsewhere, to dispute about the shadows of justice or the images that cast those shadows, and to wrangle over the notions of what is right in the minds of men who have

---

[3]This verse, spoken by the ghost of Achilles, suggests that the Cave is comparable with Hades, the Greek underworld.

[4]An allusion to the fate of Socrates.

never beheld Justice itself.

It is not at all strange.

No; a sensible man will remember that the eyes may be confused in two ways — by a change from light to darkness or from darkness to light; and he will recognize that the same thing happens to the soul. When he sees it troubled and unable to discern anything clearly, instead of laughing 160 thoughtlessly, he will ask whether, coming from a brighter existence, its unaccustomed vision is obscured by the darkness, in which case he will think its condition enviable and its life a happy one; or whether, emerging from the depths of ignorance, it is dazzled by excess of light. If so, he will rather feel sorry for it; or, if he were inclined to laugh, that would be less ridiculous than to laugh at the soul which has come down from the light.

That is a fair statement.

If this is true, then, we must conclude that education is 170 not what it is said to be by some, who profess to put knowledge into a soul which does not possess it, as if they could put sight into blind eyes. On the contrary, our own account signifies that the soul of every man does possess the power of learning the truth and the organ to see it with; and that, just as one might have to turn the whole body round in order that the eye should see light instead of darkness, so the entire soul must be turned away from this changing world, until its eye can bear to contemplate reality and that supreme splendor which we have called the 180 Good. Hence there may well be an art whose aim would be to effect this very thing, the conversion of the soul, in the readiest way; not to put the power of sight into the soul's eye, which already has it, but to ensure that, instead of looking in the wrong direction, it is turned the way it ought to be.

Yes, it may well be so.

It looks, then, as though wisdom were different from those ordinary virtues, as they are called, which are not far removed from bodily qualities, in that they can be 190 produced by habituation and exercise in a soul which has not possessed them from the first. Wisdom, it seems, is certainly the virtue of some diviner faculty, which never loses its power, though its use for good or harm depends on the direction towards which it is turned. You must have noticed in dishonest men with a reputation for sagacity the shrewd glance of a narrow intelligence piercing the objects to which it is directed. There is nothing wrong with their power of vision, but it has been forced into the service of evil, so that the keener its sight, the more harm it works. 200

Quite true.

And yet if the growth of a nature like this had been pruned from earliest childhood, cleared of those clinging overgrowths which come of gluttony and all luxurious pleasure and, like leaden weights charged with affinity to this mortal world, hang upon the soul, bending its vision downwards; if, freed from these, the soul were turned round towards true reality, then this same power in these very men would see the truth as keenly as the objects it is turned to now. 210

Yes, very likely.

Is it not also likely, or indeed certain after what has been said, that a state can never be properly governed either by the uneducated who know nothing of truth or by men who are allowed to spend all their days in the pursuit of culture?

The ignorant have no single mark before their eyes at which they must aim in all the conduct of their own lives and of affairs of state; and the others will not engage in action if they can help it, dreaming that, while still alive, they have been translated to the Island of the Blest. 220

Quite true.

It is for us, then, as founders of a commonwealth, to bring compulsion to bear on the noblest natures. They must be made to climb the ascent to the vision of Goodness, which we called the highest object of knowledge; and, when they have looked upon it long enough, they must not be allowed, as they now are, to remain on the heights, refusing to come down again to the prisoners or to take any part in their labors and rewards, however much or little these may be worth. 230

Shall we not be doing them an injustice, if we force on them a worse life than they might have?

You have forgotten again, my friend, that the law is not concerned to make any one class specially happy, but to ensure the welfare of the commonwealth as a whole. By persuasion or constraint it will unite the citizens in harmony, making them share whatever benefits each class can contribute to the common good; and its purpose in forming men of that spirit was not that each should be left to go his own way, but that they should be instrumental in 240 binding the community into one.

True, I had forgotten.

You will see, then, Glaucon, that there will be no real injustice in compelling our philosophers to watch over and care for the other citizens. We can fairly tell them that their compeers in other states may quite reasonably refuse to collaborate: there they have sprung up, like a self-sown plant, in despite of their country's institutions; no one has fostered their growth, and they cannot be expected to show gratitude for a care they have never received. "But," we 250 shall say, "it is not so with you. We have brought you into existence for your country's sake as well as for your own, to be like leaders and king-bees in a hive; you have been better and more thoroughly educated than those others and hence you are more capable of playing your part both as men of thought and as men of action. You must go down, then, each in his turn, to live with the rest and let your eyes grow accustomed to the darkness. You will then see a thousand times better than those who live there always; you will recognize every image for what it is and know what 260 it represents, because you have seen justice, beauty, and goodness in their reality; and so you and we shall find life in our commonwealth no mere dream, as it is in most existing states, where men live fighting one another about shadows and quarrelling for power, as if that were a great prize; whereas in truth government can be at its best and free from dissension only where the destined rulers are least desirous of holding office."

Quite true.

Then will our pupils refuse to listen and to take their 270 turns at sharing in the work of the community, though they may live together for most of their time in a purer air?

No; it is a fair demand, and they are fair-minded men. No doubt, unlike any ruler of the present day, they will think of holding power as an unavoidable necessity.

Yes, my friend; for the truth is that you can have a well-governed society only if you can discover for your future rulers a better way of life than being in office; then only will power be in the hands of men who are rich, not in gold, but in the wealth that brings happiness, a good and wise life. 280 All goes wrong when, starved for lack of anything good in their own lives, men turn to public affairs hoping to snatch from thence the happiness they hunger for. They set about fighting for power, and this internecine conflict ruins them and their country. The life of true philosophy is the only one that looks down upon offices of state; and access to power must be confined to men who are not in love with it; otherwise rivals will start fighting. So whom else can you compel to undertake the guardianship of the commonwealth, if not those who, besides understanding 290 best the principles of government, enjoy a nobler life than the politician's and look for rewards of a different kind?

There is indeed no other choice . . . .

———————◆———————

The "Allegory of the Cave" illustrates some key ideas in the teachings of Plato. The first of these is *idealism*, the theory that reality lies in the realm of ideas rather than in the realm of matter. Platonic idealism implies a dualistic (mind and matter) model of the universe: The mind belongs to the world of the eternal Forms, while the body belongs to the sensory or material world. Imprisoned in the body, the *psyche* forgets its once-perfect knowledge of the Forms. It is, nevertheless, capable of recovering its prenatal intelligence. The business of philosophy is to educate the *psyche*, to draw it out of its material prison so that it can regain perfect awareness of reality.

Plato's concept of an unchanging force behind the flux of our perceptions looks back to the theories of Heraclitus, while his description of the Forms resembles Pythagorean assertions of the unchanging reality of number. It is not without significance that Plato's Theory of Forms has been hailed in modern physics: The celebrated twentieth-century German physicist Werner Heisenberg argued that the smallest units of matter are not physical objects in the ordinary sense; rather, he asserted, they are "forms," or ideas that can be expressed unambiguously only in mathematical language. In constructing the Theory of Forms, Plato may also have been influenced by Far Eastern religious thought. His distinction between the realm of the senses and a higher realm is reminiscent of the Hindu belief that the illusory world of matter stands apart from Ultimate Being or Brahman (see chapter 2). In contrast with Hinduism, however, Plato did not view enlightenment as escape from the material world. Rather, he perceived the mind's ascent to knowledge as a prerequisite of individual well-being and the attainment of the good life here on earth. Plato believed, moreover, that such enlightenment was essential to achieving a just state and a healthy society. Unlike the Hindu philosophers, whose mystical ascent to enlightenment was accomplished through withdrawal from the world, meditation, and self-denial, Plato defended a practical system of education by which individuals might arrive at knowledge of the Good. That educational system is expounded in the *Republic*.

In Plato's utopian community, education is the intellectual preparation for life. The ideal state, which permits no private property and little family life, educates all individuals (male and female) equally. The roles citizens ultimately assume within the state – as laborers, soldiers, or rulers – are consistent with their mental and physical abilities. According to Plato, those who are the most fit intellectually – those who have most fully recovered a knowledge of the Forms – are obliged to act as "king-bees" in the communal hive. (Plato might have been surprised to discover that the ruling bee in a hive is female.) The life of contemplation carried with it heavy responsibilities, for in the hands of the philosopher-kings lay "the welfare of the commonwealth as a whole." In this point of view, Plato seems to echo the teachings of his sixth-century-b.c.e. predecessor, Confucius, who argued that social justice is the responsibility of the ruler – the moral model for the state (see chapter 3).

Aristotle and the Life of Reason

Among Plato's students at the Academy was a young Macedonian named Aristotle, whose contributions to philosophy ultimately rivaled those of his teacher. After a period of travel in the eastern Mediterranean and a brief career as tutor to the young prince of Macedonia (the future Alexander the Great), Aristotle returned to Athens and founded a school known as the Lyceum. Aristotle's habit of walking up and down as he lectured gave him the nickname the "peripatetic philosopher." His writings – for the most part lecture notes compiled by his students – were more practically oriented than Plato's and covered a wider range of subjects. Aristotle did not accept the Theory of Forms, insisting that form and matter could not exist independently of each other. He rejected Plato's notion of an eternal *psyche* or soul, but suggested that a portion of the soul, identified with reason (and with the impersonal force he called the Unmoved Mover), might be immortal.

Aristotle's interests spanned many fields, including those of biology, physics, politics, poetry, drama, logic, and ethics. The son of a physician, Aristotle's formative education led him to gather specimens of plant and animal life and classify them according to their physical similarities and differences. Over five hundred different animals, some of which Aristotle himself dissected, are mentioned in his zoological treatises. Though he did little in the way of modern scientific experimentation, Aristotle's practice of basing conclusions on careful observation advanced the **empirical method** – a method of inquiry dependent on direct experience. To all enterprises, Aristotle applied the principles of objectivity, clarity, and consistency; he addressed political life, literature, and human conduct in the same analytic manner that he classified plants and animals. Before writing the *Politics*, he examined the constitutions of more than 150 Greek city-states. And in the *Poetics*, he defined the various genres of literary expression (see chapter 6). In the fields of biology, astronomy, and physics, Aristotle's conclusions (including many that were incorrect) remained unchallenged for centuries. Based, for instance, on his description of procreation as the imposition of life-giving form (the male) on chaotic matter (the female), scholars for centuries considered woman an imperfect and incomplete version of man.

Aristotle's application of scientific principles to the reasoning process resulted in the science of logic. The exercise of logic required the division of an argument into individual terms, followed – in Socratic fashion – by an examination of the meaning of those terms. Aristotle formulated the **syllogism**, a deductive scheme that presents two premises from which a conclusion may be drawn. The syllogism provided a procedure for reasoned thought without reference to specific content (Figure **5.3**).

Aristotle made lasting contributions to the field of **ethics**, that branch of philosophy that sets forth the principles of human conduct. He began his inquiry by examining human values. Is not happiness or "the good life" (the Greek word *eudaimonia* means both) the only human value that may be considered an end in itself, rather than a means to any other end? Is not happiness the one goal to which all human beings aspire? If so, then how does one achieve it? The answer, said Aristotle, lies in fulfilling one's unique function. The function of a thing, that which best defines it, is synonymous with its excellence or virtue (in Greek, the word *arete* denotes both). The excellence of the eye, for instance, lies in how well it performs the function of

seeing. The excellence of a knife depends on how well it cuts. The unique function of the human being, argued Aristotle, is the ability to reason; hence, the excellence of the individual lies in the exercise of reason.

In the *Ethics*, edited by Aristotle's son Nicomachus, Aristotle presents the Theory of the Good Life and describes the Nature of Happiness. He explains that action in accordance with reason is necessary for the acquisition of excellence or virtue. Ideal conduct, suggests Aristotle, lies in the Golden Mean, the middle ground between any two extremes of behavior. Between cowardice and recklessness, for instance, one should seek the middle ground – courage; between boastfulness and timidity, one should court modesty. The Doctrine of the Mean rationalized the classical search for moderation and balance.

READING 1C

From Aristotle's *Nicomachean Ethics*

Every art and every scientific inquiry, and similarly every   1
action and purpose, may be said to aim at some good.
Hence the good has been well defined as that at which all
things aim. But it is clear that there is a difference in the
ends; for the ends are sometimes activities, and
sometimes results beyond the mere activities. Also, where
there are certain ends beyond the actions, the results are
naturally superior to the activities . . . .

If it is true that in the sphere of action there is an end
which we wish for its own sake, and for the sake of which   10
we wish for everything else, and that we do not desire all
things for the sake of something else (for, if that is so, the
process will go on *ad infinitum*, and our desire will be idle
and futile) it is clear that this will be the good or the
supreme good. Does it not follow then that the knowledge
of this supreme good is of great importance for the conduct
of life, and that, *if we know it*, we shall be like archers who
have a mark at which to aim, we shall have a better chance
of attaining what we want? But, if this is the case, we must
endeavor to comprehend, at least in outline, its nature,   20
and the science or faculty to which it belongs . . . .

It seems not unreasonable that people should derive
their conception of the good or of happiness from men's
lives. Thus ordinary or vulgar people conceive it to be
pleasure, and accordingly approve a life of enjoyment. For
there are practically three prominent lives, the sensual,
the political, and, thirdly, the speculative. Now the mass
of men present an absolutely slavish appearance, as
choosing the life of brute beasts, but they meet with
consideration because so many persons in authority share   30
the tastes of Sardanapalus.[1] Cultivated and practical
people, on the other hand, identify happiness with honor,
as honor is the general end of political life. But this
appears too superficial for our present purpose; for honor
seems to depend more upon the people who pay it than

THE SYLLOGISM

All men are mortal.
a:b
Socrates is a man.
c:a
Therefore, Socrates
is mortal.
∴c=b

Figure 5.3 The Syllogism.

---

[1] The legendary king of Assyria, known for his sensuality.

upon the person to whom it is paid, and we have an intuitive feeling that the good is something which is proper to a man himself and cannot easily be taken away from him. It seems too that the reason why men seek honor is that they may be confident of their own goodness. Accordingly they seek it at the hands of the wise and of those who know them well, and they seek it on the ground of virtue; hence it is clear that in their judgment at any rate virtue is superior to honor . . . .

We speak of that which is sought after for its own sake as more final than that which is sought after as a means to something else; we speak of that which is never desired as a means to something else as more final than the things which are desired both in themselves and as means to something else; and we speak of a thing as absolutely final, if it is always desired in itself and never as a means to something else.

It seems that happiness preeminently answers to this description, as we always desire happiness for its own sake and never as a means to something else, whereas we desire honor, pleasure, intellect, and every virtue, partly for their own sakes (for we should desire them independently of what might result from them) but partly also as being means to happiness, because we suppose they will prove the instruments of happiness. Happiness, on the other hand, nobody desires for the sake of these things, nor indeed as a means to anything else at all . . . .

Perhaps, however, it seems a truth which is generally admitted, that happiness is the supreme good; what is wanted is to define its nature a little more clearly. The best way of arriving at such a definition will probably be to ascertain the function of Man. For, as with a flute-player, a statuary, or any artisan, or in fact anybody who has a definite function and action, his goodness, or excellence seems to lie in his function, so it would seem to be with Man, if indeed he has a definite function. Can it be said then that, while a carpenter and a cobbler have definite functions and actions, Man, unlike them, is naturally functionless? The reasonable view is that, as the eye, the hand, the foot, and similarly each . . . . part of the body has a definite function, so Man may be regarded as having a definite function apart from all these. What then, can this function be? It is not life; for life is apparently something which man shares with the plants; and it is something peculiar to him that we are looking for. We must exclude therefore the life of nutrition and increase. There is next what may be called the life of sensation. But this too, is apparently shared by Man with horses, cattle, and all other animals. There remains what I may call the practical life of the rational part of *Man's being*. But the rational part is twofold; it is rational partly in the sense of being obedient to reason, and partly in the sense of possessing reason and intelligence. The practical life too may be conceived of in two ways, viz., *either as a moral state, or as a moral activity:* but we must understand by it the life of activity, as this seems to be the truer form of the conception.

The function of Man then is an activity of soul in accordance with reason, or not independently of reason . . . .

Our present study is not, like other studies, purely speculative in its intention; for the object of our inquiry is not to know the nature of virtue but to become ourselves virtuous, as that is the sole benefit which it conveys. It is

necessary therefore to consider the right way of performing actions, for it is actions as we have said that determine the character of the resulting moral states . . . .

The first point to be observed then is that in such matters as we are considering[,] deficiency and excess are equally fatal. It is so, as we observe, in regard to health and strength; for we must judge of what we cannot see by the evidence of what we do see. Excess or deficiency of gymnastic exercise is fatal to strength. Similarly an excess or deficiency of meat and drink is fatal to health, whereas a suitable amount produces, augments and sustains it. It is the same then with temperance, courage, and the other virtues. A person who avoids and is afraid of everything and faces nothing becomes a coward; a person who is not afraid of anything but is ready to face everything becomes foolhardy. Similarly he who enjoys every pleasure and never abstains from any pleasure is licentious; he who eschews all pleasures like a boor is an insensible sort of person. For temperance and courage are destroyed by excess and deficiency but preserved by the mean state . . . .

The nature of virtue has been now generically described. But it is not enough to state merely that virtue is a moral state, we must also describe the character of that moral state.

It must be laid down then that every virtue or excellence has the effect of producing a good condition of that of which it is a virtue or excellence, and of enabling it to perform its function well. Thus the excellence of the eye makes the eye good and its function good, as it is by the excellence of the eye that we see well. Similarly, the excellence of the horse makes a horse excellent and good at racing, at carrying its rider and at facing the enemy. If then this is universally true, the virtue or excellence of man will be such a moral state as makes a man good and able to perform his proper function well. We have already explained how this will be the case, but another way of making it clear will be to study the nature or character of this virtue.

Now in everything, whether it be continuous or discrete, it is possible to take a greater, a smaller, or an equal amount, and this either absolutely or in relation to ourselves, the equal being a mean between excess and deficiency. By the mean in respect of the thing itself, or the absolute mean, I understand that which is equally distinct from both extremes; and this is one and the same thing for everybody. By the mean considered relatively to ourselves I understand that which is neither too much nor too little; but this is not one thing, nor is it the same for everybody. Thus if 10 be too much and 2 too little we take 6 as a mean in respect of the thing itself; for 6 is as much greater than 2 as it is less than 10, and this is a mean in arithmetical proportion. But the mean considered relatively to ourselves must not be ascertained in this way. It does not follow that if 10 pounds of *meat* be too much and 2 be too little for a man to eat, a trainer will order him 6 pounds, as this may itself be too much or too little for the person who is to take it; it will be too little [for instance] for Milo,[2] but too much for a beginner in gymnastics. It will be the same

---

[2]A famous athlete from the Greek city-state of Crotona in southern Italy. As a teenager, he began lifting a calf each day, until, as both his strength and the calf grew, he could lift a full-grown bullock.

with running and wrestling; *the right amount will vary with the individual*. This being so, everybody who understands his business avoids alike excess and deficiency; he seeks and chooses the mean, not the absolute mean, but the mean considered relatively to ourselves. 160

Every science then performs its function well, if it regards the mean and refers the works which it produces to the mean. This is the reason why it is usually said of successful works that it is impossible to take anything from them or to add anything to them, which implies that excess or deficiency is fatal to excellence but that the mean state ensures it. Good artists too, as we say, have an eye to the mean in their works. But virtue, like Nature herself, is more accurate and better than any art; virtue therefore will aim at the mean; — I speak of moral virtue, as it is moral virtue 170 which is concerned with emotions and actions, and it is these which admit of excess and deficiency and the mean. Thus it is possible to go too far, or not to go far enough, in respect of fear, courage, desire, anger, pity, and pleasure and pain generally, and the excess and the deficiency are alike wrong; but to experience these emotions at the right times and on the right occasions and towards the right persons and for the right causes and in the right manner is the mean or the supreme good, which is characteristic of virtue. Similarly there may be excess, deficiency, or the 180 mean, in regard to actions. But virtue is concerned with emotions and actions, and here excess is an error and deficiency a fault, whereas the mean is successful and laudable, and success and merit are both characteristics of virtue.

Virtue then is a state of deliberate moral purpose consisting in a mean that is relative to ourselves, the mean being determined by reason, or as a prudent man would determine it.

———————◆———————

SUMMARY

The Greek philosophers made the speculative leap from supernatural to natural explanations of the cosmos and its operations. Such pre-Socratic philosopher-scientists as Thales, Heraclitus, and Pythagoras set forth theories describing the basic stuff of nature and the ground of being. Among the most significant of the naturalist philosophers was Democritus, who advanced the atomic theory of matter.

The Sophists and the humanist philosophers Socrates, Plato, and Aristotle moved "beyond physics" to probe the intellectual limits of human knowledge and define the nature of moral action. The Sophists argued that all knowledge and hence all virtue was relative, while their greatest critic, Socrates, held that there were absolute standards for moral conduct. To be virtuous, argued Socrates, one must know the meaning of "virtue," hence his untiring application of the dialectical method to the search for wisdom.

Plato and Aristotle were the two Greek philosophers who exercised the greatest influence on Western culture. In the *Republic,* Plato explained how virtue might be cultivated for the mutual benefit of state and citizen. Plato's Theory of Forms laid the basis for philosophical idealism and for the separation of mind and matter. Plato's high regard for education established the sanctity of the intellectual life. More practically oriented than the eloquent Plato, Aristotle investigated a wide variety of subjects ranging from logic and zoology to the art of poetry and the science of statecraft. In his *Ethics,* Aristotle defined the Golden Mean and argued that the good life was identical with the life of reason.

Like the ancient Egyptians and Mesopotamians, the Greek populace at large preserved the fabulous myths that celebrated their gods and goddesses. Greek philosophers, however, had little use for these stories. Rather, these "lovers of wisdom" cultivated the modes of reason and deductive thinking that lie at the heart of Western rationalism. By doing so, they made an immeasurable contribution to the humanistic tradition.

GLOSSARY

allegory a literary device in which objects, persons, or actions are equated with secondary, figurative meanings that underlie their literal meaning

empirical method a method of inquiry dependent on direct experience or observation

ethics that branch of philosophy that sets forth the principles of human conduct

syllogism a deductive scheme of formal argument, consisting of two premises from which a conclusion may be drawn

SUGGESTIONS FOR READING

Barnes, Jonathan. *Aristotle*. Oxford: Oxford University Press, 1982.

Dover, K. J. *Greek Popular Morality in the Time of Plato and Aristotle*. Berkeley, Calif.: University of California Press, 1980.

Gadamer, Hans-Georg. *The Idea of the Good in Platonic-Aristotelian Philosophy*, trans. by P. C. Smith. New Haven, Conn.: Yale University Press, 1986.

Guthrie, W. K. C. *The Greek Philosophers: From Thales to Aristotle*. New York: Harper, 1960.

Lear, Jonathan. *Aristotle: The Desire to Understand*. New York: Oxford University Press, 1993.

Vlastos, Gregory. *Socrates, Ironist and Moral Philosopher*. Ithaca, N.Y.: Cornell University Press, 1991.

Warner, Rex. *The Greek Philosophers*. New York: New American Library, 1958.

6
The Classical Style in the Arts

What we have come to call the "classical style" in the arts reached its perfection during the Golden Age of Greece (ca. 480-430 B.C.E), the fifty-year period between the Persian and Peloponnesian wars. During the fourth century B.C.E., after Philip of Macedonia conquered Greece, his son Alexander the Great carried Greek language and culture into Asia and the Far East, thus "Hellenizing" a vast part of the civilized world. The Romans absorbed Greek culture and, by imitation and adaption, ensured its survival. In music and literature, as in the visual arts, the Greeks provided models that the Romans would transmit to the West.* Most of the freestanding sculptures of the Greek masters survive only in Roman replicas, and what remains is a fraction of what once existed. The balance fell to the ravages of time and barbarian peoples, who ground down marble statues to make mortar and melted down bronze pieces to mint coins and cast cannons. Despite these losses, the ancient classical conception of beauty – in literature, music, and the visual arts, but most manifestly in sculpture and architecture – has dominated Western cultural expression.

Evidence of the vitality of the classical style is found in the regular occurrence of classical revivals or neoclassical ("new classical") movements throughout Western history. Such revivals were often part of a conscious attempt to recapture the best qualities of Greco-Roman civilization. To examine the main characteristics of ancient Greek art, literature, and music is to gain insight into the reasons why the classical style continued to be imitated throughout the history of Western culture and to understand why that style became the touchstone by which all creative expression was to be judged for centuries.

The Classical Style
Order and Proportion

The classical style reflects a search – similar to that which motivated the early Greek philosophers – for an underlying natural order. We have already seen how Pythagoras, in his pursuit of fundamental natural laws, advanced the idea that numbers determined all aspects of nature. In support of his theory that the laws of proportion were embedded in nature, Pythagoras demonstrated that relationships between musical sounds could be numerically expressed. Plucking a taut string produced a certain pitch; pinching that string in the middle and plucking either side produced a sound exactly consonant and one **octave** higher than the original note. Dividing the string into still other lengths by the same process produced sounds in further proportional relationships. If music was governed by numerical ratios, was not the universe as a whole subject to the laws of harmony? And, if indeed nature itself followed these laws, then should not artists imitate them?

Such hypotheses lay at the heart of the Greek artist's search for order and proportion. Among architects and sculptors of the Golden Age a **canon** or system of proportion was in use, and although little survives in the way of Greek literary evidence, Roman sources preserve information that helps us to understand that canon. Among these sources, the best guide to the classical style as practiced during the Golden Age is the work of the Roman architect and engineer, Vitruvius Pollio (?–26 B.C.E.), whose *Ten Books on Architecture* record many of the aesthetic principles and structural techniques used by the ancient Greeks. According to Vitruvius, the construction of a building and the relationship between its parts must follow the proportions of the human body. Without proportion, that is, the correspondence among the various parts of the whole, there can be no design, argued Vitruvius. And without design, there can be no art.

---

*The Roman contribution to the classical style is discussed in chapter 7.

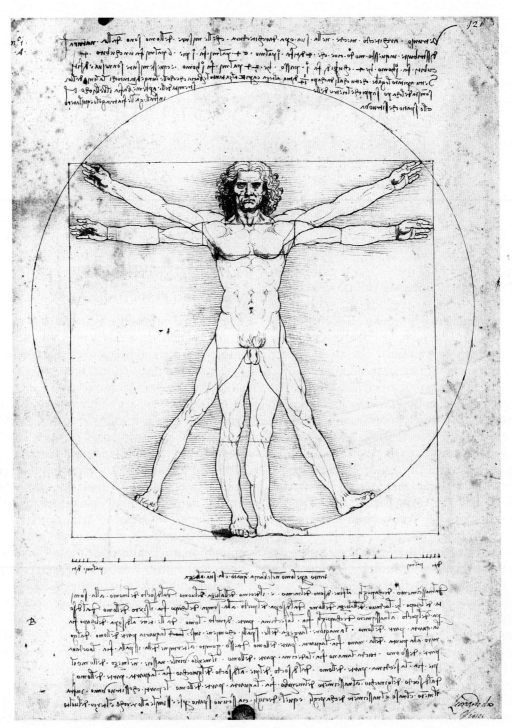

Figure 6.1 Leonardo da Vinci, *Proportional Study of a Man in the Manner of Vitruvius*, ca. 1487. Pen and ink, 13½ × 9⅝ in. Galleria dell' Accademia, Venice.

To help them imitate nature in its correct proportions, Greek artists applied a single standard of measurement – a *module* – to govern the work of art. The length of the module was not absolute, but varied according to the subject matter. In the human body, for instance, the distance between the chin to the top of the forehead, representing one-tenth of the whole body height, constituted a module by which body measurements might be figured. The fifth-century-B.C.E. sculptor Polycleitus, himself the author of a manual on proportion, is said to have provided the canon described by Vitruvius. During the Renaissance, Leonardo da Vinci (see chapter 17) rendered the human figure according to the Vitruvian canon, an image that has become a symbol of the centrality of the human being in the ideally proportioned universe (Figure 6.1).

READING 17
From Vitruvius' *Principles of Symmetry*

On Symmetry: In Temples and in the Human Body

1 The Design of a temple depends on symmetry, the principles of which must be most carefully observed by the architect. They are due to proportion . . . . Proportion is a correspondence among the measures of the members of an entire work, and of the whole to a certain part selected as standard. From this result the principles of symmetry. Without symmetry and proportion there can be no principles in the design of any temple; that is, if there is no precise relation between its members, as in the case of those of a well shaped man.

2 For the human body is so designed by nature that the face, from the chin to the top of the forehead and lowest roots of the hair, is a tenth part of the whole height; the open hand from the wrist to the tip of the middle finger is just the same; the head from the chin to the crown is an eighth, and with the neck and shoulder from the top of the breast to the lowest roots of the hair is a sixth; from the middle of the breast to the summit of the crown is a fourth. If we take the height of the face itself, the distance from the bottom of the chin to the under side of the nostrils is one third of it; the nose from the underside of the nostrils to a line between the eyebrows is the same; from there to the lowest roots of the hair is also a third, comprising the forehead. The length of the foot is one sixth of the height of the body; of the forearm, one fourth; and the breadth of the breast is also one fourth. The other members, too, have their own symmetrical proportions, and it was by employing them that famous painters and sculptors of antiquity attained to great and endless renown.

3 Similarly, in the members of a temple there ought to be the greatest harmony in the symmetrical relations of the different parts to the general magnitude of the whole. Then again, in the human body the central point is naturally the navel. For if a man be placed flat on his back, with hands and feet extended, and a pair of compasses centered at his navel, the fingers and toes of his two hands and feet will touch the circumference of a circle described therefrom. And just as the human body yields a circular outline, so too a square figure may be found from it. For if we measure the distance from the soles of the feet to the top of the head, and then apply that measure to the outstretched arms, the breadth will be found to be the same as the height, as in the case of plane surfaces which are perfectly square.

4 Therefore, since nature has designed the human body so that its members are duly proportioned to the frame as a whole, it appears that the ancients had good reason for their rule, that in perfect buildings the different members must be in exact symmetrical relations to the whole general scheme. Hence, while transmitting to us the proper arrangements for buildings of all kinds, they are particularly careful to do so in the case of temples of the gods, buildings in which merits and faults usually last forever . . . .

———————◆———————

Humanism and Idealism

Classical Greek art is humanistic not only because it observes fundamental laws derived from the human physique, but because it is distinguished by a preoccupation with the beauty of the human figure and the life of the human being. This is the case in painting as much as it is in sculpture and architecture.

Since almost all evidence of Greek wall painting has disappeared, decorated vases are our principal source of information about Greek painting. During the first three hundred years of Greek art (ca. 900–750 B.C.E), artists decorated their ceramic wares with complex geometric patterns organized according to the shape of the vessel (Figure 6.2). Thereafter, scenes from mythology, literature, and everyday life came to dominate the central zone of the vase (Figures 6.3, 6.27). Wine and water jugs, plates and bowls document a keen enjoyment of the human enterprises of dancing, drinking, warring, game playing, and conversation. In these more representational scenes, only the most minimal physical setting is provided for the action of

Figure 6.2 Pitcher with "Geometric" decoration, ca. 740 B.C.E. Height 8½ in. Reproduced by courtesy of the Trustees of the British Museum, London.

Figure 6.3 Exekias, Black Amphora with Achilles and Ajax Playing Dice, ca. 530 B.C.E. Height 24in. Vatican Museums, Rome.

the figures, and abstract motifs are confined to the rim, handle, or foot of the vessel. The principles of clarity and order so apparent in the early geometric style (see Figure 6.2) are preserved in the decoration of later vases, where a startling clarity of design is produced by the interplay of light and dark areas of figure and ground (see Figures 6.3, 6.4).

During the Geometric and Archaic phases of Greek art (ca. 750–480 B.C.E.), a style of decoration prevailed in vase painting in which black figures appeared against the red color of the clay. By the fifth century B.C.E., the black-figured style was replaced by one in which the human figure was left the color of the clay and the ground was painted black (see Figures 6.4, 6.28). The so-called red-figured style allowed artists to make human figures more lifelike by delineating physical

Figure 6.4 Epictetus, Cup (detail), ca. 510 B.C.E. Diameter 13 in. Reproduced by courtesy of the Trustees of the British Museum, London.

details on the buff-colored surface. At the same time, vase-painters added only those details that contributed to the overall design. They also positioned the figures to complement the shape of the vessel. Thus, again, they idealized or modified the imagery in accordance with preconceived standards of beauty.

Three-dimensional Greek sculpture provides equally impressive examples of the classical style.

Nowhere is the Greek affection for the natural beauty of the human body so evident as in Hellenic sculpture, where the male nude form assumed major importance as a subject. Freestanding Greek sculptures served basically the same purposes as Mesopotamian votive statues: They paid perpetual homage to the gods. But they also might depict the gods themselves, commemorate the dead, or honor the victors of the athletic games.

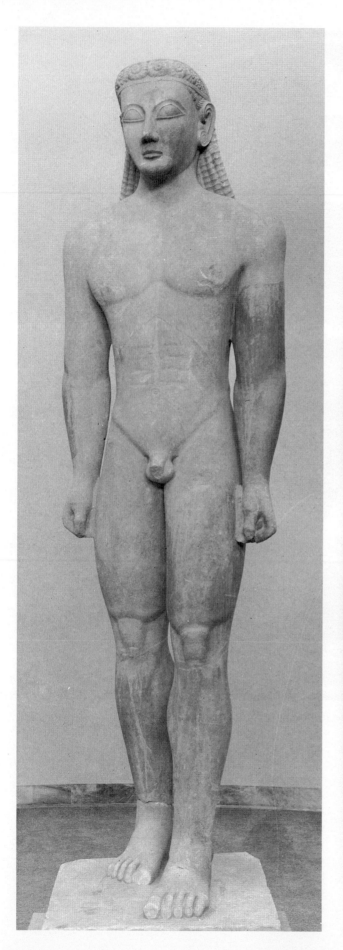

Since warriors and athletes usually wore few clothes, nudity was both appropriate to representation and a reflection of Greek pride in the human body; the fig leaves that cover the genitals of some Greek sculptures are additions dating from the Christian era. The assertion that the Greeks modeled their gods upon themselves is perhaps best illustrated in these life-size, freestanding sculptures, among which one cannot

Figure 6.5 *Kouros* of Sounion, ca. 600 B.C.E. Marble, height 10 ft. National Archeological Museum, Athens.

Figure 6.6 *Calf-Bearer*, ca. 575–550 B.C.E. Marble, height 5 ft. 6 in. Acropolis Museum, Athens. © Hirmer Fotoarchiv.

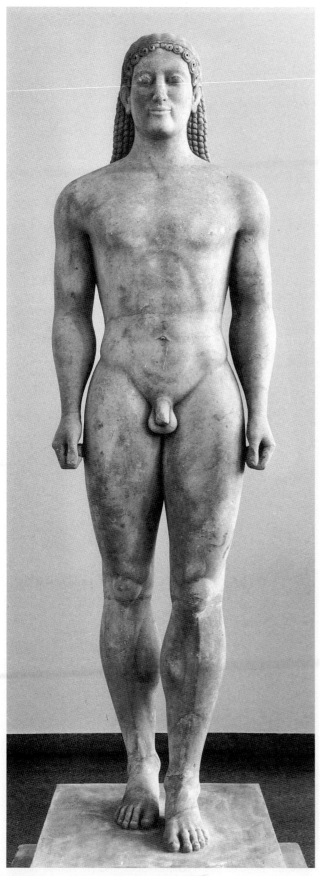

Figure 6.7 Kroisos from Anavyssos, ca. 525 B.C.E. Marble with traces of paint, height 6 ft. 4½ in. National Archeological Museum, Athens. Photo: Alison Frantz.

easily distinguish the gods from the ordinary human beings.

In the finest examples of classical sculpture, the quest for realism, or fidelity to nature, is offset by the will to idealize, that is, to modify form in accordance with preconceived standards of perfection. But the achievement of this delicate balance was a slow process, one that had its beginnings early in Greek history. During the Archaic phase of Greek sculpture, freestanding representations of the male youth (*kouros*) still resembled the blocklike statuary of ancient Egypt (see Figure 3.4). The *kouros* from Sounion (ca. 600 B.C.E) is rigidly posed, with arms close to its sides and its body weight distributed equally on both feet (Figure **6.5**). Like most Archaic statues, the figure retains the rigid verticality of tree trunks from which early Greek sculptures were carved. It also bears a blissful smile that, in contrast with the awe-filled countenances of Mesopotamian votive statues (see Figure 2.13), reflects the buoyant optimism of the early Greeks.

Produced some fifty years after the Sounion *kouros*, the *Calf-Bearer* (ca. 550 B.C.E) is more gently and more realistically modeled — note especially the trapezoidal muscles of the torso and the sensitively carved bull calf (Figure **6.6**). The hollow eyes of the youth once held inlays of semiprecious stones (such as mother-of-pearl, gray agate, and lapis lazuli) that must have given the face a strikingly realistic appearance. Such lifelike effects were further enhanced by the colored paints that — now almost totally gone — once enlivened the lips, hair, and other parts of the figure. A quarter of a century later, the robust likeness of a warrior named Kroisos (found marking his grave) shows close anatomical attention to knee and calf muscles. Like his Archaic ancestors, he strides aggressively forward, but his forearms now turn in toward his body, and his chest, arms, and legs swell with powerful energy (Figure **6.7**). By the early fifth century B.C.E., a major transformation occurred. With the Kritios Boy, the Greek sculptor arrived at a more natural positioning of the human body: The sensuous torso turns on the axis of the spine, and the weight of the body shifts from equal distribution on both legs to greater weight on the left leg (Figure **6.8**). (This counterpositioning of the human figure would be called *contrapposto* by Italian Renaissance artists.) The muscles of the Kritios Boy are no longer geometrically schematized, but protrude subtly at anatomical junctures. And the figure is no longer smiling, but instead, solemn and contemplative. The new poised stance, along with a complete mastery of human anatomy and proportion, are features of the early classical style, a style that culminates during the Greek Golden Age (or High Classical Era) in the freestanding sculptures of Polycleitus and Phidias, the two leading sculptors of that time.

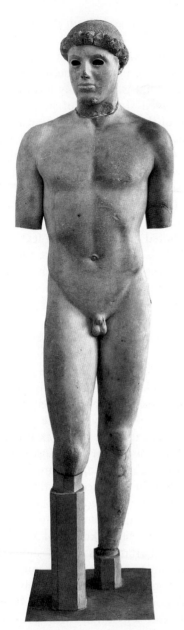

Figure 6.8 Kritios Boy, ca. 480 B.C.E. Marble, height 34 in. Acropolis Museum, Athens. © Hirmer Fotoarchiv.

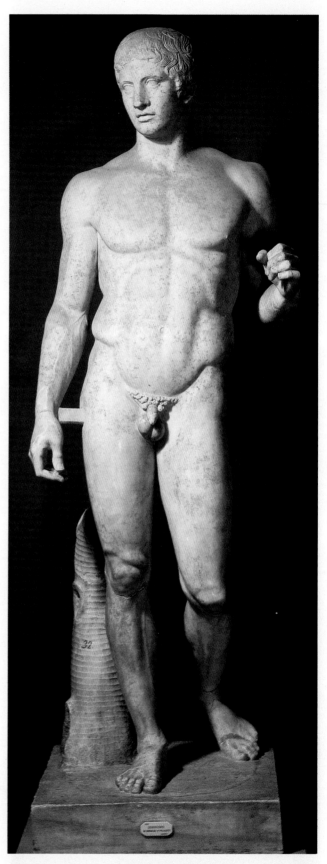

Figure 6.9 Polycleitus, *Doryphorus (Spear-Bearer)*, Roman marble copy after a bronze Greek original of ca. 450–440 B.C.E. Height 6 ft. 11 in. National Museum, Naples. Alinari/Art Resource, New York.

In the *Doryphorus* (*Spear-Bearer*) executed by Polycleitus around 440 B.C.E but known to us only in Roman copies, a sense of confidence and robust well-being prevails (Figure 6.9). The physical form unites motion and repose, dynamic energy and poised restraint – qualities of the ideal warrior-athlete. Similarly, the bronze statue of Zeus hurling a thunderbolt, the work of an unknown sculptor, captures the absolute confidence and physical vitality of the foremost god of the Greek pantheon (Figure 6.10). The Greeks invented the *cire-perdu* (lost-wax) method of bronze casting by which this piece was made. This process involves making a wax model and covering it with clay which is fired to form a mold; when the wax melts

Figure 6.10 Zeus (or Poseidon), ca. 460 B.C.E. Bronze, height 6 ft. 10 in. National Archeological Museum, Athens. Photo: © Erich Lessing/Art Resource, New York.

away, the mold is filled with molten metal. Bronze casting allowed artists to depict vigorous action and include greater detail than was possible in the more restrictive medium of marble. Dynamically posed – the artist has deliberately exaggerated the length of the god's arms – the figure fixes the decisive moment when every muscle in the body is tensed and focused on achieving the mark.

Greek and Roman sculptors often made marble copies of popular bronze-cast figures. The *Discobolus* (*Discus Thrower*), originally executed in bronze by Myron around 450 B.C.E, but surviving only in a variety

of Roman marble copies, is one such example (Figure 6.11). Like the statue of Zeus, it captures the moment before the action, when intellect guides the physical effort to follow. Indeed, these figures seem to epitomize the classical ideal (articulated by Aristotle) of will dominated by reason.

The evolution of the female figure (*kore*) underwent a somewhat different course from that of the male. Early *korai* were fully clothed and did not appear in the nude until the fourth century B.C.E. Female figures of the Archaic period were ornamental, columnar, and (like their male counterparts) smiling (Figure

Figure 6.11 Myron, _Discobolus (Discus Thrower)_, reconstructed Roman marble copy of a bronze Greek original of ca. 450 B.C.E. Height 5 ft. 1 in. Museo Nazionale delle Terme, Rome. © Hirmer Fotoarchiv.

6.12). Not until the late classical period (430–323 B.C.E.) did sculptors begin to produce the sensuous nudes that so inspired Hellenistic, Roman, and (centuries later) Renaissance artists. Regarded by the Romans as the finest statue in the world, the _Aphrodite of Cnidos_ (Figure 6.13) by Praxiteles established a model for the ideal female form: tall and graceful, with small breasts and broad hips. Praxiteles' figure exhibits a subtle counterposition of shoulders and hips, smooth body curves, and a face that bears a dreamy, melting gaze. The Cnidian _Aphrodite_ is a Roman copy of a Greek

original, and the marble bar bracing the hip suggests that the original may have been executed in bronze. Nevertheless, the statue preserves the famous Praxitelean practice of carving marble to emphasize its translucent shimmer.

Classical Greek sculpture is lifelike in appearance, but it deviates from ordinary life by enforcing an ideal or perfect vision of reality. Socrates best described the idealizing process when he advised the painter Parrhasius to reach beyond the flawed world of appearances by selecting and combining the most beautiful details of

Figure 6.12 *Kore* from Chios (?), ca. 520 B.C.E. Marble with traces of paint, height approx. 22 in. (lower part missing). Acropolis Museum, Athens.

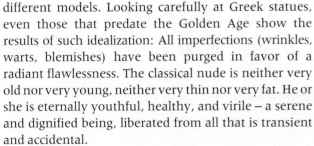

Figure 6.13 (right) Praxiteles, *Aphrodite of Cnidos*, Roman marble copy of marble Greek original of ca. 350 B.C.E. Height 6 ft. 8 in. Vatican Museums, Rome.

different models. Looking carefully at Greek statues, even those that predate the Golden Age show the results of such idealization: All imperfections (wrinkles, warts, blemishes) have been purged in favor of a radiant flawlessness. The classical nude is neither very old nor very young, neither very thin nor very fat. He or she is eternally youthful, healthy, and virile – a serene and dignified being, liberated from all that is transient and accidental.

Idealization usually employed simplification of form in favor of geometric clarity. Hence the muscles of Zeus' stomach in Figure 6.10 were made to approximate symmetrical trapezoids, and the strands of his hair and beard conform to a distinctive pattern of parallel wavy lines. As we have seen, similar efforts toward geometric idealization characterized the decoration of Greek vases. The synthesis of humanism and idealism in the representation of the freestanding nude was one of the great achievements of Greek art. Indeed, the Hellenic conception of the nude became the standard, and ideal by which centuries of Western artists and critics assessed the beauty of the human form.

Figure 6.14 Ictinus and Callicrates, west end of the Parthenon, Athens, 448–432 B.C.E. Pentelic marble, height of columns 34 ft. Photo: Sonia Halliday, Weston Turville.

Figure 6.15 Plan of the Parthenon, Athens.

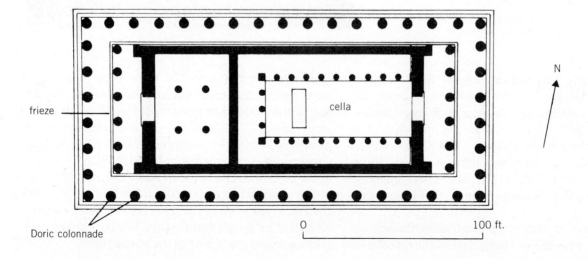

frieze

cella

N

Doric colonnade

0   100 ft.

Greek Architecture: The Parthenon

The great monuments of classical architecture were designed to serve the living, not – as in Egypt – the dead. In contrast with the superhuman scale of the Egyptian pyramid and the Mesopotamian ziggurat, the Greek temple – as Vitruvius observed – was proportioned according to the human body. Greek theaters (see Figure 4.8) celebrated life here on earth rather than the life in the hereafter, while Greek temples served as shrines for the gods and depositories for civic and religious treasures. Both theaters and temples functioned as public meeting places. Like the ziggurat, the Greek temple was a communal symbol of reverence for the gods, but while the ziggurat enforced the separation of priesthood and populace, the Greek temple united religious and secular domains.

The outstanding architectural achievement of Golden Age Athens is the Parthenon (Figures **6.14** and **6.15**), a temple dedicated to Athena, the goddess of war, the patron of the arts and crafts, and the personification of wisdom. The name Parthenon derives from the Greek word *parthenos* meaning "virgin," a popular epithet for Athena. Built in glittering Pentelic marble upon the ruins of an earlier temple burned during the Persian Wars, the Parthenon overlooks Athens from the highest point on the Acropolis (Figure 6.16). Commissioned by Pericles, the architects Ictinus and Callicrates set to work on the design of the Parthenon, while the sculptor Phidias (?–415 B.C.E) directed and supervised its construction over a period of over ten years, from 448 to 432 B.C.E. In the tradition of Egyptian builders, Greek architects used no mortar. Rather, they employed bronze clamps and dowels to fasten the meticulously cut marble segments.

The Parthenon represents the apex of a long history of post-and-lintel temple construction in which a quest for harmony and proportion – much like that which characterized Greek sculpture – came to perfection. The plan of the Parthenon, a rectangle delimited on all four sides by a colonnaded walkway, reflects the reverence for clarity and symmetry that is typical of the classical style (see Figure 6.15). Freestanding columns (each 34 feet tall) make up the exterior, while two further rows of columns on the east and west ends of the temple provide inner **porticos** (see Figure 6.21). The interior of the Parthenon is divided into two rooms, a central hall (or *cella*), which held the cult statue of Athena, and a smaller room used as a treasury. It was here that the much-disputed Delian League funds were stored. Entirely elevated on a raised platform, the Parthenon invited the individual to move around it as if it were a monumental piece of sculpture – a victory monument to honor Athens' role in the Persian Wars.

Figure 6.16 Model of the classical acropolis at Athens. American School of Classical Studies at Athens: Agora Excavations.

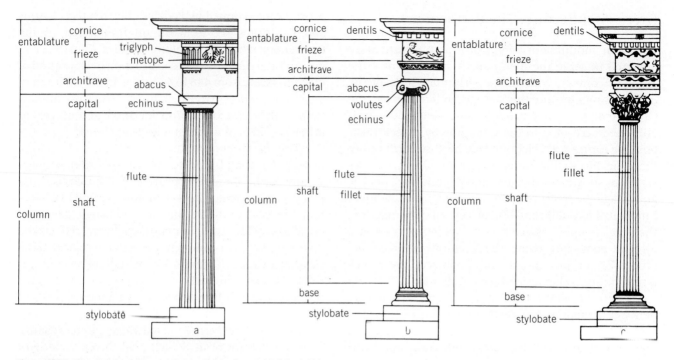

Figure 6.17 The Greek orders: (a) Doric; (b) Ionic; and (c) Corinthian.

Figure 6.18 Callicrates, Temple of Athena Nike, Athens, ca. 427–424 B.C.E. Acropolis Museum, Athens. Photo: Alison Frantz.

Figure 6.19 Theodorus of Phokaia, Tholos of the Sanctuary of Athena Pronaia, Delphi, Greece, ca. 390 B.C.E. Marble and limestone, cella diameter 28 ft. 2⅝ in. The Mansell Collection, London.

Greek architects developed three **orders**: the Doric, the Ionic, and (in Hellenistic times) the Corinthian (Figure **6.17**), each of which prescribes a fundamental set of structural and decorative parts that stand in fixed relation to each other. Each order differs in details and in the relative proportions of the parts. The Parthenon is of the Doric order. This order, which originated on the Greek mainland, is severe and rugged in style. In the Parthenon, however, it reached its most refined expression. The Ionic order, originating in Asia Minor and the Aegean Islands, is more delicate and ornamental. Its slender columns terminate in capitals with paired volutes or scrolls. The Ionic order is employed in some of the small temples on the Acropolis (Figure **6.18**). The Corinthian order, the most ornate of the orders, is characterized by capitals consisting of acanthus leaves. It is found in **tholos** (circular) sanc-

tuaries and shrines (Figure **6.19**), as well as in the larger temples that were popular during Hellenistic and Roman times.

If an ideal system governed the parts of the Greek building, a similar set of laws determined its proportions. The precise canon of proportion adopted by Phidias for the construction of the Parthenon is still, however, the subject of debate. Most architectural historians agree that a module was used, but whether the module was geometric or numerical, and whether it followed a specific ratio – such as the famous "Golden Section," a figure based on a 3:5 ratio – has never been resolved. The question is further complicated by the fact that there are virtually no straight lines in the entire building. Its Doric columns, for instance, swell out near the center to counter the optical effect of thinning that occurs when the normal eye views an uninterrupted

Figure 6.20 Ictinus and Callicrates, the Parthenon, Athens, 448–432 B.C.E. Pentelic marble, height of columns 34 ft. Photo: Gloria K. Fiero.

The Sculpture of the Parthenon

The marble sculptures of the Parthenon, produced by Phidias and the members of his workshop between 438 and 432 B.C.E., appeared in three main areas: in the **pediments** of the roof **gables**, on the **metopes** or square panels between the beam ends under the roof, and in the area along the outer wall of the *cella* (Figure **6.21**). Brightly painted, as were also some of the structural portions of the building, the Parthenon sculptures relieved the eye from the stark angularity of the post-and-lintel structure. In subject matter, the decorative portions of the temple paid homage to the patron deity of Athens. The east pediment sculptures represent the birth of Athena with gods and goddesses in attendance (Figures **6.22**, **6.23**). The west pediment shows the contest between Poseidon and Athena for domination of Athens. The ninety-two metopes illustrate scenes of combat between the Greeks (the bearers of civilization) and Giants, Amazons, and Centaurs (the forces of barbarism; Figure **6.24**). Carved in high relief, each metope is a masterful depiction of two figures, one

Figure 6.21 Sculptural and architectural detail of the Parthenon.**Frieze**, a decorative band along the top of a wall; **metopes**, segmented spaces on a frieze; **pediment**, a gable.

set of parallel lines. All columns tilt slightly inward. Corner columns are thicker than the others to compensate for the attenuating effect produced by the bright light of the sky against which the columns are viewed, but also to ensure their ability to carry the weight of the terminal segments of the superstructure (Figure **6.20**). The top step of the platform on which the columns rest is not parallel to the ground, but rises four and a quarter inches at the center, allowing for rainwater to run off the convex surface even as it corrects the optical impression of sagging along the extended length of the platform. Consistently, the architects of the Parthenon corrected negative optical illusions produced by strict conformity to geometric regularity. Avoiding rigid systems of proportion, they took as their primary consideration the aesthetic and functional integrity of the building. Today the Parthenon stands as a noble ruin, the victim of an accidental gunpowder explosion in the seventeenth century, followed by centuries of vandalism and modern air pollution.

Figure 6.22 Reconstruction of east pediment of the Parthenon, central section. Acropolis Museum, Athens.

Figure 6.23 Three Goddesses: Hestia, Dione, Aphrodite, from east pediment of the Parthenon, Athens, ca. 437–432 B.C.E. Marble, over life-size. Reproduced by courtesy of the Trustees of the British Museum, London.

Figure 6.24 Lapith Overcoming a Centaur, south metope 27, Parthenon, Athens, 447–438 B.C.E. Marble relief, height 4 ft. 5 in. Reproduced by courtesy of the Trustees of the British Museum, London.

human and the other bestial, locked in combat. As fitting a temple honoring the Goddess of Wisdom, the sculptural program of the Parthenon celebrates the victory of intellect over barbarism.

Completing Phidias' program of architectural decoration for the Parthenon is a **frieze** (a carved band of sculpture) that winds around the outer wall of the *cella* where the wall meets the roofline. The 524-foot-long frieze depicts the Panathenaic Festival, a celebration held every four years in honor of the goddess Athena. Hundreds of figures – horsemen (Figure **6.25**), water bearers, musicians, and votaries – are shown filing in calm procession toward an assembled group of gods

and goddesses (Figure **6.26**). The figures move with graceful rhythms, in tempos that could well be translated into music. To satisfy a viewpoint from below, Phidias graded the relief by cutting the figures more deeply at the top than at the bottom. Once brightly painted and ornamented with metal details, the final effect must have been impressively lifelike. Housed today in the British Museum in London, where it is hung at approximately eye level, the Parthenon frieze loses much of its illusionistic subtlety. Nevertheless, this masterpiece of the Greek Golden Age reveals the harmonious reconciliation of realism and idealism that is the hallmark of the classical style.

Figure 6.25 A Group of Young Horsemen from the north frieze of the Parthenon, Athens, 447–438 B.C.E. Marble, height 3 ft. 7 in. Reproduced by courtesy of the Trustees of the British Museum, London.

Figure 6.26 East frieze from the Parthenon, Athens, ca. 437–432 B.C.E. Marble. © TAP Services, Greece.

The Classical Style in Drama

The Parthenon reflects the classical tendency to modify the visual world according to preconceived laws of harmony and proportion. In Greek literary invention, a similar imperative was at work. In the *Poetics*, Aristotle described the "proper construction" of the plot in tragic drama: He emphasized the importance of a balanced arrangement of parts and adherence to proportions governed by human reason. The play, he pointed out, should not be so lengthy as to exceed the human capacity to remember all aspects of the story. A single action made up of several closely connected incidents without irrelevant additions should comprise the plot. Moreover, tragic action should involve an error in judgment made by an individual who is (in Aristotle's words) "better than the ordinary man," but with whom we nevertheless empathize. The emphasis on proportioned construction, as revealed in the following excerpt, is reminiscent of Vitruvius' *Principles of Symmetry* (see Reading 17).

READING 18
From Aristotle's *Poetics*

... let us now consider the proper construction of the Fable or Plot, as that is at once the first and the most important thing in Tragedy. We have laid it down that a tragedy is an imitation of an action that is complete in itself, as a whole of some magnitude; for a whole may be of no magnitude to speak of. Now a whole is that which has beginning, middle, and end. A beginning is that which is not itself necessarily after anything else, and which has naturally something else after it; an end is that which is naturally after something itself, either as its necessary or usual consequent, and with nothing else after it; and a middle, that which is by nature after one thing and has also another after it. A well-constructed Plot, therefore, cannot either begin or end at any point one likes; beginning and end in it must be of the forms just described. Again: to be beautiful, a living creature, and every whole made up of parts, must not only present a certain order in its arrangement of parts, but also be of certain definite magnitude. Beauty is a matter of size and order, and therefore impossible either (1) in a very minute creature, since our perception becomes indistinct as it approaches instantaneity; or (2) in a creature of vast size — one, say, 1,000 miles long — as in that case, instead of the object being seen all at once, the unity and wholeness of it is lost to the beholder. Just in the same way, then, as a beautiful whole made up of parts, or a beautiful living creature, must be of some size, but a size to be taken in by the eye, so a story or Plot must be of some length, but of a length to be taken in by the memory.... The truth is that, just as in the other imitative arts one imitation is always of one thing, so in poetry the story, as an imitation of action, must represent one action, a complete whole, with its

several incidents so closely connected that the transposal or withdrawal of any one of them will disjoin and dislocate the whole. For that which makes no perceptible difference by its presence or absence is no real part of the whole.... The perfect Plot, accordingly, must have a single, and not (as some tell us) a double issue; the change in the hero's fortunes must be not from misery to happiness, but on the contrary from happiness to misery; and the cause of it must lie not in any depravity, but in some great error on his part; ... As Tragedy is an imitation of personages better than the ordinary man, we in our way should follow the example of good portrait-painters, who reproduce the disctinctive features of a man, and at the same time, without losing the likeness, make him handsomer than he is....

———◆———

If we apply Aristotle's formal recommendations to Sophocles' *Antigone* (see chapter 4), we arrive at a closer understanding of the "unities" of action and time that characterized Greek tragedies. The action of *Antigone* rests upon a single incident, the rash decision of Creon and its consequences. The events of the play occur within a single place and are acted out within a time span comparable to their enactment in real life. Every episode in the play is relevant to the central action. The neoclassical playwrights of the seventeenth century viewed the unities of time and action as the essential conditions for successful drama, to which they added "unity of place." Clearly, as specific rules of proportion and order governed Greek painting, sculpture, and architecture, so did these rules guide the Greek dramatist's art.

The Classical Style in Poetry

In classical Greece, as in other parts of the ancient world, distinctions between various forms of artistic expression were neither clear-cut nor definitive. A combination of the arts prevailed in most forms of religious ritual and in public and private entertainment. In *Antigone*, for instance, choric pantomime and dance complemented dramatic poetry. And in processions and festivals, music, poetry, and the visual arts served a common purpose. The intimate relationship between music and poetry is revealed in the fact that many of the words we use to describe **lyric** forms, such as the *ode* and the *hymn*, are also musical terms. The word *lyric*, meaning "accompanied by the lyre," describes verse that was meant to be sung, not read silently. Lyric poems were designed to give voice to personal emotions and innermost feelings.

Hellenic culture produced an impressive group of lyric poets, the greatest of whom was Sappho. Sappho lived during the early sixth century B.C.E., but her personal life remains a mystery. Born into an aristocratic family, she seems to have married, mothered a daughter, and produced some nine books of poetry, of which only fragments remain. She settled on the island of Lesbos, where she led a group of young women dedicated to the cult of Aphrodite. At Lesbos, Sappho trained women in the production of highly self-conscious love poetry and music. Her own poems, many of which come to us in a fragmentary state, are filled with passion and tenderness. They offer a glimpse of a body of poetry that inspired Sappho's contemporaries to regard her as "the female Homer." Ancient and modern poets alike admired Sappho for her powerful economy of expression and her inventive combinations of sense and sound – features that are extremely difficult to convey in translation. The first of the two poems reproduced below is representative of Sappho's many lyrics that express her erotic affection for the women of the Lesbian cult. Since bisexuality was common among ancient Greek men and women, such sentiments would not have been considered unnatural in Sappho's time. The second poem – a terse and pensive lyric – reflects the intense spirit of this-worldliness that characterized classical culture.

READING 19
Sappho's Poems

He is more than a hero

He is a god in my eyes –   1
the man who is allowed
to sit beside you – he

who listens intimately
to the sweet murmur of   5
your voice, the enticing

laughter that makes my own
heart beat fast. If I meet
you suddenly, I can't

speak – my tongue is broken;   10
a thin flame runs under
my skin; seeing nothing,

hearing only my own ears
drumming, I drip with sweat;
trembling shakes my body   15

and I turn paler than
dry grass. At such times
death isn't far from me.

————————◆————————

We know this much

Death is an evil;   1
we have the gods'
word for it; they too
would die if death
were a good thing.   5

————————◆————————

While Sappho's lyric poems conveyed deeply personal sentiments, other types of lyrics, called **odes**, offered exalted praise. Odes honoring Greek athletes bear strong similarities to songs of divine praise, such as the Egyptian "Hymn to the Aten" (see chapter 2), the Hebrew Psalms, and Greek invocations. But the sentiment that is expressed in the excerpt from an ode written by the noted Greek poet Pindar (ca. 522–440 B.C.E.) is firmly planted in the secular world. The ode, written to honor Alcimidas of Aegina for his victory in the boys' division of wrestling, argues that gods and men share a common origin, but that the closest human beings can come to immortality lies in the exercise of "greatness of mind or of body." Pindar narrows the gap between hero-athletes and their divine prototypes. Though mortal limitations separate human beings from the ageless and undying gods, yet, says Pindar, our best efforts raise us to superhuman heights.

READING 20
From Pindar's *Nemean Ode VI*

Single is the race, single   1
Of men and of gods;
From a single mother we both draw breath.
But a difference of power in everything
Keeps us apart;   5
For the one is as nothing, but the brazen sky
Stays a fixed habitation for ever.
Yet we can in greatness of mind
Or of body be like the Immortals,
Though we know not to what goal   10
By day or in the nights
Fate has written that we shall run.

. . . .

————————◆————————

The Classical Style in Music

The word *music* derives from *muse*, the Greek word for any of the nine mythological daughters of Zeus and the Goddess of Memory who governed the arts and the sciences. Music, which, as Pythagoras indicated, might be expressed as mathematical ratios, was considered a science as well as an art. Although music played a major

Figure 6.27 Achilles Painter, white-ground lekythos (detail): "Muse on Mount Helicon," ca. 440–430 B.C.E. Height of vase 14½ in. Staatliche Antikensammlungen und Glyptothek, Munich.

Figure 6.28 "Young Girls Dancing Around the Altar," interior of red-figure bowl, ca. 450 B.C.E. The Hermitage, Leningrad. Note the elegantly curved chair (a Greek invention) on which the aulos player sits. The cithara player stands at the altar.

role in Greek life, it is impossible for us to know what Greek music sounded like. The ancient Greeks invented no system of notation with which to record instrumental or vocal music. Apart from written and visual descriptions of musical performances, there exist only a few fourth-century-B.C.E. treatises on music theory and some primitively notated musical fragments. From these collective sources we can gather that both vocal[◊] and instrumental music were common-

place and that contests between musicians, like those between playwrights, were a regular part of public life. Vase paintings reveal that the principal musical instruments of ancient Greece were the **lyre**, the **cithara** — both belonging to the harp family and differing only in shape, size, and number of strings (Figure **6.27**) — and the *aulos*, a flute or reed pipe (see Figures 6.4, **6.28**). Along with percussion devices often used to accompany dancing, string and wind musical instruments were inherited from Egypt.

The Greeks devised a system of **modes**, or types of scales characterized by fixed patterns of pitch and tempo within the octave. (The sound of the ancient Greek Dorian mode is approximated by playing the eight white keys of the piano beginning with the white key two notes above middle C.) Modified variously in Christian times, the modes were preserved in Gregorian Chant and Byzantine church hymnology (see chapter 9). Although the modes themselves may have been inspired by the music of ancient India, the diatonic **scale** — most familiar to Westerners as the series of notes C, D, E, F, G, A, B, C — originated in Greece. Greek music lacked harmony as we know it. It was thus **monophonic** — that is, confined to a single, unaccompanied line of melody.

From earliest times, music was believed to exercise great spiritual influence and even magical power. Greek and Roman mythology describes gods and heroes who used music to heal or destroy, while the Pythagorean view that musical ratios evinced an unchanging cosmic order inspired the belief that one who made music was literally "in tune with" the universe. Even the planets, which Pythagoras described as a series of spheres moving at varying speeds in concentric orbits around the earth, were said to produce a special harmony, the so-called music of the spheres. The Greeks believed, moreover, that music had a moral influence, a principle often referred to as the "Doctrine of Ethos." The "Doctrine of Ethos" asserted that some modes strengthened the will, while others undermined the development of character. In the *Republic*, Plato encouraged the use of the Dorian mode, which settled the temper and inspired courage, while he condemned the Lydian mode, which aroused sensuality. Because of music's potential for affecting character and mood, both Plato and Aristotle recommended that music used in the education of young children be regulated by law. As with other forms of classical expression, music was deemed inseparable from its moral effects.

The Diffusion of the Classical Style: The Hellenistic Age *(323–30 B.C.E.)*

The failure of the Greek city-states to live in unity and peace ultimately led to the spread of Hellenic culture throughout the civilized world. The fourth century

B.C.E. was a turbulent era marked by rivalry and warfare among the Greek city-states. Manipulating the shifting confederacies and internecine strife to his advantage, Philip, King of Macedonia, came to dominate all of Greece. When he was assassinated in 336 B.C.E., his twenty-year-old son Alexander (356–323 B.C.E.) assumed the throne. A student of Aristotle, Alexander brought to his role as ruler the same kind of far-reaching ambition and imagination that his teacher had exercised in the intellectual realm. Alexander was a military genius: Within twelve years, he created an empire that stretched from Greece to the borders of modern India (Map **6.1**). To all parts of his empire, but especially to the cities he founded – many of which he named after himself – Alexander carried Greek language and culture. Greek art and literature made a major impact on civilizations as far east as India, where it influenced Buddhist art and Sanskrit literature (see chapter 9).

Alexander carved out his empire with the help of an army of thirty-five thousand Greeks and Macedonians equipped with weapons that were superior to any in the ancient world. Siege machines such as catapults and battering rams were used to destroy the walls of the most well-defended cities of Asia Minor, Egypt, Syria, and Persia. Finally, in northwest India, facing the

Map 6.1 The Hellenistic World.

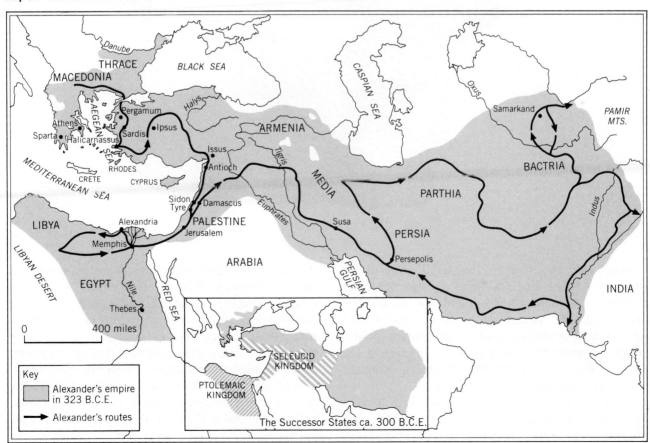

Figure 6.29 Head of Alexander from Pergamum, Hellenistic portrait, ca. 200 B.C.E. Marble, height 16 in. Archaeological Museum, Istanbul.

prospect of confronting the formidable army of the King of Ganges and his force of five thousand elephants, Alexander's troops refused to go any further. Shortly thereafter, the thirty-two-year-old general died, probably of malaria. His empire disintegrated into three main segments: Egypt ruled by the Ptolemy dynasty, Asia under the leadership of Persia, and Greece-Macedonia.

The era that followed, called Hellenistic ("Greek-like"), lasted from 323 to 30 B.C.E., after which time Rome dominated the Aegean. The defining features of the Hellenistic Age were cosmopolitanism, urbanism, and the blending of Greek, Persian, and east Asian cultures. Trade routes linked Arabia, east Africa, and the Near East, bringing great wealth to the cities of Alexandria, Antioch, Pergamum, and Rhodes (see Map 6.1). Alexandria, which replaced Athens as a cultural center, boasted a population of more than one million people and a library of half a million books (the collection was destroyed by fire when Julius Caesar besieged the city in 47 B.C.E.). The Hellenistic Age made important advances in geography, astronomy, and mathematics. Euclid, who lived in Alexandria during the late fourth century B.C.E., systematized the theorems of plane and solid geometry, while Archimedes of Syracuse, who flourished a century later, invented the compound pulley and laid the foundations for calculus.

In the vast and unstable Hellenistic world, there developed four principal schools of thought: Skepticism, Cynicism, Epicureanism, and Stoicism – all of which stressed the personal needs and emotions of the individual over and above the good of the community or state. The Skeptics denied the possibility of discovering truth. They argued for the suspension of all intellectual judgment. The Cynics held that spiritual satisfaction derived from nonattachment to societal values and conventions, including material wealth. The Epicureans taught that happiness depended on avoiding bodily excesses. And the Stoics, who believed that an impersonal Divine Will governed nature, found tranquility of mind in the acceptance of one's circumstances. The aim of the Stoic was to bring the individual will into harmony with the will of nature. All four of these philosophies constituted a practical departure from the Hellenic quest for universal truth.

The shift from city-state to empire that accompanied the advent of the Hellenistic Era was reflected in larger, more monumental forms of architecture and in such utilitarian structures as lighthouses and libraries. Circular sanctuaries (see Figure 6.19) and colossal temples with triumphant decorative friezes were particularly popular in the fourth century B.C.E. and thereafter. In sculpture, a new emphasis on personality gave rise to portraits that were more lifelike and less idealized than those of the Hellenistic Era. Such portraits as the marble head of the ruler Alexander (Figure 6.29) manifest the new taste for fleeting mood and momentary expression. The large number of sensuous female nude sculptures carved in the tradition of Praxiteles (see Figure 6.13) attests to the Hellenistic fondness for erotic expression. Perhaps the most notable example of the new sensuousness, however, is the male nude figure known as the *Apollo Belvedere* (Figure 6.30), a Roman copy of a Hellenistic statue that was destined to exercise a major influence in Western art from the moment it was recovered in Rome in 1503. A comparison of this figure with its Hellenic counterpart, the *Spear-Bearer* (see Figure 6.9), reveals how far Hellenistic sculpture had moved in the direction of a more animated, effeminate, and self-conscious style. At the same time, the broadening of subject matter to include young children, old, and even deformed people, reflects a relaxation of classical idealism. The carving techniques of Hellenistic sculptors show a high degree of technical virtuosity and a love of dynamic contrasts of light and dark. These features, plus a bold display of

Figure 6.30 Apollo Belvedere. Roman marble copy of a Greek original, late fourth century B.C.E. Height 7 ft. 4 in. Vatican Museums, Rome.

vigorous movement, are evident in the larger-than-life **Nike** (the Greek personification of Victory) erected at Rhodes to celebrate a naval triumph over Syria (Figure 6.31). The deeply cut drapery of the *Nike of Samothrace* clings sensuously to her body as she strides into the wind, like some gigantic, winged ship's prow.

The work that best sums up the Hellenistic aesthetic is the remarkable *Laocoön and His Sons* (Figure 6.32), a piece carved out of a single block of marble. The sculpture recreates the dramatic moment when Laocoön, priest of Apollo, and his two sons are attacked by sea serpents sent by the gods as punishment for Laocoön's effort to warn the Trojans against the Greek

Figure 6.31 Pythocritos of Rhodes,
Nike of Samothrace, ca. 190 B.C.E.
Marble, height 8 ft. Louvre, Paris.
© Hirmer Fotoarchiv.

Figure 6.32 Agesander, Polydorus, and Athenodorus of Rhodes, *Laocoön and His Sons*, second to first century B.C.E. or first century C.E. Marble, height 7 ft. 10½ in. Vatican Museums, Rome.

ruse – a wooden horse filled with armed soldiers – that brought an end to the Trojan War. The tortuous pose, strained muscles, and anguished face of the doomed priest create a sense of turbulence and agitation that contrasts sharply with the tranquility and restraint of classical art. Indeed, the *Laocoön* is a memorable symbol of an age in which classical idealism had already become part of history.

SUMMARY

No style in the history of the arts has been more influential than that produced during the Greek Golden Age. The classical style, as it emerged in the fifth century B.C.E, reflects the Hellenic devotion to rational laws of proportion, order, clarity, and balance. The classical style is also characterized by humanism, a this-worldly belief in the dignity and inherent worth of human beings, and by idealism, that is, the commitment to an underlying standard of perfection. The human body and human experience are central to all the arts of classical Greece. In the paintings found on Greek vases, as in the evolution of the freestanding nude figure, Hellenic artists achieved a sublime balance between fidelity to appearance and the idealization of form.

The monument that best mirrors the classical synthesis of humanism, idealism, and the search for proportional harmony is the Parthenon, the temple built atop the Acropolis to honor Athens' patron goddess of wisdom and war. In the use of the Doric order, the integration of technical refinements, and the intelligent application of architectural decoration, the Parthenon stands as one of the most noble buildings in the history of architecture.

The Hellenic synthesis of humanism and idealism, harnessed to an impassioned quest for order and proportion, also characterized literature and music. Aristotle's definition of tragedy emphasized human needs and limitations. The lyric poetry of Sappho and Pindar made the human being the basic measure of all earthly experience. And Greek music, based on a proportional system of modes, was held to influence the moral condition of the listener.

During the fourth century B.C.E. Alexander the Great spread Greek language and culture throughout a vast, though short-lived, empire that reached from Macedonia to India. During the turbulent Hellenistic Age, as metaphysics gave way to science and practical philosophy, the classical style moved in the direction of heroic realism and expressive emotion. Nevertheless,

GLOSSARY

aulos   a wind instrument used in ancient Greece; it had a double reed (held inside the mouth) and a number of finger holes and was always played in pairs, that is, with the performer holding one in each hand; a leather band was often tied around the head to support the cheeks, thus enabling the player to blow harder (see Figures 6.4 and 6.28)

canon   rule, model, or standard; often used to describe the system of proportion governing composition

cire-perdu   (French, "lost-wax") a bronze-casting method in which a figure is modeled in wax, then enclosed in a clay mold that is fired; the wax melts, and molten metal is poured in to replace it

cithara   a large version of the lyre (having seven to eleven strings) and the principal instrument of ancient Greek music

contrapposto   (Italian, "counterpoised") a position assumed by the human body in which one part is turned in opposition to another part

frieze   in architecture, a sculptured or ornamented band

gable   the triangular section of a wall at the end of a pitched roof

kouros   (Greek, "youth"; pl. *kouroi*) a youthful male figure, usually depicted nude in ancient Greek sculpture; the female counterpart is the *kore* (pl. *korai*), that is, maiden

lyre   any one of a group of plucked stringed instruments; in ancient Greece usually made of tortoise shell or horn and therefore light in weight

lyric   literally, "accompanied by the lyre," hence, verse that is meant to be sung rather than spoken; usually characterized by individual and personal emotion

metope   the square panel between the beam ends under the roof of a structure (see Figure 6.17)

mode   a type of musical scale characterized by a fixed pattern of pitch and tempo within the octave; because the Greeks associated each of the modes with a different emotional state, it is likely that the mode involved something more than a particular musical scale, perhaps a set of rhythms and melodic turns associated with each scale pattern

monophony   (Greek, "one voice") a musical texture consisting of a single, unaccompanied line of melody

Nike   the Greek goddess of victory

octave   the series of eight tones forming any major or minor scale

ode   a type of lyric poem expressing exalted emotion and usually written in honor of a person or special occasion

order   in classical architecture, the parts of a building that stand in fixed and constant relation to each other; the three classical orders are the Doric, the Ionic, and the Corinthian (see Figure 6.17)

pediment   the triangular space forming the gable of a two-pitched roof in classical architecture; any similar triangular form found over a portico, door, or window

portico   a porch with a roof supported by columns

scale   (Latin, *scala*, "ladder") a series of tones arranged in ascending or descending consecutive order; the *diatonic* scale, characteristic of Western music, consists of the eight tones (or series of notes C, D, E, F, G, A, B, C) of the twelve-tone octave; the *chromatic* scale consists of all twelve tones (represented by the twelve piano keys, seven white and five black) of the octave, each a semitone apart

tholos   a circular structure, generally in classical Greek style and probably derived from early tombs

Hellenistic (and thereafter, Roman) heirs to the classical style perpetuated its fundamental humanism and its technical sophistication. Indeed, for centuries to come, Western culture would pay homage to artists who — like newly liberated prisoners from Plato's mythical cave — threw off the chains that bound them to the imperfect world of the senses and exalted an ideal vision of reality.

MUSIC LISTENING SELECTION

Cassette I Selection 1. Anonymous, "Seikolos Song." Greek, ca. 50 C.E.

SUGGESTIONS FOR READING

Boardman, John and David Finn. *The Parthenon and its Sculptures*. Austin, Tex.: University of Texas Press, 1985.

Cook, R. M. *Greek Art*. Baltimore, Md.: Penguin, 1976.

Carpenter, Rhys. *The Architecture of the Parthenon*. Baltimore: Penguin, 1972.

————. *The Esthetic Basis of Greek Art*. Bloomington, Ind.: Indiana University Press, 1968.

Francis, E. D. *Image and Idea in Fifth Century Greece: Art and Literature after the Persian Wars*. New York: Routledge, 1990.

Pedley, John G. *Greek Art and Archeology*. Englewood Cliffs, N.J.: Prentice-Hall, 1993.

Pollit, J. J. *Art and Experience in Classical Greece*. Cambridge: Cambridge University Press, 1971.

Walbank, F. W. *The Hellenistic World*, rev. ed. Cambridge, Mass.: Harvard University Press, 1993.

7

The World of Imperial Rome

"In the second century of the Christian Era, the empire of Rome comprehended the fairest part of the earth, and the most civilized portion of mankind. The frontiers of that extensive monarchy were guarded by ancient renown and disciplined valor. The gentle, but powerful, influence of laws and manners had gradually cemented the union of the provinces." So wrote the eighteenth-century historian Edward Gibbon, who voiced universal and abiding respect for the longest-lasting and most complex empire in Western history. The rise and fall of the Roman Empire is too long and complex a story to be told in these pages. Rather, the main focus of this chapter will be Rome's contribution to the humanistic tradition in the context of Roman imperialism.

The world of imperial Rome was the stage upon which another great empire, that of China, rose to power. Although China and Rome traded through Asian intermediaries, it is unlikely that the two cultures influenced each other directly. Nevertheless, China – in the first centuries of the first millennium C.E. – presents fascinating parallels with that of Rome, and the Chinese cultural legacy bears heavily on the Eastern contribution to the global humanistic tradition. Chinese culture will receive greater attention in chapter 14, but the unique aspects of imperial China and the curious similarities between the Han and Roman Empires demand mention here.

Rome's Early History

Rome's origins are discovered among tribes of Iron Age folk called Latins, who invaded the Italian peninsula just after the beginning of the first millennium B.C.E. By the mid-eighth century B.C.E., these people had founded the city of Rome in the lower valley of the Tiber River, a spot strategically located for control of the Italian peninsula and for convenient access to the Mediterranean Sea (Map **7.1**). While central Italy became the domain of the Latins, the rest of the peninsula received a continuous infusion of eastern Mediterranean people, including Etruscans, Greeks, and Phoenicians, who brought with them cultures richer and more complex than that of the Latins. The Etruscans, who established themselves in northwest Italy, were experts in the arts of metallurgy, town building, and city planning. The Greeks, who colonized the tip of the Italian peninsula and Sicily, were masters of philosophy and the arts. And the Phoenicians, who settled on the northern coast of Africa, brought westward their alphabet and their commercial and maritime skills. From all of these people, but especially from the first two groups, the Latins learned and absorbed elements that enhanced their own civilization: from the Etruscans, the fundamentals of urban planning, chariot racing, the toga, bronze and gold crafting, and the most ingenious structural principle of Near Eastern architecture – the arch. And from the Greeks, the Romans borrowed a pantheon of gods and goddesses, linguistic and literary principles, and the aesthetics of the classical style. As the Romans absorbed Etruscan and Greek culture, so Rome drew these and other peoples into what would become the most powerful world-state in ancient history.

The Roman Republic (509–30 B.C.E.)

For three centuries, Etruscan kings ruled the Latin population, but after the Latins overthrew the Etruscans in 509 B.C.E., monarchy gave way to a government "of the people" (*res publica*). The hardworking agricultural population of ancient Rome consisted of a powerful class of large landowners, the *patricians*, and a more populous class of small farmers called *plebeians*. Although the plebeians constituted the membership of a Popular Assembly and conferred both civil and military authority (the *imperium*) upon two executive officers, or *consuls*, they had little voice in government. The wealthy patricians – life members of the Roman Senate – controlled lawmaking. But step by step, the

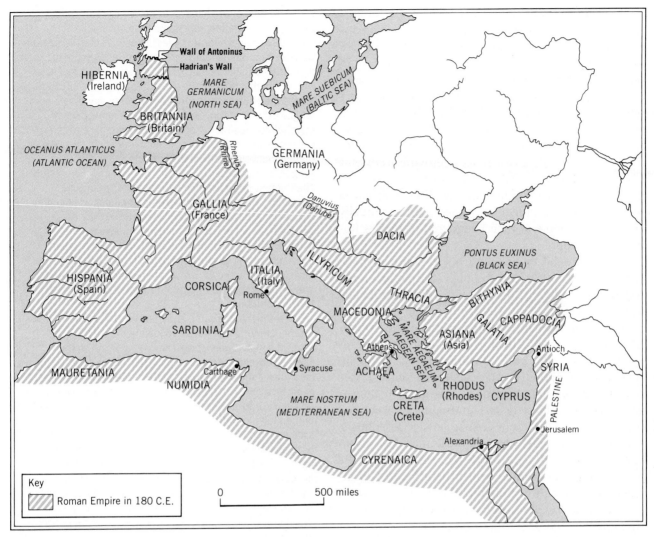

Map 7.1 The Roman Empire in 180 C.E.

plebeians gained increasing political influence. Using as leverage their role as soldiers in the Roman army and their power of veto, exercised through plebeian leaders called *tribunes*, the plebeians made themselves heard. Eventually, they won the right to intermarry with the patricians, to hold the office of consul, and finally, in 287 B.C.E., the privilege of making laws. The stern and independent population of Roman farmers arrived at *res publica* by peaceful means. But no sooner had Rome become a Republic than it adopted expansionist policies that eroded these democratic achievements.

The Rise of Roman Imperialism

Obedience to the Roman state and service in its powerful army were essential to the life of the early Republic. Both contributed to the rise of Roman imperialism, which proceeded by means of long wars of conquest similar to those that had marked the history of earlier empires. After expelling the last of the Etruscan kings, Rome extended its power over all parts of the Italian peninsula. And by the middle of the third century B.C.E., having united all of Italy by force or negotiation, Rome stood poised to conquer the Mediterranean. A longstanding distrust of the Phoenicians, and rivalry with the city of Carthage, Phoenicia's commercial stronghold in northeastern Africa, led Rome into the Punic (Latin for "Phoenician") Wars — a 150-year-period of intermittent violence that ended with the destruction of Carthage in 147 B.C.E. From this point on, Rome assumed naval and commercial leadership in the western Mediterranean. But the ambitions of army generals and the impetus of a century of warfare contributed to sustaining Roman imperialism. Rome seized every opportunity for conquest, and by the end of the first century B.C.E., the Empire included most of North Africa, the Iberian peninsula, Greece, Egypt, much of the Near East, and the territories constituting present-day Europe all the way to the Rhine River (see Map 7.1).

Despite the difficulties presented by the task of governing such far-flung territories, the Romans proved to be efficient administrators. They demanded from their foreign provinces taxes, soldiers to serve in the Roman army, tribute, and slaves. Roman governors, appointed by the Senate from among the higher ranks of the military, ruled within the conquered provinces. Usually, local customs and even local governments were permitted to continue unmodified, for the Romans considered tolerance of provincial customs politically practical. The Romans, however, introduced the Latin language and Roman law: They built paved roads, freshwater aqueducts, bridges, and eventually granted the people of their conquered territories Roman citizenship.

Rome's highly disciplined army was the back-bone of the empire. During the Republic, the Roman army consisted of citizens who served two-year terms, but by the first century C.E., the military had become a profession to which all free men might devote twenty-five years (or more) of their lives. Since serving for this length of time allowed a non-Roman to gain Roman citizenship for himself and his children, military service acted as a means of Romanizing foreigners. The Roman army was the object of fear and admiration among those familiar with Rome's rise to power. Josephus, a Jewish historian who witnessed the Roman destruction of Jerusalem in 70 C.E., described the superiority of the Roman military machine, which he estimated to include more than three hundred thousand armed men. According to Josephus, Roman soldiers performed as though they "had been born with weapons in their hands." The efficiency of the army, reported Josephus, was the consequence of superior organization and discipline. The following description of a Roman military camp offers an example of the admiration and awe with which non-Romans viewed Roman might. It also describes the nature of that "perfect discipline" and dedication to duty that characterized the Roman ethos and Roman culture in general.

READING 21

Josephus' *Description of the Roman Army*

. . . one cannot but admire the forethought shown in this   1
particular by the Romans, in making their servant class
useful to them not only for the ministrations of ordinary life
but also for war. If one goes on to study the organization of
their army as a whole, it will be seen that this vast empire
of theirs has come to them as the prize of valor, and not as
a gift of fortune.

For their nation does not wait for the outbreak of war to
give men their first lesson on arms; they do not sit with
folded hands in peace time only to put them in motion in   10
the hour of need. On the contrary, as though they had been
born with weapons in hand, they never have a truce from
training, never wait for emergencies to arise. Moreover,
their peace maneuvers are no less strenuous than veritable
warfare; each soldier daily throws all his energy into his
drill, as though he were in action. Hence that perfect ease
with which they sustain the shock of battle: no confusion
breaks their customary formation, no panic paralyzes, no
fatigue exhausts them; and as their opponents cannot
match these qualities, victory is the invariable and certain   20
consequence. Indeed, it would not be wrong to describe
their maneuvers as bloodless combats and combats as
sanguinary maneuvers.

The Romans never lay themselves open to a surprise
attack; for, whatever hostile territory they may invade, they
engage in no battle until they have fortified their camp.
This camp is not erected at random or unevenly; they do
not all work at once or in disorderly parties; if the ground is
uneven, it is first levelled; a site for the camp is then
measured out in the form of a square. For this purpose the   30
army is accompanied by a multitude of workmen and of
tools for building.

The interior of the camp is divided into rows of tents. The
exterior circuit presents the appearance of a wall and is
furnished with towers at regular intervals; and on the
spaces between the towers are placed "quick-firers,"
catapults, "stone-throwers," and every variety of artillery
engines, all ready for use. In this surrounding wall are set
four gates, one on each side, spacious enough for beasts of
burden to enter without difficulty and wide enough for   40
sallies of troops in emergencies. The camp is intersected
by streets symmetrically laid out; in the middle are the
tents of the officers, and precisely in the center the
headquarters of the commander-in-chief, resembling a
small temple. Thus, as it were, an improvised city springs
up, with its market-place, its artisan quarter, its seats of
judgment, where captains and colonels adjudicate upon
any differences which may arise . . . .

Once entrenched, the soldiers take up their quarters in
their tents by companies, quietly and in good order. All   50
their fatigue duties are performed with the same
discipline, the same regard for security; the procuring of
wood, food-supplies, and water, as required — each party
has its allotted task . . . . The same precision is maintained
on the battle-field: the troops wheel smartly round in the
requisite direction, and, whether advancing to the attack
or retreating, all move as a unit at the word of command.

When the camp is to be broken up, the trumpet sounds a
first call; at that none remain idle: instantly, at this signal,
they strike the tents and make all ready for departure. The   60
trumpets sound a second call to prepare for the march: at
once they pile their baggage on the mules and other beasts
of burden and stand ready to start, like runners breasting
the cord on the race-course. They then set fire to the
encampment, both because they can easily construct
another [on the spot], and to prevent the enemy from ever
making use of it . . . .

Then they advance, all marching in silence and in good
order, each man keeping his place in the ranks, as if in face
of the enemy . . . . By their military exercises the Romans   70
instil into their soldiers fortitude not only of body but also
of soul; fear, too, plays its part in their training. For they
have laws which punish with death not merely desertion of

the ranks, but even a slight neglect of duty; and their generals are held in even greater awe than the laws. For the high honors with which they reward the brave prevent the offenders whom they punish from regarding themselves as treated cruelly.

This perfect discipline makes the army an ornament of peace-time and in war welds the whole into a single body; so compact are their ranks, so alert their movements in wheeling to right or left, so quick their ears for orders, their eyes for signals, their hands to act upon them. Prompt as they consequently ever are in action, none are slower than they in succumbing to suffering, and never have they been known in any predicament to be beaten by numbers, by ruse, by difficulties of ground, or even by fortune; for they have more assurance of victory than of fortune. Where counsel thus precedes active operations, where the leaders' plan of campaign is followed up by so efficient an army, no wonder that the Empire has extended its boundaries on the east to the Euphrates, on the west to the ocean,[1] on the south to the most fertile tracts of Libya, on the north to the Ister[2] and the Rhine. One might say without exaggeration that, great as are their possessions, the people that won them are greater still . . . .

◆

The Roman Empire and the Pax Romana *(30 B.C.E.–180 C.E.)*

By the beginning of the first millennium C.E., Rome had become the watchdog of the ancient world. Roman imperialism, however, brought with it changes within the Republic itself. By its authority to handle all military matters, the Senate became increasingly powerful, as did the army, which dominated the overseas provinces. As precious metals, booty, and slaves from foreign conquests brought additional wealth to army generals and influential patricians, corruption became widespread. The captives of war were brought back to Rome and auctioned off to the highest bidders, usually patrician landowners, whose farms soon became large-scale plantations (*latifundia*) worked by slaves. Increased agricultural productivity gave greater economic advantage to large landowners who might easily undersell the lesser landowners and drive them out of business. Increasingly, the small farmers were forced to sell their farms to neighboring patricians in return for the right to remain on the land. Or they simply moved to the city to join, by the end of the first century B.C.E., a growing unemployed population. The disappearance of the small farmer signaled the decline of the Republic.

As Rome's rich citizens grew richer and its poor citizens poorer, the patricians fiercely resisted efforts to redistribute wealth more equally. As reform measures failed and political rivalries increased, Rome fell victim to the ambitions of army generals, who, having conquered in the name of Rome, now turned to conquering Rome itself. The first century B.C.E. was an age of military dictators, whose competing claims to power fueled civil wars. The Republic crumbled as blood confrontations replaced reasoned compromises.

In 46 B.C.E., an extraordinary army commander named Gaius Julius Caesar (Figure 7.1) triumphantly entered the city of Rome and established a dictatorship. Caesar, who had spent nine years conquering Gaul (present-day France and Belgium), was as shrewd in politics as he was brilliant in war. His campaigns are described in his prose *Commentaries on the Gallic War*. A superb organizer, Caesar took strong measures to restabilize Rome: He codified the laws, regulated taxation, reduced debts, sent large numbers of the unem-

Figure 7.1 Bust of Julius Caesar, first century B.C.E. Marble, height 3 ft. 2 in. National Archeological Museum, Naples. The Mansell Collection, London.

---

[1] The Atlantic.
[2] The Roman name for the Danube River.

...tariat to overseas colonies, and inaugu-
...works projects. He also granted citizenship
...ns and reformed the Western calendar to
...5¼ days and twelve months (one of which
– July – he named after himself). Threatened by
Caesar's populist reforms and his contempt for republican institutions, his senatorial opponents, led by Marcus Junius Brutus, assassinated him in 44 B.C.E. Despite
Caesar's inglorious death, the name *Caesar* would be
used as an official title by all his imperial successors well
into the second century C.E., as well as by many
modern-day dictators.

Figure 7.2 Augustus of Primaporta, early first century C.E., after a
bronze of ca. 20 B.C.E. Marble, height 6 ft 8 in. Vatican Museums,
Rome.

In 43 B.C.E., Caesar's grandnephew and adopted
son Octavian (63 B.C.E.–14 C.E.) usurped the consulship
and gained the approval of the Senate to rule for life
(Figure **7.2**). Although Octavian put an end to the civil
wars of the preceding century, he revived neither the
political nor the social equilibrium of the early Republic. He shared power with the Senate – which named
him Augustus ("the Revered") – but retained the right
to veto legislation. Thus, for all intents and purposes,
Rome's Republic was defunct, and Rome lay in the
hands of a military autocrat. Nevertheless, Octavian's
reign ushered in an era of peace and stability, a *Pax
Romana* (literally, peace between nationalities of the
Roman Empire; 30 B.C.E. to 180 C.E.), during which
time Rome enjoyed commercial contact with all parts of
the civilized world, including China and India. The *Pax
Romana* was a time of great artistic and literary productivity. A great patron of the arts, Augustus boasted that
when he came to power he found Rome a city of brick,
but left it a city of marble. This era also saw the rise of a
new religion, Christianity, which Rome would ultimately help to spread throughout the West (see chapters 8 and 9).

Following the death of Octavian, Rome continued
to be ruled by army generals (*imperators*, hence the title
"emperor"). Since there was no machinery for succession to the imperial throne, emperors held office until
they either died or were assassinated. Of the twenty-six
emperors that ruled Rome during the fifty-year period
between 335 and 385 C.E., only one died a natural
death. Government by and for the people had been the
hallmark of Rome's early history, but the enterprise of
imperialism ultimately overtook and consumed
Rome's lofty republican ideals.

The Roman System of Law and Order

Against this backdrop of conquest and dominion, it is
no surprise that Rome's contributions to the humanistic tradition were practical rather than theoretical. The
sheer size of the Roman Empire inspired an extraordinary program of bridge and road building, but it also
necessitated the development of a system of law and
order that became Rome's most original and influential
achievement.

Roman law (the Latin *jus* means both "law" and
"justice") evolved out of the practical need to unify a
world-state, rather than – as with the ancient Greeks –
out of a dialectic concerning the role of the citizen
within the *polis*. Familiar with the laws of Solon, the
Romans published their first civil code, the Twelve
Tables of Law, in 450 B.C.E. They placed these laws on
view in the Forum, the public meeting area for the
civic, religious, and commercial activities of Rome. The
Twelve Tables of Law provided Rome's basic legal code

for almost a thousand years. To this body of law were added the acts of the Assembly and the Senate and the edicts of the emperors. For some five hundred years, *praetors* (magistrates who administered justice) and *jurisconsults* (experts in the law) interpreted the laws, providing common-sense solutions to private disputes. Their interpretations constituted a body of "case law." In giving consideration to individual needs, these magistrates cultivated the concept of equity, which puts the spirit of the law above the letter of the law. The decisions of Roman jurists became precedents that established comprehensive guidelines for future judgments. Thus, Roman law was not fixed, but was an evolving body of opinions on the nature and dispensation of justice.

Early in Roman history, the law of the land (*jus civile*) applied only to Roman citizens, but as Roman citizenship was extended to the provinces, so too was the law. Law that embraced a wider range of peoples and customs, the law of the people (*jus gentium*), assumed a universal spirit that reflected compromises between conflicting customs and traditions. The law of the people was, in effect, a law based on universal and natural principles. The body of Roman law came to incorporate the decisions of the jurists, the acts passed by Roman legislative assemblies, and the edicts of Roman emperors. In the sixth century c.e., two hundred years after the division of the Empire into eastern and western portions and a hundred years after the collapse of Rome, the Byzantine (East Roman) Emperor Justinian codified this huge body of law, thereafter known as the *Corpus Juris Civilis*. The Roman system of law influenced the development of codified law in all European countries with the exception of England.

The Building of an Empire

Like its laws, Rome's architecture grew out of the practical need to unify and manage large groups of people. To link the provinces between the Atlantic Ocean and the Euphrates River, Roman engineers built fifty thousand miles of paved roads, most of which led to the Eternal City of Rome.

Bridges and tunnels defied natural barriers, while aqueducts brought fresh water to Rome's major cities. The aqueducts, some of which delivered well over forty million gallons of water per day to a single site, were among the most important of Rome's public works. The need to house, govern, and entertain large numbers of citizens inspired the construction of tenements, meeting halls, and ampitheaters. Superb engineers, the Romans utilized the principle of the arch, the knowledge of which they inherited from the Etruscans. These building techniques permitted the Romans to

enclose great volumes of uninterrupted space – a clear technical advance over the post-and-lintel construction used by the Greeks in buildings like the Parthenon (see Figure 6.15). The Romans adapted the arch innovatively: They placed arches back to back to form barrel **vaults**, at right angles to each other to form cross or groined vaults, and around a central point to form a dome (Figure 7.3). These inventive combinations allowed the Romans to contain larger areas of space than any had ever done so before – indeed, if architecture is defined as the enclosure of interior space, then the Romans were the first true architects. In building techniques, too, the Romans were both practical and innovative: They filled elaborate stone foundations with concrete (a combination of sand, lime, rubble, and water) and finished exterior surfaces with veneers of marble, tile, bronze, or plaster. The Roman invention of concrete made possible cheap, large-scale construction.

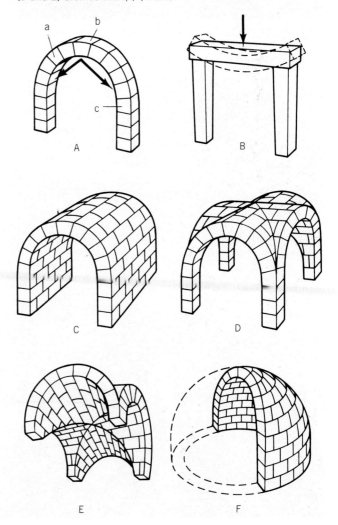

Figure 7.3 Arch principle and arch construction.
(A) Arch consisting of *voussoirs*, wedge-shaped blocks (a,b,c,);
(B) Post and lintel; (C) Barrel or tunnel vault;
(D and E) Groined vault; (F) Dome.

Figure 7.4 Pont du Gard, near Nîmes, France, ca. 20–10 B.C.E. Stone, height 162 ft.

Figure 7.5 Reconstruction of fourth-century-C.E. Rome by I. Gismondi. Museum of Roman Civilization, Rome.

Figure 7.6 Colosseum, Rome (aerial view), 70–82 C.E.
Photo: Fototeca Unione.

The Romans considered architecture and engineering as one and the same discipline. Vitruvius' *Ten Books on Architecture* (see chapter 6) places chapters on architecture alongside those on hydraulic systems, city planning, and mechanical devices. The function of a building determined its formal design, and the design of villas, theaters, and temples received the same careful

attention that was given to hospita
as Josephus reports – military camp
excelled in such large-scale enginee
nine-hundred-foot-long Pont du Gar
five-mile-long aqueduct that brough
city of Nîmes in southern France (F
six-ton stones and assembled wit
structure reflects the practical use of arches at three levels, the bottom row supporting a bridge and the second row undergirding the top channel through which water ran by gravity until it reached its destination.

The sheer magnitude of such Roman amphitheaters as the Circus Maximus, which seated two hundred and fifty thousand spectators (Figure **7.5**, foreground), and the Colosseum, which covered six acres and accommodated fifty thousand (Figure **7.6**), is a reminder that during the first century C.E. Rome's population exceeded one million people. These structures reflect the Roman taste for mass entertainments that included chariot races, mock sea battles, gladiatorial contests, and a variety of violent and brutal blood sports. In the Colosseum, arches are framed on the exterior by engaged columns (Figure **7.7**), an ingenious combination of arch and post-and-lintel motifs that was later widely imitated by Italian Renaissance architects. The long-range influence of this Roman amphitheater is apparent in the design of many modern sports arenas.

Figure 7.7 Outer wall of the Colosseum, Rome, 70–82 C.E. Alinari/Art Resource, New York.

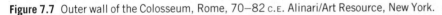

Figure 7.9 Plan and section of the Pantheon. (After Sir Banister Fletcher.) From Horst de la Croix and Richard Tansey, *Art through the Ages*, sixth edition, © 1975 by Harcourt Brace Jovanovich, Inc., reprinted by permission of the publisher.

The architectural ingenuity of the Romans is best illustrated in structures that feature vast, dramatic spatial interiors, such as the Pantheon. A Roman temple dedicated to the seven planetary deities, the Pantheon was built in the early second century C.E.. Its monumental exterior – once covered with a veneer of marble and bronze – features a portico with eight Corinthian columns originally elevated on a flight of stairs that are now buried beneath the city street (Figure 7.8). One of the few buildings from Classical Antiquity to have remained almost intact, the Pantheon boasts a nineteen-foot-thick rotunda that is capped by a solid dome consisting of five thousand tons of concrete (Figure 7.9). The interior of the dome, once painted blue and gold to resemble the vault of heaven, is pierced by a thirty-foot-wide *oculus*, or "eye," that invites light and air (Figure 7.10). The proportions of the Pantheon observe the classical principles of symmetry and harmony as described by Vitruvius (see Reading 17): The height from the floor to the apex of the dome (143 feet) equals the diameter of the rotunda. The Pantheon has inspired more works of architecture than any other classical monument. It awed and delighted such eminent late eighteenth-century neoclassicists as Thomas Jefferson, who used it as the model for many architectural designs, including that of the Rotunda of the University of Virginia (Figure 7.11).

Figure 7.10 Thomas Jefferson, The Rotunda, University of Virginia, Charlottesville, Virginia, 1822–1826. Photo: Virginia State Library, Richmond.

Figure 7.11 Giovanni Paolo Panini, *The Interior of the Pantheon*, ca. 1734–1735. Oil on canvas, 4 ft. 2½ in. × 3 ft. 3 in. National Gallery of Art, Washington, D.C. Samuel H. Kress Collection.

Figure 7.12 Maison Carrée, Nîmes, France, ca. 19 B.C.E.

Figure 7.13 Thomas Jefferson, Virginia State Capitol. Working in Paris with C.L.A. Clérisseau, Jefferson had this model made. The model arrived in Richmond in 1786. Virginia State Library, Richmond.

While the Pantheon is distinctly Roman in spirit, other Roman buildings imitated Greek models. The Roman temple in Nîmes, France, for instance, known as the Maison Carrée, stands like a miniature Greek temple atop a high podium (Figure **7.12**). A stairway and a colonnaded portico accentuate the single entranceway and give the building a frontal "focus" that is usually lacking in Greek temples. The Corinthian order (see Figure 6.17) appears in the portico, and engaged columns are featured in the exterior wall. The epitome of classical refinement, the Maison Carrée inspired numerous European and American copies. Indeed, the Virginia State Capitol, designed by Thomas Jefferson in the late eighteenth century, offers clear evidence of the use of this Roman classical temple to convey a sense of dignity, stability, and authority (Figure **7.13**).

Figure 7.14 Restoration of the Baths of Caracalla in Rome, 211–217 C.E. Engraving. The Bettmann Archive.

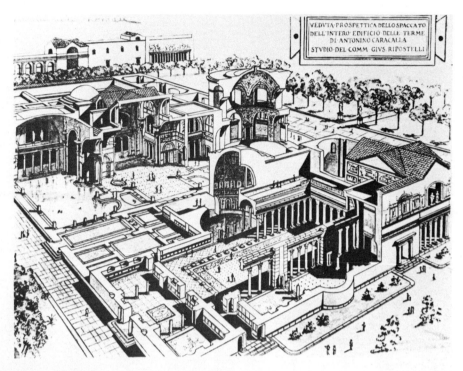

Figure 7.15 Great Bath, Roman bath complex, Bath, England, 54 C.E. Part of the finest group of Roman remains in England, this sumptuous pool is still fed by natural hot springs. The Mansell Collection, London.

If structures such as the Pantheon and the Maison Carrée answered the spiritual needs of the Romans, the Baths of Caracalla satisfied some of their temporal requirements (Figure 7.14). Elaborate structures fed by natural hot springs (Figure 7.15), the Roman spas were places for health-improvement and recreation that provided a welcome refuge from the noise and grime of the city streets. In addition to rooms in which pools of water were heated to varying degrees, the baths might include steam rooms, exercise rooms, art galleries, reading rooms, and chambers for physically intimate relaxation. The popularity of the baths is reflected in the fact that by the third century C.E. there were more than nine hundred of them in the city of Rome. The Roman baths centered on a **basilica**, a rectangular colonnaded hall commonly used for public assemblies.

Figure 7.16 Basilica of Maxentius, Rome, begun 306–310 C.E., completed by Constantine after 313 C.E. Scala/Art Resource, New York.

Basilicas also served as courts of law, meeting halls, and marketplaces. Consisting of a central nave and side aisles and usually featuring a semicircular recess called an **apse** the basilica might be roofed by wooden beams or – as in the Basilica of Maxentius (Figure 7.16) – by gigantic stone vaults. This vast meeting hall, completed by the Emperor Constantine in the fourth century C.E., was 300 feet long and 215 feet wide and boasted brick-faced concrete walls some twenty feet thick. In floor plan and construction features, the Roman basilica became the model for the Early Christian Church in the West.

Roman Sculpture

Like most imperialistic cultures that preceded them, the Romans advertised their military achievements in monumental works of art. Among Rome's classic expressions of power were triumphal arches and victory columns, monuments raised to commemorate the conquests of Roman rulers. More than sixty triumphal arches in Rome alone – and many more throughout the empire – bear witness to the grandeur of the Roman world-state and the success of its military machine. A typical example is the Arch of Titus in Rome, erected to immortalize that emperor's conquest of Jerusalem in

70 C.E. (Figure 7.17). The marble-faced concrete vault of the arch is elevated between two massive piers that bear engaged Corinthian columns and an **attic** or superstructure carrying a commemorative inscription. Narrative relief panels on the interior sides of the vault depict a triumphal procession celebrating the destruction of Jerusalem and the pillaging of the Temple of Solomon (Figure 7.18). Wearing laurel wreaths of victory, Roman soldiers march through a city gate carrying spoils of victory that include a menorah, the seven-branched candlestick used in Jewish religious services. Subtly carved in various depths from low to high relief, the scene evokes the illusion of deep space. Even in its damaged state, *The Spoils of Jerusalem* remains a vivid portrayal of conquest and triumph, and a product of an age that depended on realistic narrative relief – as we today depend on photography and film – to document historical events.

While triumphal arches served as visual propaganda for Rome's military exploits, monumental sculpture glorified Roman rulers. The freestanding, larger-than-life marble statue of Augustus from Primaporta (see Figure 7.2), his arm raised in a gesture that symbolizes imperial authority, is a prime example of Roman heroic portraiture. The conventional stance and anatomical proportions of the figure look back to

Figure 7.17 Arch of Titus, Rome, ca. 81 C.E. Marble, height approx. 50 ft., width approx. 40 ft.

Figure 7.18 Spoils from the Temple in Jerusalem. Relief from the Arch of Titus, Rome, ca. 81 C.E. Marble, height approx. 7 ft. Alinari/Art Resource, New York.

Figure 7.19 Equestrian statue of Marcus Aurelius, ca. 161–180 C.E. Bronze, over life-size. Piazza del Campidoglio, Rome.

Polycleitus' *Doryphorus* (see Figure 6.9). Augustus wears a breastplate that celebrates his victory over the Parthians, while at his feet appear Cupid and a dolphin, symbols of his alleged descent from Venus, the mother of Rome's legendary founder, Aeneas. This portrait, like those commonly found on Roman coins, is a combination of idealization (particularly obvious in the handsome face and muscular, well-proportioned physique) and realistic detail (most evident in the treatment of breastplate and toga).

During the second century, the tradition of heroic portraiture assumed an even more magisterial stamp in the image of the ruler on horseback: the **equestrian** statue (Figure **7.19**). The equestrian portrait of the Roman Emperor Marcus Aurelius depicts the general addressing his troops with the same gesture of imperial authority observed in the statue of Augustus in Figure 7.2. The body of a conquered warrior once lay under the raised right hoof of the spirited charger, whose veins and muscles seem to burst from beneath his bronze skin.

The Roman taste for realism is perhaps best realized in the three-dimensional portraits of Roman men and women. In contrast to the idealized portrait busts of Golden Age Greece (see Figures 4.7, 5.1) Roman portrait busts reflect far greater fidelity to nature. So lifelike are some examples that scholars suspect they may have been executed from wax death masks. Roman portraits tend to reflect the character of the sitter, a fact perhaps related to the ancient Roman custom of honoring the *genius* or indwelling spirit of the dead ancestor, whose image was placed on a shrine

Figure 7.20 Head of a Bearded Man, ca. 250 C.E. Marble, life-size. Collection of the J. Paul Getty Museum, Malibu, California.

Figure 7.21 Flavian Woman, ca. 80 C.E. Marble, life-size. Collection of the J. Paul Getty Museum, Malibu, California.

dedicated to the household gods. The marble portrait bust of Julius Caesar reveals a determined man in his mid-forties (see Figure 7.1). It is the record of a particular person at a particular time in his life. A second example, the head of an anonymous bearded man whose face is accented by a furrowed brow and solemn mouth, betrays deep anxiety and doubt (Figure **7.20**). And the face of the square-jawed aristocratic woman, whose wig or hairdo surely required the fastidious application of the curling iron, discloses the proud confidence of a Roman matron (Figure **7.21**). Whether cast in bronze, or carved in marble or terracotta, these psychologically penetrating studies are often as unflattering as they are honest. Moreover, they are typically Roman in their lack of idealization and their affection for literal detail.

Roman Painting

A similar kind of realism appears in the remarkable frescoes with which the Romans decorated their country villas. Possibly inspired by Greek murals, of which only few examples survive, Roman artists painted the walls of their houses with scenes drawn from literature, religion, and everyday life. Among the finest examples of Roman frescoes are those found in and near Pompeii and Herculaneum, two south Italian cities that were destroyed in 79 C.E. in the volcanic eruption of Mount Vesuvius. Preserved by the volcanic lava left by the eruption, the area's elegant suburban homes – each

Figure 7.22 Atrium, House of the Silver Wedding, Pompeii, Italy, first century C.E. Alimari/Art Resource, New York.

Figure 7.23 Bedroom from the Villa of P. Fannius Synistor, Boscoreale, first century B.C.E. Mosaic floor, couch, and footstool come from other Roman villas of later date. Fresco on lime plaster, 8 ft. 8½ in. × 19 ft. 1⅞ in. × 10 ft. 11½ in. The Metropolitan Museum of Art, New York, Rogers Fund, 1903 (03.14.13). Photo: Schecter Lee.

constructed around an **atrium** (a large central hall open to the sky) – are valuable sources of information concerning the life-styles of wealthy Romans (Figure 7.22).

At a villa in Boscoreale, about a mile north of Pompeii, the floors of some rooms consist of **mosaics** (surface decorations made by embedding small pieces of stone or glass into cement surfaces), while the walls are painted to look like windows that open onto gardens or urban vistas (Figure 7.23). Such illusionistic paintings are a kind of pleasant visual trickery known by the French phrase *trompe l'oeil* ("fool the eye"). Designed to tantalize the eye, they reveal the Roman artist's familiarity with empirical perspective (the technique of making oblique lines move toward an imaginary vanishing point) and other devices designed to create a convincing illusion of three-dimensional space on a two-dimensional surface. In another first century B.C.E. Roman villa, frescoes illustrating the adventures of the Greek hero Odysseus feature spacious landscapes peopled with tiny figures (Figure 7.24). Bathed in light and shade, the naturalistically modeled figures cast shadows to indicate their physical presence in space. Apparent in Roman landscapes is an affection for the countryside and for the pleasures of nature – a phenomenon referred to as the "Arcadian Spirit." Such landscapes echo **pastoral** themes made famous in Greek and Latin poems that celebrated the life of innocence and simplicity led by the shepherds of Arcadia, a mountainous region on the Greek mainland. The yearning for bucolic freedom, expressive of the Roman disenchantment with city life, would reappear frequently in the literature and art of the West, especially during periods of rising urbanization.

Roman Music

While the visual resources of Roman civilization are manifold, the absence of surviving examples in music make it almost impossible to evaluate the Roman

Figure 7.24 Ulysses in the Land of the Lestrygonians, part of the Odyssey Landscapes, second-style ("architectural") wall painting from a house in Rome, late first century B.C.E. Height approx. 5 ft. Vatican Library, Rome.

contribution in this area of the arts. Passages from the writings of Roman historians suggest that Roman music theory was adopted from the Greeks, as were most Roman instruments. In drama, musical interludes replaced the Greek choral odes, a change that suggests the growing distance between drama and its ancient ritual function. Music was, however, essential to most forms of public entertainment and played an important role in military life. For the latter, the Romans developed brass instruments, such as trumpets and horns, and drums for military processions.

Roman Philosophic Thought

The practical-minded Romans made no original contributions to the field of philosophy. Educated Romans admired the writings of Aristotle, as well as the speculations of the Epicureans and the Stoics. The poet Lucretius (95–55 B.C.E.) popularized the materialistic view of the universe held by Democritus and the Epicureans. Since all things, including human souls, were made of atoms, he explains in his poem *On the Nature of Things*, there is no reason to fear death: "We shall not feel because we shall not be."

In the vast, impersonal world of the Roman Empire, many thinkers cultivated attitudes of resignation and detachment popular among Hellenistic proponents of Stoicism. Like their third-century-B.C.E. forebears, Roman Stoics believed that impersonal Providence or Fortune governed the world, and that happiness lay in one's ability to accept one's fate. The Stoic belief in the equality of all human beings within nature, was an attitude that had a distinctly humanitarian effect on both Roman jurisprudence and Christian teaching. Stoics rejected any emotional attachments that might enslave them. The ideal spiritual condition and the one most conducive to contentment, according to the Stoic point of view, depended on the subjugation of the emotions to reason.

The common-sense philosophy of Stoicism encouraged the Roman sense of duty found in the writings of Cicero, Virgil, and Horace. Stoicism was especially popular among such intellectuals as the noted playwright and essayist Lucius Annaeus Seneca (ca. 55 B.C.E.–41 C.E.) and the Emperor Marcus Aurelius (121–180 C.E.), both of whom wrote stimulating treatises on the subject. Seneca's *On Tranquility of Mind*, an excerpt from which follows, argues that one may achieve peace of mind by avoiding burdensome responsibilities, gloomy companions, and excessive wealth. Just as the Roman baths provided a physical retreat from the noise and grime of city life, so Stoicism offered a reasoned retreat from psychic pain and moral despair, a practical set of solutions to the daily strife between the self and society.

READING 22

From Seneca's *On Tranquility of Mind*

... our question, then, is how the mind can maintain a consistent and advantageous course, be kind to itself and take pleasure in its attributes, never interrupt this satisfaction but abide in its serenity, without excitement or depression. This amounts to tranquility. We shall inquire how it may be attained 1

A correct estimate of self is prerequisite, for we are generally inclined to overrate our capacities. One man is tripped by confidence in his eloquence, another makes greater demands upon his estate than it can stand, another 10 burdens a frail body with an exhausting office. Some are too bashful for politics, which require aggressiveness; some are too headstrong for court; some do not control their temper and break into unguarded language at the slightest provocation; some cannot restrain their wit or resist making risky jokes. For all such people retirement is better than a career; an assertive and intolerant temperament should avoid incitements to outspokenness that will prove harmful.

Next we must appraise the career and compare our 20 strength with the task we shall attempt. The worker must be stronger than his project; loads larger than the bearer must necessarily crush him. Certain careers, moreover, are not so demanding in themselves as they are prolific in begetting a mass of other activities. Enterprises which give rise to new and multifarious activities should be avoided; you must not commit yourself to a task from which there is no free egress. Put your hand to one you can finish or at least hope to finish; leave alone those that expand as you work at them and do not stop where you intend they should. 30

In our choice of men we should be particularly careful to see whether they are worth spending part of our life on and whether they will appreciate our loss of time; some people think we are in their debt if we do them a service. Athenadorus said he would not even go to dine with a man who would not feel indebted for his coming. Much less would he dine with people, as I suppose you understand, who discharge indebtedness for services rendered by giving a dinner and count the courses as favors, as if their lavishness was a mark of honor to others. Take away 40 witnesses and spectators and they will take no pleasure in secret gormandizing.

But nothing can equal the pleasures of faithful and congenial friendship. How good it is to have willing hearts as safe repositories for your every secret, whose privity you fear less than your own, whose conversation allays your anxiety, whose counsel promotes your plans, whose cheerfulness dissipates your gloom, whose very appearance gives you joy! But we must choose friends who are, so far as possible, free from passions. Vices are 50 contagious; they light upon whoever is nearest and infect by contact. During a plague we must be careful not to sit near people caught in the throes and burning with fever, because we would be courting danger and drawing poison in with our breath; just so in choosing friends we must pay attention to character and take those least tainted. To mingle the healthy with the sick is the beginning of disease. But I would not prescribe that you become attached to or attract no one who is not a sage. Where would you find him? We have been searching for him for centuries. Call the least bad man the best. You could not have a more opulent choice, if you were looking for good men, than among the Platos and Xenophons[1] and the famous Socratic brood, or if you had at your disposal the age of Cato,[2] which produced many characters worthy to be his contemporaries (just as it produced many unprecedentedly bad, who engineered monstrous crimes. Both kinds were necessary to make Cato's quality understood: he needed bad men against whom he could make his strength effective and good men to appreciate his effectiveness). But now there is a great dearth of good men, and your choice cannot be fastidious. But gloomy people who deplore everything and find reason to complain you must take pains to avoid. With all his loyalty and good will, a grumbling and touchy companion militates against tranquility.

We pass now to property, the greatest source of affliction to humanity. If you balance all our other troubles — deaths, diseases, fears, longings, subjection to labor and pain — with the miseries in which our money involves us, the latter will far outweigh the former. Reflect, then, how much less a grief it is not to have money than to lose it, and then you will realize that poverty has less to torment us with in the degree that it has less to lose. If you suppose that rich men take their losses with greater equanimity you are mistaken; a wound hurts a big man as much as it does a little. Bion[3] put it smartly: a bald man is as bothered when his hair is plucked as a man with a full head. The same applies to rich and poor, you may be sure; in either case the money is glued on and cannot be torn away without a twinge, so that both suffer alike. It is less distressing, as I have said, and easier not to acquire money than to lose it, and you will therefore notice that people upon whom Fortune never has smiled are more cheerful than those she has deserted . . . .

All life is bondage. Man must therefore habituate himself to his condition, complain of it as little as possible, and grasp whatever good lies within his reach. No situation is so harsh that a dispassionate mind cannot find some consolation in it. If a man lays even a very small area out skillfully it will provide ample space for many uses, and even a foothold can be made livable by deft arrangement. Apply good sense to your problems; the hard can be softened, the narrow widened, and the heavy made lighter by the skillful bearer . . . .

◆

Latin Prose Literature

The Roman literary contribution reveals a masterful use of Latin prose and a tendency to inform or instruct. Rome gave the West its first geographies and encyclopedias, as well as some of its finest biographies, histories, and manuals of instructions. In these genres in particular, the Romans demonstrated their practical talents as collectors and organizers of factual material. And although Roman historians tended to glorify Rome and Roman leadership, their attention to detail often surpassed that of the Greek historians. One of Rome's greatest historians, Titus Livius ("Livy," ca. 59 B.C.E.–17 C.E.), wrote a history of Rome from the eighth century B.C.E. to his own day. Although only a small portion of Livy's original 142 books survive, this monumental work — commissioned by Octavian himself — constitutes our most reliable account of political and social life in the days of the Roman Republic.

The Romans were masters in the writing of **epistles** (letters) and in **oratory**, that is, the art of public speaking. In both of these areas, the statesman Marcus Tullius Cicero (106–43 B.C.E.) excelled. A contemporary of Julius Caesar, Cicero produced more than nine hundred letters — sometimes writing three a day to the same person — and more than one hundred speeches and essays. Clarity and eloquence were the hallmarks of Cicero's prose style, which became the model for literary expression among Renaissance humanists (see chapter 16). While Cicero was familiar with the theoretical works of Aristotle and the Stoics, his letters reflect a profound concern for the political realities of his own day. In his lifetime, Cicero served Rome as consul, statesman, and orator, and his carefully reasoned speeches helped to shape public opinion. He admired Julius Caesar's literary style but opposed his dictatorship. (Amicably, Caesar assured Cicero: "It is nobler to enlarge the boundaries of human intelligence than those of the Roman Empire.") As we see in the following excerpt from Cicero's essay *On Duty*, he considered public service the noblest of human activities — one that demanded the exercise of personal courage equal to that required in military combat.

READING 23

From Cicero's *On Duty*

. . . that moral goodness which we look for in a lofty, high-minded spirit is secured, of course, by moral, not by physical, strength. And yet the body must be trained and so disciplined that it can obey the dictates of judgment and reason in attending to business and in enduring toil. But that moral goodness which is our theme depends wholly upon the thought and attention given to it by the mind. And, in this way, the men who in a civil capacity direct the affairs of the nation render no less important service then they who conduct its wars: by their statesmanship oftentimes wars are either averted or terminated; sometimes also they are declared. Upon Marcus Cato's[1]

---

[1]A Greek historian and biographer who lived ca. 428–354 B.C.E.
[2]Marcus Porcius Cato (234–149 B.C.E.), known as "the Censor," a Roman champion of austerity and simplicity.
[3]A Greek poet who lived around 100 B.C.E.

---

[1]Known as "the Censor," the Roman senator Cato (234–149 B.C.E.) repeatedly demanded the total destruction of Carthage.

counsel, for example, the Third Punic War was undertaken, and in its conduct his influence was dominant, even after he was dead. And so diplomacy in the friendly settlement of controversies is more desirable than courage in settling them on the battlefield; but we must be careful not to take that course merely for the sake of avoiding war rather than for the sake of public expediency. War, however, should be undertaken in such a way as to make it evident that it has no other object than to secure peace.

But it takes a brave and resolute spirit not to be disconcerted in times of difficulty or ruffled and thrown off one's feet, as the saying is, but to keep one's presence of mind and one's self-possession and not to swerve from the path of reason.

Now all this requires great personal courage; but it calls also for great intellectual ability by reflection to anticipate the future, to discover some time in advance what may happen whether for good or for ill, and what must be done in any possible event, and never to be reduced to having to say "I had not thought of that."

These are the activities that mark a spirit strong, high, and self-reliant in its prudence and wisdom. But to mix rashly in the fray and to fight hand to hand with the enemy is but a barbarous and brutish kind of business. Yet when the stress of circumstances demands it, we must gird on the sword and prefer death to slavery and disgrace.

As to destroying and plundering cities, let me say that great care should be taken that nothing be done in reckless cruelty or wantonness. And it is a great man's duty in troublous times to single out the guilty for punishment, to spare the many, and in every turn of fortune to hold to a true and honorable course. For whereas there are many, as I have said before, who place the achievements of war above those of peace, so one may find many to whom adventurous, hot-headed counsels seem more brilliant and more impressive than calm and well-considered measures.

We must, of course, never be guilty of seeming cowardly and craven in our avoidance of danger; but we must also beware of exposing ourselves to danger needlessly. Nothing can be more foolhardy than that. Accordingly, in encountering danger we should do as doctors do in their practice: in light cases of illness they give mild treatment; in cases of dangerous sickness they are compelled to apply hazardous and even desperate remedies. It is, therefore, only a madman who, in a calm, would pray for a storm; a wise man's way is, when the storm does come, to withstand it with all the means at his command, and especially when the advantages to be expected in case of a successful issue are greater than the hazards of the struggle.

The dangers attending great affairs of state fall sometimes upon those who undertake them, sometimes upon the state. In carrying out such enterprises, some run the risk of losing their lives, others their reputation and the good-will of their fellow-citizens. It is our duty, then, to be more ready to endanger our own than the public welfare and to hazard honor and glory more readily than other advantages . . . .

———————◆———————

As Cicero indicates, Roman education emphasized civic duty and aimed at training the young for active roles in civic life. To the careers of law and political administration, the art of public speaking was essential. Indeed, in the provinces, where people of many languages mingled, oratory was the ultimate form of political influence. Since the art of public speaking was the distinctive mark of the educated Roman, the practical skills of grammar and rhetoric held an important place in Roman education. One of the greatest spokesmen for the significance of oratory in public life was the Roman historian and politician, P. Cornelius Tacitus (ca. 55–120 C.E.). Tacitus' *Dialogue on Oratory* describes the role of public speaking in ancient Roman life. It bemoans the passing of a time when "eloquence led not only to great rewards, but was also a sheer necessity."

READING 24

From Tacitus' *Dialogue on Oratory*

. . . great oratory is like a flame: it needs fuel to feed it, movement to fan it, and it brightens as it burns.

At Rome too the eloquence of our forefathers owed its development to [special] conditions. For although the orators of today have also succeeded in obtaining all the influence that it would be proper to allow them under settled, peaceable, and prosperous political conditions, yet their predecessors in those days of unrest and unrestraint thought they could accomplish more when, in the general ferment and without the strong hand of a single ruler, a speaker's political wisdom was measured by his power of carrying conviction to the unstable populace. This was the source of the constant succession of measures put forward by champions of the people's rights, of the harangues of state officials who almost spent the night on the hustings,[1] of the impeachments of powerful criminals and hereditary feuds between whole families, of schisms among the aristocracy and never-ending struggles between the senate and the commons.[2] All this tore the commonwealth in pieces, but it provided a sphere for the oratory of those days and heaped on it what one saw were vast rewards. The more influence a man could wield by his powers of speech, the more readily did he attain to high office, the further did he, when in office, outstrip his colleagues in the race for precedence, the more did he gain favor with the great, authority with the senate, and name and fame with the common people. These were the men who had whole nations of foreigners under their protection, several at a time; the men to whom state officials presented their humble duty on the eve of their departure to take up the government of a province, and to whom they paid their respects on their return; the men who, without

———————

[1] The speaker's platform.
[2] The Popular Assembly.

any effort on their own part, seemed to have praetorships and consulates at their beck and call; the men who even when out of office were in power, seeing that by their advice and authority they could bend both the senate and the people to their will. With them, moreover, it was a conviction that without eloquence it was impossible for anyone either to attain to a position of distinction and prominence in the community, or to maintain it; and no wonder they cherished this conviction, when they were called on to appear in public even when they would rather not, when it was not enough to move a brief resolution in the senate, unless one made good one's opinion in an able speech, when persons who had in some way or other incurred odium, or else were definitely charged with some offence, had to put in an appearance in person, when, moreover, evidence in criminal trials had to be given not indirectly or by affidavit, but personally and by word of mouth. So it was that eloquence not only led to great rewards, but was also a sheer necessity; and just as it was considered great and glorious to have the reputation of being a good speaker, so, on the other hand, it was accounted discreditable to be inarticulate and incapable of utterance . . . .

40

50

———————————— ◆ ————————————

Roman Poetry

While the Romans excelled in didactic prose, they also produced some of the world's finest verse. Under the patronage of Octavian, Rome enjoyed a Golden Age of Latin literature whose most notable respresentative was Virgil (70–19 B.C.E.). Rome's foremost poet-publicist, Virgil wrote a semilegendary epic that took as its theme Rome's destiny as world ruler. The *Aeneid* was not the product of an oral tradition, as were the Homeric epics, but was written in an effort to equal the Greek epics. The hero of Virgil's poem is Rome's mythical founder, the Trojan-born Aeneas, who undergoes a series of adventures that test his Stoic sense of duty over and above his desire for personal fulfillment. The first six books of the *Aeneid* recount Aeneas' journey from Troy to Italy and his love affair with the beautiful Carthagian princess, Dido. The second six books describe the Trojan conquest of Latium and the establishment of the Roman state. No summary of this verse masterpiece can represent adequately the monumental impact of the work that would become the foundation for education in the Latin language. Yet the following two excerpts capture the spirit of Virgil's vision. In the first, Aeneas, pressed to fulfil his divine mission, takes leave of the passionate Dido; the second passage, drawn from a long monologue spoken by the ghost of Aeneas' father, sums up the unique character of the Roman achievement.

READING 25

From Virgil's *Aeneid* (Books Four and Six)

[Mercury, the divine herald, urges Aeneas to leave Carthage and proceed to Italy.]

Mercury wastes no time: — "What are you doing,   1
Forgetful of your kingdom and your fortunes,
Building for Carthage? Woman-crazy fellow,
The ruler of the Gods, the great compeller
Of heaven and earth, has sent me from Olympus
With no more word than this: what are you doing,
With what ambition wasting time in Libya?
If your own fame and fortune count as nothing,
Think of Ascanius[1] at least, whose kingdom
In Italy, whose Roman land, are waiting   10
As promise justly due." He spoke, and vanished
Into thin air. Apalled, amazed, Aeneas
Is stricken dumb; his hair stands up in terror,
His voice sticks in his throat. He is more than eager
To flee that pleasant land, awed by the warning
Of the divine command. But how to do it?
How get around that passionate queen?[2] What opening
Try first? His mind runs out in all directions,
Shifting and veering. Finally, he has it,
Or thinks he has: he calls his comrades to him,   20
The leaders, bids them quietly prepare
The fleet for voyage, meanwhile saying nothing
About the new activity; since Dido
Is unaware, has no idea that passion
As strong as theirs is on the verge of breaking,
He will see what he can do, find the right moment
To let her know, all in good time. Rejoicing,
The captains move to carry out the orders.

    Who can deceive a woman in love? The queen
Anticipates each move, is fearful even   30
While everything is safe, foresees this cunning,
And the same trouble-making goddess, Rumor,
Tells her the fleet is being armed, made ready
For voyaging. She rages through the city
Like a woman mad, or drunk, the way the Maenads[3]
Go howling through the night-time on Cithaeron[4]
When Bacchus' cymbals summon with their clashing.
She waits no explanation from Aeneas;
She is the first to speak: "And so, betrayer,
You hoped to hide your wickedness, go sneaking   40
Out of my land without a word? Our love
Means nothing to you, our exchange of vows,
And even the death of Dido could not hold you.
The season is dead of winter, and you labor
Over the fleet; the northern gales are nothing —
You must be cruel, must you not? Why, even,
If ancient Troy remained, and you were seeking
Not unknown homes and lands, but Troy again,
Would you be venturing Troyward in this weather?

---

[1] Aeneas' son.
[2] Dido, Queen of Carthage.
[3] "Mad women," the votaries of Bacchus (Dionysus).
[4] A mountain range between Attica and Boetia.

I am the one you flee from: true? I beg you   50
By my own tears, and your right hand — (I have nothing
Else left my wretchedness) — by the beginnings
Of marriage, wedlock, what we had, if ever
I served you well, if anything of mine
Was ever sweet to you, I beg you, pity
A falling house; if there is room for pleading
As late as this, I plead, put off that purpose.
You are the reason I am hated; Libyans,
Numidians, Tyrians, hate me; and my honor
Is lost, and the fame I had, that almost brought me   60
High as the stars, is gone. To whom, O guest —
I must not call you husband any longer —
To whom do you leave me? I am a dying woman;
Why do I linger on? Until Pygmalion,
My brother, brings destruction to this city?
Until the prince Iarbas leads me captive?
At least if there had been some hope of children
Before your flight, a little Aeneas playing
Around my courts, to bring you back, in feature
At least, I would seem less taken and deserted."   70
    There was nothing he could say. Jove bade him keep
Affection from his eyes, and grief in his heart
With never a sign. At last, he managed something: —
"Never, O Queen, will I deny you merit
Whatever you have strength to claim; I will not
Regret remembering Dido, while I have
Breath in my body, or consciousness of spirit.
I have a point or two to make. I did not,
Believe me, hope to hide my flight by cunning;
I did not, ever, claim to be a husband,   80
Made no such vows. If I had fate's permission
To live my life my way, to settle my troubles
At my own will, I would be watching over
The city of Troy, and caring for my people,
Those whom the Greeks had spared, and Priam's palace
Would still be standing; for the vanquished people
I would have built the town again. But now
It is Italy I must seek, great Italy,
Apollo orders, and his oracles
Call me to Italy. There is my love,   90
There is my country. If the towers of Carthage,
The Libyan citadels, can please a woman
Who came from Tyre,[5] why must you grudge the Trojans
Ausonian land?[6] It is proper for us also
To seek a foreign kingdom. I am warned
Of this in dreams: when the earth is veiled in shadow
And the fiery stars are burning, I see my father,
Anchises, or his ghost, and I am frightened;
I am troubled for the wrong I do my son,
Cheating him out of his kingdom in the west,   100
And lands that fate assigns him. And a herald,
Jove's[7] messenger — I call them both to witness —
Has brought me, through the rush of air, his orders;
I saw the god myself, in the full daylight,
Enter these walls, I heard the words he brought me.

Cease to inflame us both with your complainings;
I follow Italy not because I want to."

[In the Underworld described in Book 6, Aeneas encounters the soul of his father, Anchises, who foretells the destiny of Rome.]

"Others, no doubt, will better mould the bronze
To the semblance of soft breathing, draw from
   marble,
The living countenance; and others please   110
With greater eloquence, or learn to measure
Better than we, the pathways of the heavens,
The risings of the stars: remember, Roman,
To rule the people under law, to establish
The way of peace, to battle down the haughty,
To spare the meek. Our fine arts, these forever."

———————◆———————

While Virgil is best known for the *Aeneid*, he also wrote **eclogues**, pastoral poems that glorify the natural landscape and its rustic inhabitants. Virgil's *Eclogues* found inspiration in the pastoral sketches of Theocritus, a third-century-B.C.E. Sicilian poet. Other Roman poets besides Virgil looked to Greek prototypes. The Roman poet Catullus (ca. 84–54 B.C.E.), for instance, wrote intimate love lyrics reminiscent of Sappho's, but often laced with biting wit. However, passion and personal feeling were not typical of Latin literature, which generally inclined more toward moralizing, synthesizing, and satirizing. Publius Ovidius Naso, or Ovid (43 B.C.E.–17 C.E.), produced the *Metamorphoses*, a vast collection of stories about Greek and Roman gods who experience supernatural transformation. He also wrote a witty guide to the seduction of women, *The Art of Love*, which swelled an already large classical canon of misogynic, or antifemale, literature. In *The Art of Love*, which offers vivid glimpses into everyday life in Rome, Ovid argues that the greatest human crimes issue from women's lust, which, according to the poet, is "keener, fiercer and more wanton" than men's.

Roman poets were at their most typical when they were moralizing. Octavian's poet laureate, Quintus Horatius Flaccus, better known as Horace (65–8 B.C.E.), took a critical view of life. Though lacking the grandeur of Virgil and the virtuosity of Ovid, Horace composed verse that pointed up the contradictions between practical realities and philosophic ideals. Having lived through the devastating civil wars of the first century B.C.E., Horace brought a common-sense insight to the subject of war, as we see in the first of the following poems. The second poem below exemplifies the Roman taste for **satire**, a literary genre that uses humor to denouce human vice and folly. Satire – Rome's only

---

[5]A maritime city of ancient Phoenicia, ruled by Dido's father.
[6]From *Ausones*, the ancient name for the inhabitants of middle and southern Italy.
[7]Jupiter, the sky-god.

unique contribution to world literature — is a kind of moralizing in which human imperfection is not simply criticized, but rather, mocked through biting wit and comic exaggeration. *To Be Quite Frank* is a caustic description of a middle-aged lady with teenage pretensions, a characterization as unvarnished and true-to-life as most Roman portraits. Finally, in the third poem that follows, Horace reveals himself to be a Stoic with little hope for human perfection: He advises us to "seize the day" (*carpe diem*) and "learn to accept whatever is to be."

READING 26

Horace's Poems

Civil War

Why do ye rush, oh wicked folk,	1
To a fresh war?	
Again the cries, the sword, the smoke —	
What for?	
Has not sufficient precious blood	5
Been fiercely shed?	
Must ye spill more until ye flood	
The dead?	
Not even armed in rivalry	
Your hate's employed;	10
But 'gainst yourselves until ye be	
Destroyed!	
Even when beasts slay beasts, they kill	
Some other kind.	
Can it be madness makes ye still	15
So blind?	
Make answer! Is your conscience numb?	
Each ashy face	
Admits, with silent lips, the dumb	
Disgrace.	20
Murder of brothers! Of all crime,	
Vilest and worst!	
Pause — lest ye be, through all of time,	
Accursed.	

To Be Quite Frank

Your conduct, naughty Chloris, is	1
Not just exactly Horace's	
Ideal of a lady	
At the shady	
Time of life;	5
You mustn't throw your soul away	
On foolishness, like Pholoë —	
Her days are folly-laden —	
She's a maiden,	
You're a wife.	10

Your daughter, with propriety,	
May look for male society,	
Do one thing and another	
In which mother	
Shouldn't mix;	15
But revels Bacchanalian	
Are — or should be — quite alien	
To you a married person,	
Something worse'n	
Forty-six!	20
Yes, Chloris, you cut up too much,	
You love the dance and cup too much,	
Your years are quickly flitting —	
To your knitting	
Right about!	25
Forget the incidental things	
That keep you from parental things —	
The World, the Flesh, the Devil,	
On the level,	
Cut 'em out!	30

———————◆———————

Carpe Diem

Pry not in forbidden lore,	1
Ask no more, Leuconoë,	
How many years — to you? — to me? —	
The gods will send us	
Before they end us;	5
Nor, questing, fix your hopes	
On Babylonian horoscopes.	
Learn to accept whatever is to be:	
Whether Jove grant us many winters,	
Or make of this the last, which splinters	10
Now on opposing cliffs the Tuscan sea.	
Be wise; decant your wine; condense	
Large aims to fit life's cramped circumference.	
We talk, time flies — you've said it!	
Makes hay today,	15
Tomorrow rates no credit.	

———————◆———————

While Horace's satirical lyrics were, for the most part, genial, those of Rome's greatest satirist, Juvenal (ca. 55–130 C.E.), were among the most devastating ever written. Juvenal came to Rome from the provinces. In Rome, his career as a magistrate and his experience of poverty and financial failure contributed to his negative perception of Roman society, which he describes in his sixteen bitter satires as swollen with greed and corruption. Juvenal's attack on the city of Rome pictures a noisy, dirty, and crowded urban community inhabited by selfish, violent, and self-indulgent people.

READING 27A

From Juvenal's "Against the City of Rome"

"Rome, good-bye! Let the rest stay in the town if they want to,   1
Fellows like A, B, and C, who make black white at their pleasure,
Finding it easy to grab contracts for rivers and harbors,
Putting up temples, or cleaning out sewers, or hauling off corpses,
Or, if it comes to that, auctioning slaves in the market.   5
Once they used to be hornblowers, working the carneys;
Every wide place in the road knew their puffed-out cheeks and their squealing.
Now they give shows of their own. Thumbs up! Thumbs down![1] And the killers
Spare or slay, and then go back to concessions for private privies.
Nothing they won't take on. Why not? — since the kindness of Fortune   10
(Fortune is out for laughs) has exalted them out of the gutter.

. . . .

"If you're poor, you're a joke, on each and every occasion.
What a laugh, if your cloak is dirty or torn, if your toga
Seems a little bit soiled, if your shoe has a crack in the leather,
Or if more than one patch attests to more than one mending!
Poverty's greatest curse, much worse then the fact of it, is that   15
It makes men objects of mirth, ridiculed, humbled, embarrassed.
'Out of the front-row seats!' they cry when you're out of money,
Yield your place to the sons of some pimp, the spawn of some cathouse,
Some slick auctioneer's brat, or the louts some trainer has fathered   20
Or the well-groomed boys whose sire is a gladiator.

. . . .

"Here in town the sick die from insomnia mostly.
Undigested food, on a stomach burning with ulcers,
Brings on listlessness, but who can sleep in a flophouse?
Who but the rich can afford sleep and a garden apartment?   25
That's the source of infection. The wheels creak by on the narrow
Streets of the wards, the drivers squabble and brawl when they're stopped,
More than enough to frustrate the drowsiest son of a sea cow.
When his business calls, the crowd makes way, as the rich man,
Carried high in his car, rides over them, reading or writing,   30

Even taking a snooze, perhaps, for the motion's composing.
Still, he gets where he wants before we do; for all of our hurry
Traffic gets in our way, in front, around and behind us.
Somebody gives me a shove with an elbow, or two-by-four scantling.[2]
One clunks my head with a beam, another cracks down with a beer keg.   35
Mud is thick on my shins, I am trampled by somebody's big feet.
Now what? — a soldier grinds his hobnails into my toes."

. . . .

———————◆———————

If Juvenal found much to criticize among his peers, he was equally hostile toward foreigners and women. His Sixth Satire – "Against Women" – is one of the most bitter antifemale diatribes in the history of Western literature. Here, the poet laments the disappearance of the chaste Latin woman whose virtues, he submits, have been corrupted by luxury. Though Juvenal's bias against womankind strikes a personal note, it is likely that he was reflecting the public outcry against the licentiousness that was widespread in his own day. Increasingly during the second century, men openly enjoyed concubines, mistresses, and prostitutes. Infidelity among married women was on the rise, and divorce was common, as were second and third marriages for both sexes.

READING 27B

From Juvenal's "Against Women"

Where, you ask, do they come from, such monsters as these? In the old days   1
Latin women were chaste by dint of their lowly fortunes.
Toil and short hours for sleep kept cottages free from contagion,
Hands were hard from working the wood, and husbands were watching,
Standing to arms at the Colline Gate, and the shadow of Hannibal's looming.[1]   5
Now we suffer the evils of long peace. Luxury hatches
Terrors worse than the wars, avenging a world beaten down.
Every crime is here, and every lust, as they have been
Since the day, long since, when Roman poverty perished.

---

[1] To turn the thumb down was the signal to kill a wounded gladiator; to turn it up signaled that he should be spared.

[2] A piece of lumber.

[1] In 213 B.C.E. the Carthaginian general, Hannibal, Rome's most formidable enemy, was camped only a few miles outside rome, poised to attack (see Livy, xxvi:10).

Over our seven hills,[2] from that day on, they came
    pouring.   10
The rabble and rout of the East, Sybaris, Rhodes, Miletus,
Yes, and Tarentum[3] too, garlanded, drunken, shameless.
Dirty money it was that first imported among us
Foreign vice and our times broke down with
    overindulgence.
Riches are flabby, soft. And what does Venus care for   15
When she is drunk? She can't tell one end of a thing from
    another,
Gulping big oysters down at midnight, making the
    unguents
Foam in the unmixed wine, and drinking out of a conch-
    horn
While the walls spin round, and the table starts in dancing,
And the glow of the lamps is blurred by double their
    number.   20
    .   .   .   .

There's nothing a woman won't do, nothing she thinks is
    disgraceful
With the green gems at her neck, or pearls distending her
    ear lobes.
Nothing is worse to endure than your Mrs. Richbitch,
    whose visage
Is padded and plastered with dough, in the most ridiculous
    manner.
Furthermore, she reeks of unguents, so God help her
    husband   25
With his wretched face stunk up with these, smeared by
    her lipstick.
To her lovers she comes with her skin washed clean. But at
    home
Why does she need to look pretty? Nard[4] is assumed for the
    lover,
For the lover she buys all the Arabian perfumes.
It takes her some time to strip down to her face, removing
    the layers   30
One by one, till at last she is recognizable, almost,
Then she uses a lotion, she-asses' milk; she'd need herds
Of these creatures to keep her supplied on her
    northernmost journeys.
But when she's given herself the treatment in full, from the
    ground base
Through the last layer of mud pack, from the first wash to a
    poultice,   35
What lies under all this — a human face, or an ulcer?
    .   .   .   .

◆

Roman Drama

Roman tragedies were roughly modeled on those of
Greece. They were moral and didactic in intent, and
their themes were drawn from Greek or Roman history. Theatrical performances in Rome were not,
however, a religious solemnity as they were in Greece.

[2]The hills surrounding the city of Rome.
[3]Greek cities associated with luxury and vice.
[4]Spikenard, a fragrant ointment.

Rather, they were a form of entertainment offered
along with the public games that marked the major
civic festivals known as *ludi*. The *ludi* included few of
the athletic contests that were common to Greek
games. They featured instead displays of gladiatorial
combat, chariot races, animal contests, and a variety of
other violent amusements. The nature of these public
spectacles may explain why many of the tragedies
written to compete with them were bloody and ghoul-
ish in character. The lurid plays of the Stoic poet Seneca
drew crowds in Roman times and were to inspire —
some 1,500 years later — such playwrights as William
Shakespeare.

    The Romans seem to have enjoyed comedies over
tragedies, for most surviving Roman plays are comedies. Comic writers employed simple plots and broad
(often obscene) humor. The plays of Plautus (ca. 250-
184 B.C.E.) are filled with stock characters, such as the
good-hearted prostitute, the shrewish wife, and the
clever servant, who engage in farcical schemes of the
kind common to today's television situation comedies.
In the comic theater of the Romans, as in Roman
culture in general, fact took precedence over theory,
and the real, if imperfect, world was the natural setting
for all human endeavors.

Imperial China (221 B.C.E.–220 C.E.)

Just as the Roman Empire was the culminating phase of
classical civilization in the West, so the Han Empire
(206 B.C.E.–220 C.E.) represented the high point of
ancient Chinese civilization. Han China established the
intellectual and cultural foundations not only for
China, but for China's neighbors: Korea, Vietnam, and
Japan. Indeed, the Chinese still refer to themselves as
the "children of the Han."

    Han rulers expanded the empire they inherited
from their forebears, the Ch'in — the dynasty from
which the name *China* derives. Although the Ch'in
dynasty lasted only fifteen years (221–206 B.C.E.), it
was extremely effective at centralizing political power.
The Ch'in standardized the written Chinese language
and created a uniform system of weights and measures,
even dictating the widths of axles in all the wagons that
rumbled down the roads. The empire started by the
Ch'in lasted more than four centuries, despite repeated
invasions along its northern borders by the nomadic
Huns of Central Asia. To discourage invaders, the Ch'in
commissioned the construction of a 1,400-mile-long
Great Wall (Figure **7.25**), a spectacular engineering feat
that is often compared with the Roman emperor
Hadrian's Wall (only seventy-three miles long), built in
Britain some three hundred years later in an effort
to deter barbarian attacks on Rome's northernmost
borders.

Figure 7.25 Great Chinese Wall in the Pata Ling Hills, near Peking, China, begun third century B.C.E. © Paolo Koch/Photo Researchers, Inc.

Map 7.2 Han and Roman Empires.

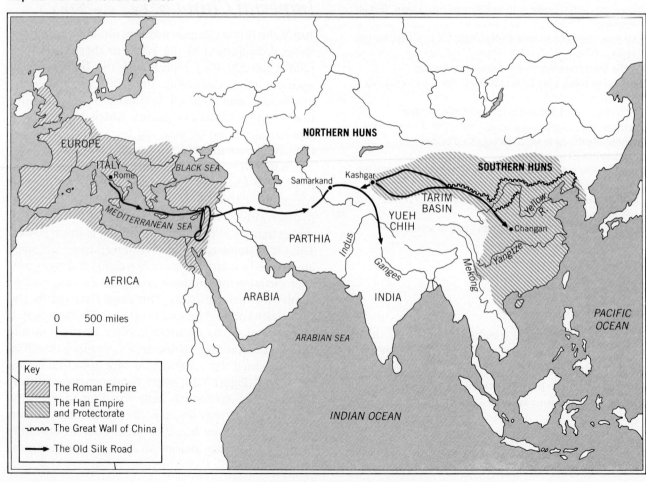

The Han dynasty ruled an empire roughly equivalent to that of Rome in power and prestige, though larger in actual population (Map **7.2**). During the Han Era, China traded with both Rome and India. In exchange for Western linen, wool, glass, and metalware, the Chinese sold silk, ivory, gems, and spices. The Romans traded by way of Asian intermediaries, who led camel caravans across a vast "Silk Road" that stretched from Asia Minor to the Pacific Ocean. China's economy depended on a large peasant class dominated by wealthy landlords. Farmers were often conscripted for war and other state projects, such as the building of the Great Wall. Like the kings of ancient China, Chinese emperors held absolute responsibility for maintaining order and harmony (see chapter 3). Rulers depended on a large, salaried bureaucracy made up of qualified civil servants. Drawn from a wealthy patrician class, these men took rigorous exams that tested their knowledge of the Chinese classics — a body of writings associated with the teachings of Confucius. The imperial bureaucracy was supported by heavy taxes levied on the peasants, whose violent revolts against prosperous landowners ultimately led to the overthrow of the Han dynasty.

The Arts in Han China

Just as the Romans borrowed the best of the cultural traditions that preceded them, so Han rulers gathered the masterworks of their forebears to pass on to future generations an authoritative, or classical, Chinese culture. The study of classic Chinese texts began during the Han Era. An imperial university founded in 124 B.C.E. drew over three thousand scholars within a one-hundred-year period. Han scholars compiled China's first dictionary; others produced some of China's finest essays, poems, rhyme-prose tales, and histories. These literary works were marked by extraordinary simplicity and refinement.

The writing of history was one of China's greatest achievements. According to tradition, Chinese court historians kept chronicles of events as far back as one thousand years before the Han Era. Unfortunately, many of these chronicles were lost in the wars and notorious "book-burnings" of the Ch'in Era. Beginning with the second century B.C.E., however, palace historians kept a continuous record of rulership. Ancient China's greatest historian Ssu-ma Ch'ien (145–90 B.C.E.), who rivals both Thucydides and Livy, produced the monumental *Shih Chi* (*Records of the Grand Historian*), a narrative account of Chinese history from earliest times through the lifetime of the author. Ssu-ma Ch'ien, himself the son of a palace historian-astronomer, served at the court of the Emperor Wu, the vigorous ruler who brought Han China to the peak of its power. In the following excerpt from the chapter on "Wealth and Commerce," Ssu-ma Ch'ien interrupts a detailed description of the economic life of the Han Empire to make some provocative comments on China's social and moral life. While economic activity follows the natural order (*li*), the author explains, morals "come as the effects of wealth." Ssu-ma Ch'ien voices the neo-Confucian idea that wealth and virtue are interdependent. A flourishing economy will encourage the people to be virtuous, while poverty leads inevitably to moral decay. Stylistically, Ssu-ma Ch'ien's *Records* display the economy and vigor of expression that characterizes the finest Han prose.

READING 28

From Ssu-ma Ch'ien's *Records of the Grand Historian*

I do not know about prehistoric times before Shennung,[1] but since the Yu and Shia dynasties [after the twenty-second century B.C.E.] during the period discussed by the historical records, human nature has always struggled for good food, dress, amusements, and physical comfort, and has always tended to be proud of wealth and ostenatation. No matter how the philosophers may teach otherwise, the people cannot be changed. Therefore, the best of men leave it alone, and next in order come those who try to guide it, then those who moralize about it, and then those [10] who try to make adjustments to it, and lastly come those who get into the scramble themselves. Briefly, Shansi produces timber, grains, linen, ox hair, and jades. Shantung produces fish, salt, lacquer, silks, and musical instruments. Kiangnan [south of the Yangtse] produces cedar, *tzu* [a hard wood for making wood blocks], ginger, cinnamon, gold and tin ores, cinnabar, rhinoceros horn, tortoise shell, pearls, and hides. Lungmen produces stone for tablets. The north produces horses, cattle, sheep, furs, and horns. As for copper and iron, they are often found in [20] mountains everywhere, spread out like pawns on a chessboard. These are what the people of China like and what provide the necessities for their living and for ceremonies for the dead. The farmers produce them, the wholesalers bring them from the country, the artisans work on them, and the merchants trade on them. All this takes place without the intervention of government or of the philosophers. Everybody exerts his best and uses his labor to get what he wants. Therefore prices seek their level, cheap goods going to where they are expensive and higher [30] prices are brought down. People follow their respective professions and do it on their own initiative. It is like flowing water which seeks the lower level day and night without stop. All things are produced by the people themselves without being asked and transported to where

---

[1] A legendary culture hero, inventor of agriculture and commerce, ca. 2737 B.C.E.

they are wanted. Is it not true that these operations happen naturally in accord with their own principles? The *Book of Chou*[2] says, "Without the farmers, food will not be produced; without the artisans, industry will not develop; without the merchants, the valuable goods will disappear; and without the wholesalers, there will be no capital and the natural resources of lakes and mountains will not be opened up." Our food and our dress come from these four classes, and wealth and poverty vary with the size of these sources. On a larger scale, it benefits a country, and on a smaller scale, it enriches a family. These are the inescapable laws of wealth and poverty. The clever ones have enough and to spare, while the stupid ones have not enough 40

Therefore, first the granaries must be full before the people can talk of culture. The people must have sufficient food and good dress before they can talk of honor. The good customs and social amenities come from wealth and disappear when the country is poor. Even as fish thrive in a deep lake and the beasts gravitate toward a deep jungle, so the morals of mankind come as effects of wealth. The rich acquire power and influence, while the poor are unhappy and have no place to turn to. This is even truer of the barbarians. Therefore it is said: "A wealthy man's son does not die in the market place," and it is not an empty saying. It is said: 50

60

The world hustles
   Where money beckons.
The world jostles
   Where profit thickens.

Even kings and dukes and the wealthy gentry worry about poverty. Why wonder that the common people and the slaves do the same? . . . [Here follows a long section on the economic products and conditions and the people's character and way of living of the different regions.] 70

Therefore you see the distinguished scholars who argue at courts and temples about policies and talk about honesty and self-sacrifice, and the mountain recluses who achieve a great reputation. Where do they go? They seek after the rich. The honest officials acquire wealth as time goes on, and the honest merchants become wealthier and wealthier. For wealth is something which man seeks instinctively without being taught. You see soldiers rush in front of battle and perform great exploits in a hail of arrows and rocks and against great dangers, because there is a great reward. You see young men steal and rob and commit violence and dig up tombs for treasures, and even risk the punishments by law, throwing all considerations of their own safety to the winds — all because of money. The courtesans of Chao and Cheng dress up and play music and wear long sleeves and pointed dancing shoes. They flirt and wink, and do not mind being called to a great distance, irrespective of the age of the men — all are attracted by the rich. The sons of the rich dress up in caps and carry swords and go about with a fleet of carriages just to show off their wealth. The hunters and the fishermen go out at night, in snow and frost, roam in the wooded valleys haunted by wild beasts, because they want to catch game. Others gamble, 80

90

have cock fights, and match dogs in order to win. Physicians and magicians practice their arts in expectation of compensation for their services. Bureaucrats play hide-and-seek with the law and even commit forgery and falsify seals at the risk of penal sentences because they have received bribes. And so all farmers, artisans, and merchants and cattle raisers try to reach the same goal. Everybody knows this, and one hardly ever hears of one who works and declines pay for it 100

◆

Ssu-ma Ch'ien's narrative describes the men and women of the Han Era as practical and this-worldly, in fact, as remarkably similar to Romans. This practical sensibility also fostered Chinese contributions in cartography, medicine, mathematics, astronomy, and technology. Among China's most notable achievements in the last of these areas were the invention of paper, the seismograph, the horse collar, the watermill, and the manufacture of silk.

Before the introduction of Buddhism into China late in the Han Era (see chapter 9), the Chinese

Figure 7.26 Tomb model of a house, Eastern Han Dynasty, first century C.E. Earthenware with unfired pigments, 52 × 33½ × 27 in. The Nelson-Atkins Museum of Art, Kansas City, Missouri (Purchase: Nelson Trust) 33–521.

---

[2]The book of documents devoted to the Chou Dynasty (1111–221 B.C.E.).

Figure 7.27 Imperial warriors, tomb of a Han Emperor, Xianyang, China, third century B.C.E. Painted terra-cotta. Photo: Robert Harding Picture Library, London.

produced no monumental architecture comparable to that of Rome. Since the Chinese built primarily in the impermanent medium of wood, no structures erected during the Han Era are still standing. Ceramic funerary models of multiroofed Chinese houses, however, give us an excellent idea of China's early architectural accomplishments (Figure **7.26**), and engineering projects such as the Great Wall testify to the high level of Chinese building skills.

During the Han Era, the visual arts flourished. Like their Shang forebears (see chapter 1), the Han excelled in bronze casting, and in the creation of sculpture in **terra-cotta** (baked clay). The most extraordinary artifacts from China's imperial era – the treasures discovered in the twenty-one-square-mile burial site of the Ch'in emperor Qin – suggest that the ceramic tradition had reached its peak in China well before the Han period. Excavated during the 1970s and 1980s, Qin's subterranean vault was found to contain an army of some eight thousand clay soldiers, equipped with actual swords, spears, and bows and arrows (Figure

7.27). The life-size warriors – no two faces of which are exactly alike – belong to a formidable military force that the Romans might have envied. In nearby tombs, bronze chariots, complete with earthenware horses and riders, offer further astonishing evidence of China's imperial might, as well as its high level of technical and artistic achievement.

SUMMARY

A genius for practical organization marked all aspects of Roman history. As Josephus observed, Roman rule was not "a gift of fortune," but the result of unflagging discipline and a devotion to duty. From its beginnings, Rome showed an extraordinary talent for adopting and adapting the best of other cultures such as those of the Greeks and Etruscans. While the Roman Republic engaged all citizens in government, power rested largely with the wealthy and influential patrician class. As Rome built an empire and assumed mastery of the civilized world, the Roman state fell increasingly into the hands of such military dictators as Julius Caesar. In the early part of the Roman Empire, Octavian ushered in a *Pax Romana*, a time of peace and high cultural productivity.

The Romans produced no original philosophy; rather, they cultivated popular schools of thought such as Stoicism, which suited the materialistic and practical Roman cast of mind. Rome's greatest accomplishments lay in the practical areas of law, language, and political life. Roman law unified the far-flung parts of the Empire and established the long-lasting principles of human freedom and individual autonomy. Rome's architectural and engineering projects, which engaged the inventive use of the arch and the techniques of concrete and brick construction, exercised an influence on all subsequent civilizations in the West. To the classical style in architecture, the Romans contributed domed and stone-vaulted types of construction that enclosed vast areas of space. Rome borrowed Hellenic models in all of the arts, but the Roman taste for realism dominated narrative relief sculpture, portrait busts, and fresco painting. These genres disclose a love for literal truth that contrasts sharply with the Hellenic effort to generalize and idealize form.

Roman literature manifests a similar bias for factual information. Roman writers gave the world its first encyclopedias, biographies, and manuals of instruction, as well as memorable essays, speeches, histories, and letters. The high moral tone and lucid language of Cicero and Tacitus characterize Roman prose at its best. In poetry, Virgil paid homage to the Roman state in the *Aeneid*, while Horace and Juvenal offered a critical view of Roman life in satiric verse, the genre that constitutes Rome's most original contribution to literature.

For almost a thousand years, the Romans held together a geographically and ethnically diverse realm, providing a large population with such a high quality of life as to move future generations to envy and praise. The Roman contribution to the classical legacy is imprinted on our language, our laws, our architecture, and our everyday modes of behavior. By transmitting Greek culture to the West and by imposing its own unique ways of life on so vast a geographic area, Rome's influence on the humanistic tradition was felt long after Roman glory and might had faded.

While Rome preserved the classical heritage in the West, the Han Empire played an equally vital role in establishing classical Chinese culture in the East. Curiously similar in many ways to the Roman Empire, the Han Empire developed an aggressive military, an educated bureaucracy, an extraordinary technology, a flourishing economy, and vigorous literary and artistic traditions that would dominate Eastern culture for centuries.

GLOSSARY

apse a vaulted semicircular recess at one or both ends of a basilica

atrium the inner courtyard of a Roman house, usually colonnaded and open to the sky

attic the superstructure or low upper story above the main order of a facade

basilica a large, colonnaded hall commonly used for public assemblies, law courts, baths, and marketplaces

eclogue a pastoral poem, usually involving shepherds in an idyllic rural setting

epistle a formal letter

equestrian mounted on horseback

imperium (Latin, "command," "empire") the civil and military authority exercised by the rulers of ancient Rome (and the root of the English words "imperialism" and "empire"); symbolized in ancient Rome by an eagle-headed scepter and the *fasces*, an ax bound in a bundle of rods

mosaic a medium by which small pieces of glass or stone are embedded in wet cement on wall and floor surfaces; any picture or pattern made in this manner

oratory the art of public speaking

pastoral pertaining to the country, to shepherds and the simple rural life; also, any work of art presenting an idealized picture of country life

res publica (Latin, "of the people") a government in which power resides in citizens entitled to vote and is exercised by representatives responsible to them and to a body of law

satire a literary genre that ridicules or pokes fun at human vices and follies

terra-cotta (Italian, "baked earth") a brownish-orange clay medium that may be glazed or painted; also called "earthenware"

trompe l'oeil (French, "fool the eye") a form of illusionistic painting that tries to convince the viewer that the image is real and not painted

vault a roof or ceiling constructed on the arch principle (see Figure 7.3)

SUGGESTIONS FOR READING

Barrow, R. H. *The Romans*. Baltimore, Md.: Penguin, 1963.

Boren, H. C. *Roman Society*. Lexington, Mass.: Heath, 1977.

Bradley, K. R. *Slaves and Masters in the Roman Empire*. Berkeley, Calif.: University of California Press, 1987.

Christ, Karl. *The Romans: An Introduction to Their History and Civilization*. Berkeley, Calif.: University of California Press, 1984.

Hanfmann, G. M. *Roman Art*. New York: Norton, 1975.

Hooper, Finley. *Roman Realities*. Detroit: Wayne State University Press, 1980.

L'Orange, H. P. *The Roman Empire: Art Forms and Civic Life*. New York: Rizzoli, 1985.

Schwartz, Benjamin. *The World of Thought in Ancient China*. Cambridge, Mass.: Harvard University Press, 1985.

Strong, Donald. *Roman Art*. Harmondsworth, England: Penguin, 1976.

Zanker, Paul. *The Power of Images in the Age of Augustus*. Ann Arbor: University of Michigan Press, 1988.

Selected General Bibliography

Baker, Herschel. *The Image of Man: A Study in the Idea of Human Dignity in Classical Antiquity; the Middle Ages, and the Renaissance*. New York: Harper, 1961.

Bentley, Jerry H. *Old World Encounters: Cross-Cultural Contacts and Exchanges in Pre-Modern Times*. New York: Oxford University Press, 1993.

Bernal, Martin. *Black Athena: The Afroasiatic Roots of Classical Civilization*. Vol. 1, *The Fabricating of Ancient Greece 1785–1985*. Vol. 2, *The Archeological and Documentary Evidence*. New Brunswick, N.J.: Rutgers University Press, 1987 and 1991.

Bugner, Ladislas, ed. *The Image of the Black in Western Art*. Vol. 1, *From the Pharaohs to the Fall of the Roman Empire*. Cambridge, Mass.: Harvard University Press, 1976.

Clark, Kenneth. *The Nude: A Study in Ideal Form*. Princeton, N.J.: Princeton University Press, 1956.

Craven, Roy C. *Indian Art: A Concise History*. London: Thames and Hudson, 1985.

De Coulanges, Fustel. *The Ancient City: A Study of the Religion, Laws, and Institution of Greece and Rome*. Baltimore, Md.: John Hopkins University Press, 1980.

De la Croix, Horst, Richard G. Tansey, and Diane Kirkpatrick. *Gardner's Art Through the Ages*, 9th ed. San Diego: Harcourt, 1991.

Finley, M. I. *Ancient Slavery and Modern Ideology*. New York: Viking, 1980.

Grout, Donald Jay. *A History of Western Music*, rev. ed. New York: Norton, 1979

Hall, James. *Dictionary of Subjects and Symbols in Art*, rev. ed. New York: Harper, 1979.

Hopfe, L. M. *Religions of the World*, 4th ed. New York: Macmillan, 1987.

Howatson, M. C., and Paul Harvey. *The Oxford Companion to Classical Literature*, 2nd ed. New York: Oxford University Press, 1989.

Kostof, Spiro. *A History of Architecture: Settings and Rituals*. New York: Oxford University Press, 1985.

———. *The City Shaped: Urban Patterns and Meanings Through History*. New York: Little, Brown & Company, 1992.

Lee, Sherman E. *A History of Far Eastern Art*, 4th ed. New York: Abrams, 1982.

Lerner, Gerda. *The Creation of Patriarchy*. New York: Oxford University Press, 1986.

Lund, Erik, Mogens Pihl, and Johannes Sløk. *A History of European Ideas*, trans. W. G. Jones. Reading, Mass.: Addison-Wesley, 1962.

May, Elizabeth, ed. *Music of Many Cultures*. Berkeley, Calif.: University of California Press, 1980.

Munro, Donald J. *The Concept of Man in Early China*. Stanford, Ca.: Stanford University Press, 1969.

Nuttgens, Patrick. *The Story of Architecture*. Englewood Cliffs, N.J.: Prentice-Hall, 1983.

O'Faolain, Julia, and Lauro Martines, eds. *Not in God's Image: Women in History from the Greeks to the Victorians*. New York: Harper, 1973.

Sedlar, J. W. *India and the Greek World: A Study in the Transmission of Culture*. Totowa, N.J.: Rowman, 1980.

Sorrell, Walter. *The Dance Through the Ages*. New York: Grosset and Dunlap, 1967.

Spencer, Harold. *The Image Maker: Man and His Art*. New York: Scribner, 1975.

Starr, Chester G. *A History of the Ancient World*, 4th ed. New York: Oxford University Press, 1991.

Sternfeld, F. W., gen. ed. *Praeger History of Western Music*. 5 vols. New York: Praeger, 1973.

Sullivan, Michael. *The Arts of China*, 3rd ed. Berkeley, Calif.: University of California Press, 1984.

Tidworth, Simon. *Theatres: An Architectural and Cultural History*. New York: Praeger, 1973.

Tregear, Mary. *Chinese Art*. London: Thames and Hudson, 1980.

Wang, Zhongshu. *Han Civilization*, trans. K. C. Chang. New Haven, Conn.: Yale University Press, 1982.

Books in Series

Daily Life in the Five Great Ages of History. The Horizon Books of Daily Life. New York: American Heritage Pub. Co., 1975.

Great Ages of Man: A History of the World's Cultures. New York: Time-Life Books, 1965–1969.

Time-Frame. 25 vols. (projected). New York: Time-Life Books, 1990–.

Credits

Calmann & King, the author, and the literature researcher wish to thank the publishers and individuals who have kindly allowed their copyright material to be reproduced in this book, as listed below. Every effort has been made to contact copyright holders, but should there be any errors or omissions, Calmann & King would be pleased to insert the appropriate acknowledgment in any subsequent edition of this publication.

CHAPTER 1

Reading 1 (p. 4): Reprinted by permission of The Museum of Modern Art, New York, from *Prehistoric Rock Pictures in Europe and Africa*, 1937.

CHAPTER 2

Reading 2 (p. 17): From "The Hymn to the Aten" in *The Literature of Ancient Egypt*, edited by William Kelly Simpson. © 1973 Yale University Press. Reprinted by permission.

Reading 3 (p. 24): From *The Epic of Gilgamesh: An English Version* by N. K. Sandars (Penguin Classics, 1960, Rev. ed. 1964), © N. K. Sandars 1960, 1964. Reprinted by permission of Penguin Books Ltd.

Reading 4A, B, C & D (pp. 29–33): From *The New Jerusalem Bible* (Reader's edition). Biblical text © 1985, Reader's edition © 1990 by Darton, Longman & Todd Ltd., and Doubleday, a division of Bantam, Doubleday, Dell Publishing Group, Inc. Used by permission of Doubleday, a division of Bantam Doubleday Dell Publishing Group, Inc.

Reading 5 (p. 36): From *The Bhagavad-Gita*, from *The Song of God: The Bhagavad-Gita*, translated by Swami Prabhavanda to Christopher Isherwood (1951). Reprinted by permission of Vedanta Press, CA.

Reading 6 (p. 38): From *The Way of Life* by Lao Tzu, translated by Raymond B. Blakney. Translation © 1955 by Raymond B. Blakney, © renewed 1983 by Charles Philip Blakney. Reprinted by permission of New American Library, a division of Penguin Books USA, Inc.

CHAPTER 3

Reading 7 (p. 45): From *The Autobiography of Rekh-mi-re* in *The Tomb of Rekh-mi-re at Thebes* by Norman de Garis Davies. Copyright 1943 by The Metropolitan Museum of Art. Reprinted by permission.

Reading 8 (p. 48): *The Hammurabi Code and the Sinaitic Legislation*, translated by Chilperic Edwards, 1971. New York: Kennikat Press.

Reading 9 (p. 41): From *The New Jerusalem Bible* (Reader's edition). Biblical text © 1985, Reader's edition © 1990 by Darton, Longman & Todd Ltd., and Doubleday, a division of Bantam, Doubleday, Dell Publishing Group, Inc. Used by permission of Doubleday, a division of Bantam Doubleday Dell Publishing Group, Inc.

Reading 10 (p. 52) Source: *The Chinese Classics (Confucius)*, pp. 64, 66, 112–113, 117. New York: John W. Lovell & Co., 1870.

CHAPTER 4

Reading 11 (p. 62): From *The Iliad of Homer*, translated by Richard Lattimore. Copyright © 1965 The University of Chicago Press. Reprinted by permission.

Reading 12 (p. 67) Source: Pericles' "Funeral Speech" from Thucydides' *History of the Peloponnesian War*, translated by Benjamin Jowett, in F. R. B. Godolphin, ed., *The Greek Historian*, 1942, pp. 648–651, Random House, Inc., New York.

Reading 13 (p. 71): © The Estate of Shamus O'Sheel.

Reading 14 (p. 80): Reprinted with the permission of Macmillan College Publishing Company from *Authyphro, Apology, Crito* by Plato, translated by F. J. Church. Copyright © 1956 by Macmillan College Publishing Company, Inc.

Reading 15 (p. 86) Source: Reprinted from *The Republic of Plato*, translated by F. M. Cornford (1941) by permission of Oxford University Press.

CHAPTER 5

Reading 16 (p. 90): From Aristotle's *Ethics*, from *The Nicomachean Ethics of Aristotle*, translated by J. E. C. Welldon. Reprinted by permission of Macmillan Ltd.

CHAPTER 6

Reading 17 (p. 95): Vitruvius, *Principles of Symmetry* from *Ten Books on Architecture*, translated by Morris Hicky Morgan. © 1960 Dover Publications Inc. Reprinted by permission.

Reading 18 (p. 112): From Aristotle, *Poetics*, translated by Ingram Bywater, in *The Works of Aristotle*, Vol. 11 (1925), ed. W. D. Ross. Reprinted by permission of Oxford University Press.

Reading 19 (p. 113): From Mary Barnard, *Sappho: A New Translation*. Copyright © 1958 The Regents of the University of California, © renewed 1984 Mary Barnard. Used by permission.

Reading 20 (p. 113) Source: From Pindar, *Nemean Ode VI*, translated by C. M. Bowa. Copyright © 1964 Oxford University Press.

CHAPTER 7

Reading 21 (p. 124): Reprinted by permission of the publishers and the Loeb Classical Library from Josephus, *The Jewish War*, Vol. II, Books 1–3, translated by S. St. J. Thackeray. Cambridge, Mass.: Harvard University Press, 1927.

Reading 22 (p. 140): From *The Stoic Philosophy of Seneca* by Moses Hadas. Copyright © 1958 by Moses Hadas. Used by permission of Doubleday, a division of Bantam Doubleday Dell Publishing Group, Inc.

Reading 23 (p. 141): Reprinted by permission of the publishers and the Loeb Classical Library from Cicero, *De Officiis*, Vol. XXI, translated by Walter Miller, Cambridge, Mass.: Harvard University Press, 1961.

Reading 24 (p. 142): Reprinted by permission of the publishers and the Loeb Classical Library, from Tacitus *Dialogue on Oratory*, from *Dialogus*, translated by W. Peterson, Cambridge, Mass.: Harvard University Press, 1958.

Reading 25 (p. 143): Reprinted with permission of Macmillan College Publishing Co. from *The Aeneid of Virgil*, translated by Rolfe Humphries, edited and with notes by Brian Wilkie. Copyright 1951 Charles Scribner's Sons.

Reading 26 (p. 145): From *Selected Poems of Horace*, introduction by George F. Whicher. Copyright 1947 Van Nostrand Reinhold. Copyright renewed 1975 Susan W. Whicher, Stephen F. Whicher and Nancy Whicher Greene as next of kin.

Reading 27A (p. 146): From "Against the City of Rome" in *The Satires of Juvenal*, translated by Rolfe Humphries. Copyright © 1958 by Indiana University Press.

Reading 27B (p. 146): From "Against Women" in *The Satires of Juvenal*, translated by Rolfe Humphries. Copyright © 1958 by Indiana University Press.

Reading 28 (p. 149) Source: Yutang, Lin, *Translations from the Chinese: The Importance of Understanding*. Cleveland: The World Publishing Company, 1960, pp. 207–210.

Index